Memoirs of a Statesman

Brian Faulkner

Memoirs of a Statesman

edited by John Houston

Weidenfeld and Nicolson
London

Contents

Illustrations

You can do three things in Irish politics: the right thing, the wrong thing, or nothing at all. I have always thought it is better to do the wrong thing than to do nothing at all.

Brian Faulkner, July 1974

Foreword

There are certain qualities—loyalty, patriotism, courage—which when they are combined in one person compel attention. That is true in any walk of life, but in particular in politics.

Brian Faulkner, as even the most prejudiced of his critics will allow, had all of them—and to spare—for he added plain speech and the ability to be flexible without compromising principle.

If it is true that politics is the 'art of the possible' it is more true of Northern Ireland than of anywhere else.

Brian was a practical man. In this autobiography the reader can follow his career in industry, where his ability and application were a great asset to the family firm.

Later, as Minister for Commerce, he used his knowledge and his imagination to help to diversify Northern Irish industry, and thus to give the economy a broader base.

With so down-to-earth and constructive a mind it was inevitable that he should be drawn further into politics and into the turmoil of problems which have haunted Ulster for so long. Deliberately he sacrificed comfort and leisure—his home life and the horses he loved—for the hard way.

I am not in a position to judge his evaluation of the political personalities of whom he writes who were on the Ulster scene during the testing years; nor would it be right—for I was a member of the British Government which decreed 'Direct Rule'—that I should comment on his criticisms of that action. Suffice it to say that Brian was totally convinced that Stormont was the best pattern of devolved government, and that it could pioneer the social reforms which were necessary to bring harmony into community life. To retain it with the ability to control law and order, he fought his corner hard and fairly.

The eventual decision by the British Government to take charge of security and to govern through a Secretary of State was a test of his loyalty, patriotism and courage. His loyalty to the principle that Northern Ireland should remain a part of the United Kingdom never wavered. His patriotism dictated that he should use all his influence as Prime Minister to keep the idea of a return to Stormont, or to something closely akin to it, alive. While his courage was revealed by his readiness to consult with, and to serve with, political opponents, and to search diligently for a constructive settlement which would cater for the interests of all the people of Ulster.

The part of the book which everyone in Northern Ireland and in the rest of the United Kingdom should read is the story of his discussion with all and sundry at and between the two conferences which were held with the British Government at Darlington and Sunningdale in 1973. For the reader who follows the tale will find that the apparently irreconcilable and the apparently unacceptable were achieved. A power-sharing Executive of the three political parties was created. It took office on 1 January 1974. It got down to work and did agree upon a programme of social advance for the province inside the framework laid down by the British Government. It operated within the principle of 'collective responsibility' and clearly had great significance for the constitutional future of Northern Ireland.

Brian Faulkner records: 'All decisions were taken by only the 11 full members of the Executive . . . in any case there was never a vote. Our decisions were taken by consensus as we all knew that we had to work together for the Executive to survive.'

There was one other event during the lifetime of the Executive which only a short time previously would have been incredible. That was agreement with Dublin on the function of the 'Council of Ireland'. Representatives of the government in Dublin met the Executive of Northern Ireland and the negotiation was one between equals.

For a time Brian Faulkner's policy of 'constructive co-operation' held the field, and nor was the break-up when it came inspired by differences on policies within the Executive. It was a recurrence of violence fomented by extremists and events outside Northern Ireland which dashed hopes yet again.

It is important to mark that fact, for when something has happened and succeeded once it can occur again.

Brian concludes: 'A politician should be judged by what he has done, and what he had tried to do . . .' He expresses the hope that his 'activities can stand that test'. The great majority of his readers will concur.

When the next opportunity comes it will need men as loyal, as patriotic, as patient, as diligent and as dedicated to peaceful co-operation as Brian Faulkner and his colleagues if settlement is to come at last.

It will be the prayer and hope of all that with a model before them good men will then succeed.

LORD HOME

Introduction

The manuscript of this book was in its final stages of preparation when Lord Faulkner was killed in a hunting accident on 3 March 1977. The previous August he had retired from active political life, saying that having gone through so many rounds of political negotiations he found it difficult 'to thrash over the same problems hour after hour and week after week the second or third time round'. In the New Year's Honours List for 1977 he received a life peerage and formally took his seat in the House of Lords on 22 February.

There then occurred one of those strange quirks of fate that seemed to draw together so many threads early in 1977. Lord Faulkner's portrait by the Ulster artist Raymond Piper, a gift from his former political colleagues, was completed. These memoirs, after two years' work, required only a final editing and typing. Lord Faulkner was happily active again in the industrial world he knew so well. His political retirement had marked the end of an epoch in Ulster politics. He was one of the last and most renowned of the new generation of thrusting young men who stood for election in the late 1940s to leave the political scene. He had also in February written an unusual personal letter to one of his closest colleagues, Reggie Magee. It is unusual because Brian Faulkner was recognized by those who knew him to be a man who hoped for the future, lived zestfully in the present, and was generally bored by the past. This letter, which shows a mood of sombre reflection on a lifetime in politics, is given particular significance by the subsequent tragedy and it is included at the end of the book with the permission of the recipient.

The countryside of Co. Down and the sport of hunting were two of Brian Faulkner's chief passions. Two weeks after taking his seat in the House of Lords he was riding with the Co. Down Staghounds at Saintfield when his horse, travelling at full gallop on a narrow country road, slipped and fell. Lord Faulkner was killed instantly. He died much as he had lived, moving at top speed, squaring up to obstacles, and taking astonishing personal risks to achieve his objectives.

There are many people whose help in the preparation of these memoirs should be acknowledged, but I can mention only a few of them here. Ken Bloomfield, Robert Ramsay, Harry Jones and William Stout have given unstintingly of their time to assist on matters of fact relating to the long periods when they were Brian Faulkner's closest official aides, and have provided stimulating recollections of many of the incidents which litter a politician's career. Leslie Morrell furnished us with astonishingly comprehensive notes of the inter-party negotiations at Stormont Castle and later at Sunningdale. Thanks are also due to the authors and publishers of the large number of books on the Ulster 'troubles', many of which were referred to at some stage but which are too numerous to list here with any accuracy. The encyclopedic *Chronology of Events' in Northern Ireland 1968–74* by Richard Deutsch and Vivien Magowan was particularly valuable in helping to sort out the complex sequence of events. Needless to say none of these gentlemen or these sources bear any responsibility for the contents of this book. The views expressed are Brian Faulkner's, any errors of fact are probably mine.

We have been fortunate in the quality of our secretarial help. Pat Keir has patiently typed transcripts of taped conversations which, because of my primitive equipment, were often scarcely audible. Sue O'Brien has, in spite of numerous last-minute changes, maintained an unparalleled enthusiasm in typing the manuscript, interpreting with accuracy and skill the illegibly scrawled notes and directions. Thanks are also due to Claire, Antonella, Julia and Joanna.

Above all, thanks are due to the Faulkner family for their help and encouragement throughout. Lady Faulkner's detailed family scrapbooks dating back over several years provided an invaluable basis for the work, and in the difficult weeks after the accident she played a vital part in the preparations for publication. I believe it is to his family that Lord Faulkner would, had he lived, have wished to dedicate this book.

JOHN HOUSTON
Editor

1
Carson's Ghost

It was an unusual place for the head of government to hold a press conference. But it had been a very unusual day at the end of a very unusual two weeks.

I stood on the low wooden steps and read a prepared statement to the crowd of pressmen and photographers who crowded around, some of them standing on the steps and the rest gathering on the tarmac of what used to be a car park at the east side of Stormont Buildings. Behind us was the all-too-necessary security hut which now masked with its prefabricated ugliness the eastern entrance into the great white marble Parliament Buildings. We all knew it was a significant day in the history of these buildings, which had been the hub of all devolved Northern Ireland Governments since they were opened in November 1932 by the Prince of Wales.

At around 8.30 on the morning of 29 May 1974 an army helicopter had landed in the paddock outside my home to convey me to the office. It was a form of transport which I did not normally use to cover the thirty-odd miles, but for more than seven days now it had been all that was available. Conditions across the Province were such that, even if there had been sufficient petrol available to keep government cars running—which there was not—an army convoy would have been required to ensure our early arrival at Stormont. Helicopter travel was a more practical proposition. All over Northern Ireland that morning members of the Executive were travelling in to their offices for a day's work none of us was looking forward to.

There was no morning mail to clear up with my Private Office, because the mail was not operating. Even the telephones were beginning to sound weak and indistinct. I held brief consultations with some of my officials, confirming only what had become obvious at the meeting of our coalition Executive the previous afternoon. The whole Province was on the brink of an unprecedented collapse of organized community life. The electricity grid was thought to be only six hours from total shutdown.

A talk with fellow Unionist members of the coalition Executive showed that most of them had come to conclusions similar to those which I had reached after a rather sleepless night. One way or another the deadlock would have to be broken. The options for doing so were limited. Only two suggested themselves to us, and we feared that only the one which was from our point of view the least attractive would work.

An early-morning meeting with all our Unionist Assemblymen underlined the gravity of the situation and the worry of our supporters. From all over the Province came stories of how the rebels were in control and the community was taking the soft option of giving them at least passive support.

At 11 a.m. we had a meeting of the Northern Ireland Executive. Only one item was on the agenda—the 'Emergency Situation'. I opened by summing up the situation. The Army was operating a minimal petrol and oil supply. The Belfast gas plant was out of operation. The power stations were dangerously near total shutdown, and even if the Army had the technical capacity to restore partial functioning there would be a total blackout for several days at least. The water supply and sewerage services were at grave risk, and the flooding of large parts of Belfast with raw sewage was a real possibility. Basic food distribution was in jeopardy. Supplies of feedstuffs to farms had stopped.

We have only two options. First we break the strike by sitting it out as long as is necessary. That involves allowing the strikers to do their worst and waiting for their supporters to realise the disaster into which they have led the Province. It will bring a great deal of hardship to thousands and will probably cause several deaths. Secondly, we can explore the possibility of negotiation, either directly or through intermediaries.

I and my Unionist colleagues are simply not prepared to sacrifice the economy of Northern Ireland and the lives of its people to maintain what is now a clearly unrealistic position. I propose that we seek the agreement of the Secretary of State to discussions through intermediaries to see how the strike can be brought to an end. Failing that we have only one option—to hand in our resignations and bring down the Executive.

A long discussion followed. The Alliance Party supported negotiations, but was adamant that there could be no question of resigning. The SDLP would agree to neither talks nor the threat of resignation. They said we were the democratically elected government of the Province and that if we gave in we would be acquiescing in what amounted to a coup. If suffering and even deaths occurred the responsibility would lie on the junta which was holding the community to ransom, and people might then come to their senses.

I could see the SDLP's point and I did not regard their tough stance as unreasonable. But I felt we simply could not, for any reason, allow the Province to descend into the anarchy which now appeared imminent. The strikers were obviously prepared to go to any lengths to bring down the Executive, the solidarity of those who had supported us initially was diminishing, and one way or another the impasse would have to be ended. Having spent the greater part of my life trying to make Northern Ireland a modern and civilized place to live, I could not conceive of allowing the economy to be wrecked for any political reason.

By 12.45 a.m. it was clear that there would be no consensus in the Executive, though there was a majority view that the Executive should open communication with the strikers, preferably by way of mediation. It was agreed that I would report that view to the Secretary of State. I did not say in summing up, but it was clearly understood by all present, that the rejection of this proposal by Mr Rees would mean the resignation of I and my colleagues in the Unionist Party.

At 1 p.m. I travelled the familiar half mile to Stormont Castle to see the Secretary of State. Ken Bloomfield, as Permanent Secretary to the Executive, came with me. Merlyn Rees, whose staff had been notified by telephone that we were coming, was waiting for us in the first-floor office with Frank Cooper, his Permanent Secretary and confidante. I told him the Executive had met and a majority favoured communication with the strikers. The Unionist members of the Executive had unanimously decided that if this was not agreed they would resign. I pointed out that he had told me the services were not capable of restarting the power stations on their own, and I was not prepared to take the risks with life which were involved in going on.

Merlyn simply said: 'Well, without the Unionists that's the end of the Executive.' He was in quite an emotional state, for he had shared our hopes for the Executive and the future of the Province, but he knew that things had gone so far now that only the end of the Executive could make Northern Ireland governable again. 'Whatever history may record of the events of the last few weeks', said Merlyn, 'it is certain that you and your colleagues will go down as people who tried very hard to do something very important for Northern Ireland.' Then he appeared to choke up. We shook hands and I left.

Back in our room in Stormont the other members of the Executive were expecting the news I brought them. The Secretary of State's acceptance of the seven Unionist resignations made the termination of the other appointments merely a question of formalities, but the SDLP and Alliance Ministers decided that they would make the gesture of refusing to hand in their resignations. For a few hours until Rees prorogued the Assembly Northern Ireland had its first ever completely non-Unionist government, in theory at least.

The five-minute meeting ended with all the members shaking hands in an atmosphere charged with emotion and despondency. Oliver Napier, the Alliance Party leader, and Gerry Fitt, the SDLP leader, were visibly upset at the collapse of all we had worked for. The minutes recorded that 'good wishes were exchanged' and 'mutual sorrow' was expressed. We all agreed that come what may we would not deviate in the future from the principles of partnership on which the Executive had been based. I was very heartened when Austin Currie, the SDLP Minister for Housing, Local Government and Planning, and once a bitter personal critic, said to me as we were shaking hands, 'Whatever happens now I have worked with you long enough to know that I will always be able to trust you.'

I spent the next twenty minutes preparing a statement and then went down to meet the hastily gathered press corps outside the building. The statement said:

We believe that Northern Ireland can only be maintained as a part of the U.K. on the basis of co-operation between Protestants and Roman Catholics, and that is why I and my party have taken part in the Executive. I cannot speak too highly of the spirit in which, as colleagues, we from the different parties have been able to conduct our business. It is however apparent to us, from the extent of support for the present stoppage, that the degree of consent needed to sustain the Executive does not at present exist. Nor as Ulstermen are we prepared to see our country undergo, for any political reason, the catastrophe which now confronts it. That is why I recommended this morning on behalf of myself and my Unionist colleagues, that some sort of dialogue between the Government and those confronting it should now take place, but the Secretary of State was unable to accept this recommendation. We have therefore offered our resignations to the Secretary of State, and have advised him to explore at once the possibility of constructing a new Administration on a basis which will command general public confidence.

As the pressmen rushed off to meet their deadlines Ken Bloomfield and I went back inside the building. We were climbing the marble staircase towards my office when Ken's proverbial restraint snapped and he broke down. He had been a leading public servant and adviser through the premierships of O'Neill, Chichester-Clark, and myself. But I had not until that moment quite understood the depth of his individual commitment to a better future for Northern Ireland.

Back in my office members of the Executive who had finished clearing their desks started to drift in for a final chat. I opened my official drinks cupboard, which the civil service always kept well stocked for my visitors. I was handing round drinks when John Hume, deputy leader of the SDLP came in. With a typical flash of dry humour he said, 'There's always drinks at a wake!'

Down in the Assembly chamber formal proceedings went ahead as usual at 2.30 p.m. with a small number of Members in attendance. Austin Currie, still technically a Minister, went to answer questions to his department on housing, but the Executive business was not moved and the Assembly was adjourned after twenty-five minutes. Most of us did not have the heart to go down and take part in proceedings which were now meaningless, and after staying in my office for about an hour we broke up and went our respective ways.

As I drove from the Parliament Buildings a crowd of triumphant strike supporters were gathering at the front near Carson's statue carrying Ulster flags and Union Jacks. For hundreds of yards down the main driveway tractors and trailers, brought as part of an organized protest by farmers, were packed tightly together. All had now heard the news of the Executive's resignation and what had been planned as another grim protest was turning into a celebration. Before leaving the office I had been told that the electricity workers were going back to work, so total social collapse had at least been averted.

I had never been so disappointed and worried about the future of Northern Ireland as when I drove away from Stormont that afternoon. Since I first arrived there in 1949 as the youngest MP and the first to be born in partitioned Ireland I had been involved in many difficult and disheartening events. But I had never been disheartened for long. There had always, even in 1972 when the Stormont Parliament was suspended after only one year of my Premiership, seemed to be some way in which one could move ahead positively and turn adversity into success. But this time it was hard to see what there remained to do except to go back and start from scratch. With a quarter of a century of Northern Ireland politics behind me that was not an option. It looked very much like the end of the political road.

We had staked everything on the attempt to bind Catholics and Protestants together in a power-sharing Executive, and lost. It was hard to believe that something with so much to offer the people of Northern Ireland could have been so wilfully destroyed. But I felt discouraged rather than bitter. I understood why many determined Ulster folk had supported the general strike. The statue of Carson round which they gathered in front of Stormont symbolized their conviction that Ulster was going through another '1912'. A plot was afoot, they believed, to deprive them of their British citizenship and push them by stages into an Irish Republic which they regarded as an alien and hostile state. So they rallied to the old slogans of 'No surrender' which had been given new relevance by the continuation of a vicious terrorist campaign directed largely against the civilian population. They had been cruelly misled and conned by all the would-be Carsons into believing that the reactions of 1912 were all that was required in 1974.

The fight for the survival of the Northern Ireland Executive was a struggle between negative and positive politics in the Province. When one looks at all the circumstances it is perhaps understandable that negative politics triumphed and brought down the Executive. People under violent attack are likely to view with suspicion an imaginative new gesture of conciliation towards those they feel to be associated with their attackers. The Executive offered so much that was positive and hopeful, but people used to feeling threatened by a neighbouring state with designs on their territory and resentful of the harsh and sometimes unjust criticism they had been subjected to by the international media found defence a more natural stance. Ulster people had learned to expect the worst, and fear overcame hope in their response to the Executive.

Against this background my colleagues and I could feel that our failure to communicate our confidence about the future under the new Constitution was not completely surprising, but that did not reduce our disappointment. We knew we had made mistakes, both in the details of some of the negotiations and our presentation of them to the public. We had suffered almost as much misrepresentation by our friends as our enemies. When physically challenged we had found ourselves stripped by Westminster of any policing powers, helpless to defend our government or enforce its laws.

But when all the qualifications about the power-sharing Executive had been entered we were still convinced that we attempted and almost succeeded in the greatest breakthrough in Irish politics this century. In all my years in politics there was no venture whose success I more wished for and which appeared to offer so much. For those pulling it down it was a pyrrhic victory; they had shown a capacity to destroy, but could they ever come remotely near to replacing it with anything offering a new basis for peaceful co-existence in Ireland? Over two years later that is a question which still waits for an answer.

2
Early Years

Ulster is home to me, and always will be. I have never wished to live anywhere else in the world, among any other people than my own Ulster people, and among the hills and loughs of County Down.

I have lived in that county since I was born on 18 February 1921 in the village of Helen's Bay on the southern shore of Belfast Lough. During my childhood we moved to a house in the Holywood Hills on the outskirts of the city, and then near to the seaside town of Bangor—first to a farm at Rathgael and then to a house where our garden ran down to the sands of Ballyholme Bay. Later the family moved to a farm on the shores of Strangford Lough near the village of Killinchy, and after I was married we bought a house near Ballynahinch—by tradition the heart of Down—before moving to our present home at Seaforde, a few miles from the mountains of Mourne. All these homes had one thing in common: there had to be a place to keep a horse.

My father's family had its roots in western Ulster, in County Tyrone, where my grandfather owned a flax mill near Cookstown. He became an alcoholic, lost his mill and his money, and died leaving my grandmother to bring up nine children. She uprooted herself and her family and moved to East Belfast, in the shadow of the shipyards, where my father, the youngest of the family, grew up.

He was, as a consequence, a life-long teetotaller. He was determined that his father's fate would not be repeated in his own family and I suppose he handed down his aversion to me. When my brother Dennis and I were children he made a bargain with us that if we didn't drink or smoke until we were twenty-one (although he was quite a heavy smoker himself!) he would give us each £100. In those days that seemed a princely sum. The bargain was made in typically Irish fashion in the back room of a pub in County Down when the local hunt was meeting there, and the man who suggested the idea to my father was the late John Miller Andrews, then Minister of Finance in the Stormont Government.

It was he who handed over the cheque when the time came, although by then he had succeeded Lord Craigavon as Northern Ireland's second Prime Minister. I am still a teetotaller. People often say to me that it must be very difficult in public life to go round the world without taking a drink, but I never found it any embarrassment. One does, however, get rather fed up with orange juice, and I am grateful to the wine waiters in many parts of the United Kingdom who know how to produce, unasked, a bottle of apple juice!

My mother was of English parents, and she brought to the partnership a touch of calm and caution, and realistic common sense. My father was the adventurer, always ready for a challenge, quick to try out something new. He built up from nothing what was to become the largest single shirt factory in the United Kingdom, the Belfast Collar Company, employing a work force of about a thousand, its trade name 'Faulat'. In those pre-war days he travelled a great deal looking for orders. He went each year to the trade fair in Leipzig, bringing back—along with some wonderful toys—new machinery for the factory, and new ideas. He was the first shirt manufacturer in the United Kingdom to introduce the conveyor-belt system in production.

As a boy I took it for granted that my future was in the factory, with my father and my brother Dennis, and each school holiday I spent more and more of my time working there. As far as I know I am the only member of the family who ever took an interest in politics. Certainly my father thought it was an unnecessary diversion from work, and discouraged me from taking up a political career.

His own capacity for taking a chance, and trying out something new, sometimes rubbed off on the rest of his family in ways that were exciting for a boy. I remember him taking me with him on the first commercial flight across the Irish Sea from Northern Ireland to Great Britain. In fact, I think we two were the only passengers, because the weather was so bad that the official party to inaugurate the flight was called off! He was recovering at the time from a bad fall in our local hunt point to point races, and I remember him hobbling out on crutches to the plane, a de Havilland Rapide. Sometimes his adventurous instincts were curtailed by my mother's caution, but he was ingenious in getting his own way. She disapproved of his efforts to encourage me to ride in horse shows—probably because of the many times she had tended his own broken bones after hunting accidents. I remember as a seven-year-old setting off with him in the car one morning, ostensibly for school as usual, but in fact to ride a pony for the first time in the show ring, at the Royal Agricultural Society's annual show in Belfast. The pony and I won first prize, but it was a pyrrhic victory. Our photograph appeared next morning in the *Northern Whig* for all to see, including my mother.

I do not remember a time when I could not ride a horse—or for that matter, sail a boat, although on that side of our family's activity it has always been my brother who is the expert. We were a family with strong ties binding us and as a boy I remember feeling very responsible for him, as my junior by four years, except when it came to boats when Dennis was always very much in charge! We took our family holidays together, sometimes to a cottage near Strangford Lough. My father used to take the back seats out of his Rover car, and we persuaded Mary, our Shetland pony, to climb in and be taken there on holiday with us. We always had some sort of a boat, and when we were older my father often took us all cruising on the west coast of Scotland.

The Ulster I knew then was rather different from today. I remember getting the tram from Newtownbreda to Inchmarlo school on the other side of Belfast, which meant changing at Castle Junction in the city centre. The Royal Ulster Constabulary pointsman on duty saw us all safely across the road. He had no need of a flak jacket, and we had never heard the noise of an exploding bomb.

After Inchmarlo I was sent to Elm Park boarding school in County Armagh. It was a good school, with a headmaster for whom I still feel admiration and gratitude. There were only about forty of us there and we were well taught, but above all we learned a lot of self-reliance. But I hated being away from home and I still remember vividly the depression that got worse and worse every day as the end of the school holidays came near.

We were a family of Ulster Presbyterians, and as such it seems a strange choice that when the time came for me to go to public school I should have been sent to St Columba's College, an Anglican foundation near the city of Dublin. But my father was determined that part of an Ulster boy's education should be outside Northern Ireland, and I chose St Columba's for the simple reason that it was nearer home than a school in Great Britain would have been. I was one of only three Nonconformists there at the time, and the only Ulster Unionist. As such I learnt to fight my corner, and to argue carefully and constructively. Argue I had to, for my best friend throughout the years there was Michael Yeats, son of the poet W. B. Yeats, and an ardent advocate of a United Ireland. I had to fight hard in all sorts of ways, for in class Michael was usually effortlessly at the top, and I came second, but only by dint of steady hard work. It was a friendship which persisted after school days. Michael and I spent a number of holidays together in the west of

Ireland and the north, cycling and staying in youth hostels. Eventually he entered politics as well, on his side of the border, and he is now a Fianna Fail Senator and a Vice-President of the European Parliament.

One of my minor difficulties at school was that I could never hit a ball, or catch it. I enjoyed rugby—I had a turn of speed and played wing—but I was lousy at cricket and the only team I managed to get in to was the hockey team. However, I edited the school magazine, and I think the thing I look back on with most pleasure during my school career was that I became the first boy to be allowed to manage the school shop. I had been horrified to find that school clothes were bought for the shop from retailers, a crazy system that offended my inherited business instincts. I went off looking for quotations and began to buy all our goods wholesale and, for the first time in its life, the school shop started to make a profit.

The very fact of being in a small minority at school intensified my awareness not only of being a Unionist Ulsterman, but also of being a Presbyterian. As a family, we went regularly to church on Sundays, and my father and mother were always interested in church work. I remember when I was very young I had a great admiration for our minister at Groomsport Church. He drove a Riley with twin carburettors and he gave me a ride in it occasionally, so anything he said was gospel as far as I was concerned! Then, as today, I had no interest in the finer points of theology. I look on Christianity as a practical religion and a guide for my way of life, and have a deep respect for and an attachment to the simple Presbyterian faith in which I was brought up. I have always had a great faith in the power of prayer, a faith which remains with me today. I look forward to Sunday service at the little country church of Magherahamlet where the Reverend Cecil Adams, upon whose good counsel and advice I often depend, delivers a sermon full of common sense as well as spiritual guidance. One legacy at least which my Anglican school has left me is that I can feel equally at home with the services of the Episcopal church as with my own.

On leaving school I went to Queen's University to read law but after one term there war broke out and the factory, which had turned to 100 per cent war production, had serious staffing problems. The production manager was in the Officer Reserve and my help was required in the firm. I had to take over from him almost immediately at the age of eighteen. We were working seven days a week, the shirts being sometimes flown out within twenty-four hours of completion. At the same time I was farming some 120 acres of land not previously tilled for generations,

on islands in Strangford Lough, for food production. It was an impossible task and I remember well looking at some young fellows queuing
for a film one Saturday afternoon as I trundled through the village with
a laden tractor, and thinking 'Where on earth do they find the time to
do that?'

It was, of course, my own decision to stay in the family factory, and
in retrospect, it was a foolish one. The only service to the country that
many people recognized was service in the armed forces. So medals and
a military rank were valuable assets for political advancement in the
post-war world, and lack of either was a serious obstacle to overcome.
This has been especially true in Northern Ireland, where the practice
of using one's wartime rank has persisted among many politicians until
very recently. But I regarded my task as a particularly useful and important part of the country's war effort. It was also important for the family
business that my father had created.

Hugh Dalton, President of the Board of Trade in London, came to
the factory in 1944 to congratulate the workers on their contribution
to the war effort. I had to introduce him to the workers from a bench
on the factory floor, giving a brief speech which must have been one of
my first outside school debates. Dalton said when making his speech
'We will have to see about getting this young man into Parliament,' and
the newspapers, who were covering the visit, reported this the next day.
But although I appreciated the compliment I did not initially take the
idea very seriously.

Altogether I spent some twenty-two years managing the factory, with
my father and my brother, until, on taking office as Minister of Commerce in the Northern Ireland Government in 1963, I decided a conflict
of interest might arise, and resigned from the family business. It was a
difficult decision to make and neither my father nor Dennis interfered
with me in making it, but I knew it would have a considerable effect on
the family. My decision to leave was instrumental in persuading them
that the firm must eventually amalgamate with a larger unit, and later
Faulat was taken over by Ladybird Ltd.

During those years, apart from learning about industry throughout
the United Kingdom and abroad from the inside, I learned more about
the working people of Ulster than I could possibly have learned from
twenty-two years in politics. Our factory was situated in the vicinity of
the Shankill and the Falls Roads, and we had a mixed work force of
Protestants and Catholics. During the years before 1969 there was the
best of good relations on the factory floor. Each 12 July the Union Jacks
came out, and nobody minded. There had, of course, been sectarian

troubles in the city. I remember during school days my father telling me once that the workers had had to be taken home in police tenders because there was rioting in the area.

I discovered at first hand that there is not in the world anyone quicker to learn a new technique, or more adaptable, than the men and women of Belfast. I also learned to appreciate their lightning humour, often tart and invariably devastating. There is no place in Ulster, in management or on the shop floor, for the man who takes himself too seriously. I could find my way blindfolded through those streets of West Belfast now so familiar to television viewers, like Agnes Street and Cambrai Street. For those of us who knew them at first hand, and the people who live there, the changes brought about by seven years of violence are incredibly tragic.

There was so much happening in the post-war world that it was difficult not to take an interest in public affairs. I had always been interested in politics at school, not in political theory but in day-to-day political affairs as reported in the newspapers, and in the political personalities involved north and south of the border and in London. Soon after the war ended there was a by-election for a Westminster seat in County Down and a good friend of mine, Charles Mullan of Newry, who had just come home from the Royal Navy, was selected as the Unionist candidate. My first election speech was on his platform. At the same time I was getting involved in the local Unionist Association in Mid-Down, and in 1947 became its honorary secretary.

Many contemporaries of my own were also getting involved. We were impatient of the old-fashioned structures and practices of the Unionist Party and we wanted to see a more modern professional approach adopted. With the indispensable assistance of Jim Bailie, then the Party Organizer, we started the Young Unionist movement, of which I became the first chairman. From then until the mid-1960s the Young Unionists were the radical and forward-looking section of the party, and produced many valuable ideas for change. Not that change came easily, then as now. A group of us were asked to write a pamphlet on party organization, on which we spent weeks of sweat and toil before we presented it to the chairman of the Standing Committee. It was turned down, and in indignation we threatened to publish it ourselves. The Chairman, Sir Clarence Graham, capitulated, the pamphlet was published and eventually became the foundation upon which a lot of the post-war Unionist Party reorganization was done.

There were a number of us in those days who started getting involved in politics—Jim Bailie, whom I have already mentioned, remained

Party Organizer for over twenty years. He and I were nearly killed when driving back from a meeting in County Fermanagh one night in the 1950s. A timber trailer crashed into my car and sliced the roof off, an experience which has given me an illogical dislike of seat belts, because had we been wearing belts that night we would have been decapitated. The meeting had been in Enniskillen with Harry West, another contemporary, who became Stormont MP for the area. He had just arrived home when he received a telephone call saying, 'Brian Faulkner and Jim Bailie are lying dead on the road!' He rushed post haste to the hospital at Enniskillen, and he said the first thing he heard was the sound of my voice demanding to be allowed to go home. Later when I resigned as Leader of the Glengall Street Unionists in 1974 Harry was elected in my place. L. P. S. ('Willie') Orr, who in 1974 relinquished his South Down seat at Westminster to Enoch Powell, after a period as Leader of the Westminster Ulster Unionist Members, also began his career at this time.

In 1946 I joined the Orange Order, the first member of my family to do so. Many people outside Northern Ireland have seen in the Order a sinister secret society of Protestants, a sort of Ku Klux Klan. But it seemed to me to be a reasonable organization which, by and large, sought to restrain the wilder elements of the Protestant community and taught justice and respect for the beliefs of one's neighbours. It overrode all divisions among the Protestant sects and denominations and provided a feeling of solidarity in reaction to the aggressive religio-political nationalism which had been, and was in the post-war years, manifesting itself in Ireland. If, like some organizations under pressure, it has retreated into the past rather than moving with the times we live in, that is the fault of its leaders, or perhaps the fault of a lack of leadership, rather than in the character of the men who compose it.

I had no thought at this time of taking up a career in politics. I was greatly interested in the subject and was speaking at quite a few Unionist meetings, but to me this was a case of putting forward my views rather than pursuing a political ambition. The man who was eventually instrumental in bringing me into the House of Commons at Stormont in 1949 as the MP for East Down (the constituency originally held in the Westminster Parliament by Sir James Craig, later Lord Craigavon) and the youngest member of the House, was Terence O'Neill. I originally met Terence when we had asked him, as the youngest Member of Stormont at that time, to be president of our Young Unionist organization. Now he came to see me at the factory to say that Colonel Gordon, the East Down Member, was not going to stand at the next election in a few months time. 'Alec told me about it today and no one else knows yet,' he said. 'I hoped you might be interested.'

That night I spoke to Colonel Gordon who gave me his support, and during the next three weeks I visited personally each of the delegates who would attend the selection meeting, accompanied by the Chairman of the local Association, James Bell of Ballynahinch, one of the finest gentlemen I ever knew. There were two other contestants, Colonel Percival Price of Saintfield and Willie Orr. When the meeting was held I was selected with an overall majority on the first count, and the election followed two months later, on 10 February 1949.

I had a straight fight with an Irish Nationalist opponent, Ned McGrady. The election of 1949 was fought almost totally, throughout Northern Ireland, on Ulster's place within the United Kingdom. That this should be so was determined by a particularly ill-judged and offensive piece of interference from the Dublin Government. In 1949 Eire had decided to leave the British Commonwealth and declare a republic (an action which drove even further wedges between Irishmen, North and South). Sean McBride, a former IRA leader, then Minister of External Affairs in Dublin (recently awarded a share in the Nobel Peace Prize for his work in Amnesty International) was helping to stir up the Nationalists inside Ulster and an all-party Anti-Partition Fund was set up. The election in Northern Ireland became notorious as the 'Chapel Gates Election' due to the decision of the Fund's organizers to hold a collection outside all Roman Catholic chapels in Ireland on the Sunday before polling day.

Against this background Unionists were well aware that a decisive answer must be given by the voters of Northern Ireland on their British citizenship. We would have been much happier in a position where the clearly declared wishes of the vast majority of the voters of Northern Ireland had been accepted, and citizenship was no longer an issue. But the decision as to the grounds upon which this election (and many other elections) were to be fought was not made by us. Those who talk critically of the 'siege mentality' of Ulstermen would do well to remember that for many years after the war siege was well and truly laid to the Province by successive Dublin Governments. In 1949, as at so many other elections before and since, the voters of Ulster proclaimed their overwhelming wish to remain within the United Kingdom.

In East Down I had a majority of 2,651 in a total poll of 13,612. After the count Mr McGrady thanked us for a clean fight and said that throughout he had recognized my 'gentlemanliness and courtesy'. There was no acrimony between us, for we each respected the other's convictions, and knew them to be sincerely held. Unfortunately, there were a few of Mr McGrady's followers in the county town of Downpatrick who did not share his feelings about the election, for during a victory parade later our lorry was attacked and some bricks and hurley sticks thrown at us. I well remember standing in the darkness of that cold February night in the centre of Downpatrick appealing to my Unionist followers to go quietly home, while on the other side of the street the local Roman Catholic priest did likewise to the Nationalists. There was an amusing sequel. About three weeks later a Downpatrick sports goods retailer appealed to me to approach the Board of Trade on his behalf to get a licence to import hurley sticks from Eire! He approached me with some diffidence, but we both appreciated the humour of the situation, and I am glad to say I was able to get him his licence.

I have in front of me the message I published for my new constituents after the election. I have put the same statement into each of my election addresses since, and it is an objective I have sincerely tried to live up to. I said: 'It will be my earnest endeavour at all times to work for the welfare of all my constituents, irrespective of creed or of the section of the community to which they belong.'

3
Backbencher to Minister

There have always seemed to be three quite separate and distinct strands running through my life, each of them important in itself: family life, political life, and hunting. It was about this time, 1950, that by force of circumstances they all intertwined at one moment, with considerable consequences. I was acting as Election Agent for Willie Orr, who was standing as a candidate for a County Down seat at Westminster for the first time. During the campaign I broke a collar-bone one day when hunting at Killinchy, so I called on a friend to drive me around the constituency—Lucy Forsythe, who like myself was born and bred in County Down and who shared my interest in politics. We had first met in the hunting field on Saturday mornings, for in those days I worked in the factory five days a week and she was working as a reporter on the *Belfast Telegraph*. On the way back from one of Willie Orr's election meetings in the mountains of Mourne I proposed to her and we were married in February 1951.

It was about this time, too, that I began to travel extensively abroad on business, and when the occasion arose, especially in the United States, I took the opportunity of presenting the case for Northern Ireland which so often went by default. I remember my very first television appearance in April 1949 on an hour-long debate in New York with an Irish–American, Judge Troy. After the debate I said to him, 'What part of Ireland do you come from?' 'County Westmeath,' he said, 'though I haven't been there since the age of three. But I do have to get an Irish vote.' I thought it was the same story with so many outside pundits on Irish affairs, not excluding some in Great Britain. I had only three supporters in the eighty-strong studio audience of Irish–Americans—the British Consul-General Francis Evans, the President of the Ulster–Irish Society of New York, and an Ulster linen salesman I had met on the boat on the way over. I think this was probably the first television appearance by any Ulster politician and so I had the opportunity from very early in my career to learn the pitfalls and the opportunities of televized political debate. The most important thing I ever learned was to forget that there was an audience of millions watching.

I returned from each of my overseas trips with an increasing sense of the inadequacy of the presentation of the Northern Ireland situation throughout the world, and I frequently raised this problem in my time as a backbencher. While the Dublin Government was disseminating propaganda against us through its embassies and (after 1955) the United Nations, we had to rely on the efforts of the United Kingdom Foreign Office, which was at times somewhat half-hearted on our behalf. I objected strongly to the adoption by the South of the title 'Republic of Ireland'. 'They have no right to the title of "Ireland" a name of which we are just as proud as they,' I said at a meeting, and I criticized the British Government for sanctioning such an arrangement.

British politicians who had seen the 1920 settlement as an interim one pending a United Ireland sometimes needed reminders that opposition to Dublin rule inside Ulster had become no less with the passing of the years. Today, when the intense passions aroused by the Border issue are in every news bulletin this seems self-evident, but twenty-five years ago events in Ireland, North or South, were of little interest in Great Britain. However, after the Irish Government's declaration of a republic and the display of Unionist opinion in the 1949 election, the Attlee Government were persuaded by the then Prime Minister of Northern Ireland, Sir Basil Brooke, later Lord Brookeborough, to enact a pledge that Northern Ireland would not cease to be part of the United Kingdom without the consent of the Parliament of Northern Ireland. It was a promise which gave Unionists a sense of belonging which lasted for over twenty years.

It was not until the late 1950s, when there was a resurgence of terrorist activity against Ulster and the IRA showed signs of trying to enforce in practice the take-over of the Province which the Dublin Government had been irresponsibly preaching in theory, that Mr Costello and Mr de Valera began to take a more conciliatory stance and to preach co-operation between the two parts of Ireland. I said then that a gesture of good faith was required, and I proposed an extradition agreement which would prevent terrorists using the Republic as a base from which to mount attacks on Northern Ireland, as they were then doing. But this was not acceptable in Dublin.

I think that in those days, before cross-border contacts became fashionable, I was one of the very few politicians in Ulster who had personal contact with Dublin politicians, and personal knowledge of the

Republic. My wife and I spent many holidays in the South, often cara-
vanning with the children in Achill or Connemara or Kerry. It was in
the early 1950s on a Fair Day in the village of Claremorris in County
Galway that I first met Mr Cosgrave, later Prime Minister (Taoiseach,
as the Dublin Premier is called in Gaelic) of the Republic. I had gone
to hear what he had to say at a political meeting in the square, and afterwards I went up to have a word with him and he invited me into the pub
for a drink. I also, of course, met and talked annually with most
members of the Southern Government in the President's box of the
Royal Dublin Society's Horse Show in August, before the present
trouble put an end to cross-border frivolities.

As a backbencher, my major concern was the social and industrial
issues confronting the Government. I made my maiden speech on the
closure of the County Down railway, a subject of serious concern to my
constituents. I also got involved in the then controversial subject of
education, only to end up being attacked by both sides. For a time I ran
a one-man campaign advocating the siting of one of the new atomic
energy plants in Northern Ireland to create employment. I was also
chairman of the Public Accounts Committee for a while.

Looking over the old Hansard accounts of Stormont debates I realize
that early in my political career I was quite dogmatic about anything
that smacked of Socialism. 'Socialism', I said, 'as a general creed is not
for the sturdy, independent Ulster men and women.' It is a view I still
hold. Nevertheless, I was probably more enthusiastic then about the
merits of unadulterated private enterprise for Northern Ireland than in
later years, after administrative experience of the problems involved at
the Ministry of Commerce.

My early views were certainly coloured by the working of the Ulster
Transport Authority, a particularly bad example of the effects of unnecessary State intervention. The existence of the UTA was not preventing the closure of railway routes, inadequate freight services and
continuing financial losses. It seemed to me that it was simply a huge
bureaucratic monopoly which was hindering the provision of an
efficient transport system. The *Daily Express* of 9 March 1956, gave me
an accolade flattering to a mere backbencher. It said I had 'triumphed
after seven years of parliamentary battling against the monopolistic
UTA, practically forcing the Government to admit his argument that
road transport can only pay under free enterprise'. Certainly the success
that followed the dissolution of the UTA made my point.

There was one event, in 1953, which was in retrospect a watershed
in my career, and sometimes I wonder what the future would have held

had I made another decision. I was asked to stand for the North Down constituency at Westminster. It was one of the few personal occasions in my life when I have been undecided about the right thing to do, and eventually—for if there is one thing I hate it is indecision—I asked the advice of my friend Brian Maginness, then the Stormont Minister of Home Affairs, and one of the wisest and most truly liberal men I have known. His advice was to stay in Northern Ireland because, as he put it, 'Stormont will remain the fulcrum of the political scene'. I took his advice, partly for the reasons he gave, and partly for domestic and business reasons.

At about the same time the Prime Minister asked me to become Parliamentary Secretary to the Ministry of Commerce. I regretfully turned down the offer, for much the same reasons that I had refused the seat at Westminster—the family business came first, and I did not think it was right to take on a job connected with industrial affairs while I was so closely involved in industry.

In 1956 I was offered and accepted the post of Chief Whip (officially Parliamentary Secretary to the Ministry of Finance) to the Unionist Party at Stormont. I had built up a wide knowledge of the party organization as a Young Unionist and as an active backbencher and in some ways I enjoyed the job. But the wheeling-and-dealing side of party politics is not, I think, something I am very good at. A lot of a Chief Whip's job is best done socializing in the Members' bar, and that is an irksome task if one is fortified only by orange juice.

While I was Chief Whip Ted Heath visited Stormont, I think for the first time, as my guest. He was then Conservative Chief Whip at Westminster and I was impressed by his sharpness of mind and force of personality. I knew he would be a force to be reckoned with in the Conservative Party. He gave me no reason to believe that he was anything but sympathetic to the Unionist point of view. I have an interesting series of photographs, the first taken on that occasion, the second when I was Minister of Commerce at Stormont and Ted Heath was President of the Board of Trade, and lastly when he was Prime Minister, and I was Prime Minister at Stormont. In each my hair has got a lot whiter, and Ted has got a little stouter.

I have never been one of those Ulster Unionists who frequented Conservative Party functions. In fact, the first time I went to a Conservative Party Conference was in 1972. My family background and business experience in Ulster had instilled in me a dislike of class-based politics. The Unionist Party had grown up as a community movement rather than a political organization, and it had retained much of its democratic all-class character. Opposition to socialism had not given me a 'management' attitude to industry. I was proud of the skills and industry of Ulster's wage earners because I knew them at first hand with their ability to adapt quickly to new techniques, and the speed with which they could turn out top-quality produce, and I said so frequently in public.

I looked on the link between the Conservative Party and the Ulster Unionist Party as important, but to me it was not so much based on doctrinaire Conservatism as on mutual interest. It existed because of the Conservative Party's historic commitment to the Union, and it continued because, as I said at the Ulster Unionist Council in 1949, 'It is the only Party that, through good times and bad, has stood by us.' The strong sense of patriotism which was such an important factor in Ulster was also seen as finding its expression through the Conservatives. That the party of those days also looked favourably on the Ulster link was made clear. Colonel Glover, then Vice-Chairman of the National Union of Conservative and Unionist Associations, said in Belfast that Ulster must remain 'one of the brightest jewels in the Queen's crown'. And in the run-up to the 1959 Westminster election Harold Macmillan sent a message to Northern Ireland which said, 'We are with you heart and soul in your determination to remain an integral part of the United Kingdom.' (Incidentally, Unionists won all twelve Northern Ireland seats.) Of all the politicians from Britain who spoke of or to the Ulster people I think Harold Macmillan was the one who most truly touched the right chord. I heard him on two occasions in Belfast, one a prepared speech and the other impromptu, and on each occasion he was given a deservedly rapturous reception.

In December 1959, I was asked by the Prime Minister to take on the Ministry of Home Affairs. I went to see him in his office when I accepted and he said to me, 'I will not interfere with the running of your Department, that is your responsibility. But I want you to keep me informed of any important decisions you take, and you can depend upon me to back you up.' This he did. One could not have asked for a more loyal or courageous chief. Lord Brookeborough had the ability to concentrate on things that were of importance; the detail he left to others. He got through his work efficiently because he knew how to delegate authority. But his greatest attribute was his ability to communicate with people. He was one of the Establishment, a soldier by vocation and a gentleman by birth. He found it as easy to talk to a welder in the shipyard as a man farming thirty acres in his own County Fermanagh.

I came to the Ministry of Home Affairs at a time when the IRA was engaged in a six-year campaign against Northern Ireland, largely in the border areas. The terrorist activity never spread to Belfast, nor did it draw any appreciable support from the Catholic community. The Ulster Special Constabulary (the 'B' Specials or USC) played a very large part in putting down this campaign. They were able to operate effectively because the campaign was confined to the countryside, where their local knowledge and vigilance were valuable, and where they could quickly operate road blocks in an emergency. In those days too, the Royal Ulster Constabulary was in the front line and suffered casualties which seemed to us tragically heavy. But the vital factor in stamping out terrorism, and one lacking in the present campaign, was the introduction of internment by the Government in Dublin parallel with its introduction in Northern Ireland and prompt co-operation between the gardai and the RUC.

The relationship between Stormont and Westminster at this time makes an interesting contrast with the one which developed later. As Minister of Home Affairs I was in charge of the counter-terrorist measures. Westminster was helpful and co-operative at all times, providing troops when they were needed for a particular operation, and making various representations to Dublin. But its role was very much a supportive one, standing aside from the day-to-day decisions.

One recurring problem for all Ministers of Home Affairs at Stormont was what to do about marches. Marches have always been an important part of politics and cultural traditions in Ireland, just as in some parts of Britain. In Ulster the Orange marches were an assertion of the Protestant and British tradition of the majority and as such were unwelcome in predominantly nationalist areas. One of my predecessors in the office said years ago that the Minister of Home Affairs couldn't be popular if he were the Archangel Gabriel himself. Certainly the exigencies of that office gave a man a tough, uncompromising, hard-line image with all those who disagreed with him, and that was usually at some time or other both sections of the Ulster population. My own attitude to parades was always that the advice of the security forces should be followed, for it is the prime responsibility of government to see that peace and order is maintained. On that basis I supported a ban by my predecessor in Home Affairs on an Orange march in Dungiven, a largely Catholic town in County Londonderry, in 1959, and authorized one the following year, when it was a parade to a religious service. So I found myself under attack by Orange militants as an appeaser of Republicans one year, and by Republicans as an Orange bigot the next.

In my own case the situation with regard to marches was sharpened by the experience of the 'Longstone Road' which has now passed into Ulster folk-lore. In the mountains of Mourne there is a country by-way known locally as the Longstone Road. Orangemen from one area wished to walk along it to link up with Orangemen from another area for their annual celebrations. The Nationalists who lived between strongly opposed the idea. As a result the parade was banned in 1952 and 1953, on police advice, and although personally I found the attitude of those who were preventing the march by threat of force offensive, I supported the ban and urged that it should be observed. When, in 1955, a decision was taken that the parade should be allowed to take place I walked in it and it passed off peacefully, under police escort, although Republicans had planted bombs the night before to blow up the famous Longstone after which the road was named. Of such things are legends made in Ireland, North and South.

During my time at Home Affairs I had the privilege of many contacts with Rab Butler, then Home Secretary. I remember seeking his advice on one of the more awesome tasks of my post—recommending to the Northern Ireland Cabinet whether to grant a reprieve to those sentenced to death (in Britain this was the responsibility of the Home Secretary alone). He told me that when he had to make decisions—several times each year—he locked himself away for forty-eight hours and read all the relevant papers. Once he had made up his mind he never allowed himself to have any regrets because he had simply been carrying out the law. But he never allowed himself to forget the responsibility involved. On the mantlepiece in his office there was always a list of those awaiting execution. I adopted a similar approach on the four occasions when this problem faced me. Two were reprieved and two were not. They were the four most difficult decisions I have ever taken, but I am convinced they were right. They helped me to learn the importance in public life of never going back on what one has done. I have never believed that society should abandon the use of the ultimate sanction, capital punishment, when the safety of its citizens is at stake.

Looking back on this period and on our attitude in the Stormont Parliament, two things stand out in my mind. First that we as a government and as a party sincerely did our best to serve the province of Northern Ireland through eighteen very difficult post-war years. It was not a period of political compromise and harsh things were said and done on both sides. But at a time when Northern Ireland was under attack both political and physical, a remarkable degree of peace and stability was maintained, and much was done to improve the material well-being of all the people.

The second thing is that we were too absorbed in our own affairs. The only real contacts with Westminster were ministerial. There was precious little other contact because Westminster was not interested in Northern Ireland and, similarly, Northern Ireland was not very interested in Westminster. The important place politically was Stormont. And I think that was a mistake, a weakness. It led politicians in Northern Ireland into illusions of self-sufficiency, of taking part in a sovereign parliament. It created unspoken separatist tendencies. It also meant that the crisis of 1969 hit an unprepared Westminster right between the eyes. Both sides must accept some responsibility for that situation.

4
Department of Commerce

The resignation of the Prime Minister, Lord Brookeborough, in 1963 came as a surprise. As far as I know it was for medical reasons, though the political pressure he had been under in preceding months may have contributed to his sudden illness. Some people, including Unionist MP Phelim O'Neill, later the leader of the Alliance Party, had been pressing publicly for a change of leader on the grounds that a more modern personality was required. But this view was not widely shared in the party, and I felt that Lord Brookeborough's dominance of the political scene and strong popular support were not things the party was ready to dispense with.

The problems caused by Lord Brookeborough's departure were sharpened by the tragic deaths of two of Ulster's most outstanding senior Unionists in the preceding years. Maynard Sinclair, Minister of Finance and effectively Deputy Prime Minister, was one of 129 people drowned when the *Princess Victoria*, the Stranraer–Larne ferry, sank off the Copeland Islands during a storm in 1953. He had been in Stormont since the late 1930s and was a highly respected and popular politician who would have been the natural successor to the Prime Minister. His death was not only a political loss. The loss also of his financial expertise and close relations with the Treasury in London was a blow to the workings of government from which it took some years to recover.

William Morrison May, a man of outstanding ability and drive, died in 1962. He entered Stormont in the same election as myself and from the neighbouring constituency of Ards. We became close friends and colleagues, making our maiden speeches on the same day on the same subject and forming a hard-working backbench partnership on financial and commercial matters which kept the Ministers on their toes. I am sure that, had he lived, he would have become Leader of the Unionist Party and Prime Minister of Northern Ireland. The deaths of those two men, both in their fifties and both with the capacity for leadership, were tragic for the Province.

I first heard the news of Lord Brookeborough's resignation when Sir Arthur Kelly, then Secretary to the Cabinet, asked me to see him and said that the Prime Minister would shortly be tendering his resignation to the Governor and indicating that his successor would be Terence O'Neill. Many different versions of how he came to be chosen have been given subsequently. The fact that the Leader emerged by a consultative process, as was done in the Conservative Party at that time, rather than by a democratic election from the Parliamentary Party, added to the speculation. Clearly, the three key figures involved were the Prime Minister, the Governor, and the then Chief Whip, Bill Craig. The last did much to ensure O'Neill's appointment and the two were close allies for some years after. But who exactly gave the decisive advice has never been made clear, though it is now well known that the three names considered were Jack Andrews, son of Lord Brookeborough's predecessor, Terence O'Neill, and myself.

I had no pretensions to the Premiership; the idea had simply not entered my mind as an immediate possibility for consideration. At that time the Ministry of Home Affairs absorbed all my activities and energies, as has always been the case with any department under my charge. To do the job properly needed single-minded concentration, and there was no time for things which were not of immediate importance. I assumed that when Brookeborough went Jack Andrews, who was widely liked, would take over. Neither I, nor many others, had thought of O'Neill as the next Premier. He was at that time the Minister of Finance, and had been in the Cabinet for seven or eight years, but he had made no real political impact and had no obvious political base. His main public activity was in the annual meetings of the World Bank, at one of which he struck up a relationship with Dr T. K. Whittaker who was to become an important Dublin contact for him. After he became Prime Minister Terence was, I think, very conscious of his political weakness and of the stronger political following in the Province which both Jack Andrews and I had.

On the day he became Prime Minister, Terence O'Neill asked me to call to see him. He told me first that he had asked Jack Andrews to be his Deputy and to take charge of the Ministry of Finance, but that I could have the choice of becoming Minister of Commerce or staying on as Minister of Home Affairs. He added that if I opted for Commerce he would ask me to take on the appointment in six months time, as he would like to take over that Ministry himself temporarily in order to familiarize himself with matters of industrial development. I said that I would like to take on the Ministry of Commerce, but that a six-month delay would not be reasonable as it would put me into a sort of limbo and waste time. About an hour later he rang my office and said that he was agreeable to my taking on Commerce immediately but he was not yet ready to appoint someone to Home Affairs. So I ended up holding the two posts briefly until the appointment of Bill Craig to Home Affairs.

The Ministry of Commerce seemed to be the job for which most of my working life had been a preparation. I had learned the weaknesses and the strengths of industry in Ulster at first hand during my twenty-two years in the family firm in Belfast and had travelled the world studying new techniques and searching out new markets. I began work with optimism, believing that I could help to develop the modern go-ahead Province emerging in the 1960s into a soundly based industrial economy.

Ulster's major asset has always been its people; on their resourcefulness and common sense our prosperity has always depended. We have few natural resources and there is a sea barrier between us and our major markets in Britain and Europe. By 1963 linen and shipbuilding, two of the major industries on which our position as the industrial part of Ireland (the 'Black North' some Southerners called us) had been based, were declining in terms of employment. In addition, people were leaving the land at the rate of about two thousand a year as agriculture, the other major industry, became mechanized and farms became larger. Diversification was urgently needed and, although a good start had been made in synthetic fibres by the attraction of firms such as Du Pont and Enkalon, much more needed to be done if we were to provide employment for those leaving the old industries, and to meet the needs of one of the most rapidly increasing populations in Western Europe.

The old saying that 'when the British economy sneezes Ulster catches pneumonia' had proved all too true in the past. In the 1930s unemployment had been running at around 20 per cent, sometimes rising as high as 25 per cent. By the 1950s it had come down to an average of around $7\frac{1}{2}$ per cent, but this was still far too high, and if we did not act it could rise higher again.

So it was obvious that a hard selling job needed to be done to attract new industries. We had to examine what exactly our assets were, ensure that they were properly developed, decide what financial assistance the Government should provide and then set about convincing industrialists all over the world that Northern Ireland was the kind of place in which they could profitably invest.

The working people of Ulster, both management and labour, were its major asset because in the 1960s no other part of Europe—except, perhaps, Southern Italy which was not a competitor then and Scotland which was a serious competitor—had immediately available the quantity and quality of workers we had in Northern Ireland, many of them, both male and female, with industrial experience and quickly adaptable to new techniques. So we rapidly set about consolidating this valuable asset, setting up government training centres providing by 1969 over two thousand places for trainees, and schemes well ahead of those anywhere else in the United Kingdom.

Coupled with this, and essential to our success, were the excellent industrial relations existing on the shop floor. As an industrialist I had good relations with the trade unions, and as Minister of Commerce I was able to build on my personal contacts with the leaders. In 1964 I almost got my fingers burned on the subject of recognition of the Northern Ireland Committee of the Irish Congress of Trade Unions by the Northern Ireland Government. O'Neill had continually postponed meetings with a deputation from the Committee and during his absence on holiday I unwisely allowed myself to be persuaded by his staff to see them. I told them what the Government line then was—that we recognized all branches of British trade unions operating in the Province, but not the Northern Ireland Committee as it was an adjunct of a Dublin trade union organization. But shortly after this the Government decided to change its policy and to recognize the Northern Ireland Committee, which had become almost autonomous. The Northern Ireland Labour Party was still a relatively small party with only four MPs at Stormont, but it had increased its support and was providing a useful— though not always very co-operative—constitutional opposition, and O'Neill was very anxious to prevent it attracting any further support. My relatively recent meeting with the deputation provided a useful stick for my critics, not all of whom were outside the party, but it never seriously damaged my relations with the unions.

In 1965 we set up the Economic Council, consisting of management, unions and government and with myself as its first chairman. It was a real step forward which helped to strengthen our happy record as a place where industrial disputes were rare and where all sides worked together to achieve prosperity. The leadership of trade unionists such as Billy Blease, Norman Kennedy and many others, men dedicated to the welfare of their members rather than any political dogma, produced a constructive relationship which meant that Ulster did not want and did not need the Industrial Relations Act applied to Great Britain in 1972. To these trade unionists much of the credit for the success achieved during these years rightfully belongs.

In 1954 the Northern Ireland Government had recognized that, even with these assets, financial inducements were necessary to offset the geographical disadvantages of our situation, and had passed the Capital Grants to Industry Act, which was a broadly based measure designed to give assistance to industry to encourage new buildings and machinery. This was a pioneering measure in the United Kingdom, since it came into effect several years before there was similar legislation for any part of Britain. Soon we were building advance factories in areas where employment was needed, so that firms coming to Northern Ireland could move right in and start production with a minimum of delay, and this practice has since been expanded. We tried to ensure that capital incentives for investment in Northern Ireland were more flexible and more attractive than for any other region in the United Kingdom or indeed in Western Europe. Thanks largely to the advantages of a devolved regional Parliament—which provided industrialists with ready access to the responsible Minister and with quick decisions—and thanks also to a helpful sovereign Parliament at Westminster this is what we succeeded in doing.

In all my relationships with the Labour Government, I found them concerned to contribute to the welfare of the people in Northern Ireland. I first met George Brown about twenty-four hours after he had been appointed as Secretary of State at the Department of Economic Affairs in 1964. I went over to London to see him. After our discussions, he said, 'Now tell me, have you met any of my colleagues in this government?' When I told him I had not yet had the pleasure, he said, 'Oh well you must certainly do so.' He tapped on his desk intercom and said, 'Ask Jim to join us,' and a few minutes later James Callaghan, then Chancellor of the Exchequer, came in. 'Now let's have the President of the Board of Trade,' said George Brown, tapping in his intercom again, and in came Douglas Jay. In the space of about fifteen minutes I had been introduced to the Chancellor of the Exchequer, the President of the Board of Trade, the Head of the DEA, and one or two junior Ministers; I was very impressed with George Brown's apparent ability to call them with the flick of a switch on his desk! I felt he was doing this for two reasons; first, because he wanted to give me a good success story of entrée to the Labour Government with which to return to Northern Ireland but, more importantly, because he was anxious that there should be a good working relationship between Stormont and Westminster. I appreciated it on both levels.

I particularly remember a visit to Northern Ireland by Roy Jenkins, then the Minister of Aviation. Naturally, the main part of his visit was an extensive tour of the Belfast aircraft factories of Short Brothers, during which I accompanied him. At the time Shorts were building the Skyvan aircraft, and the Managing Director, Bob Harvey, asked Roy Jenkins and I if we would like to go for a flight in the plane. So we took off—three of us plus the pilot—and flew across Belfast Lough and up County Antrim as far as Larne before returning to the base at Sydenham. As we got out of the plane, I turned to Harvey and said, 'That was very pleasant, she seems to go very nicely.' He replied with a smile, 'Yes, and it will be even better when we get our certificate of airworthiness!' Roy maintained his usual unruffled appearance, but I dare say it may have been his first flight in an aircraft without a certificate of airworthiness! Subsequently, the Skyvan aircraft has done very well commercially and has earned a high reputation for safety.

As Minister of Commerce I tried to inject new momentum into the job-getting drive and to direct our effort into new expanding industrial fields. I had always thought it would be tremendous if we could manufacture motor cars and farm vehicles in Northern Ireland, and it was generally agreed at the Ministry that we needed more engineering industry. However, I quickly realized that the manufacture of car components must come before the manufacture of cars, so I concentrated first on the components industry.

I went to see Henry Ford at Detroit, spending a day with him touring his production lines and holding discussions in his palatial office situated in the heart of the Ford engineering complex. He was a big, reserved man with an encyclopaedic knowledge of his world-wide operations. We had lunch in a private dining-room attached to the office. During it he turned to the British Consul-General, who had also been invited, and said, 'I am right, am I not, in thinking that Northern Ireland has the status of a British Dominion?' The Consul hastened to point out that Northern Ireland was an integral part of the United Kingdom, but the question did illustrate to me how much the Province was seen as a separate entity. I did eventually persuade Henry Ford to open a factory in Ulster, and this factory still supplies, I believe, all the carburettors and distributors for European and British Fords, and has recently announced a £2½ million expansion.

Goodyear was another 'blue chip' American firm which came to Ulster in 1966, after long negotiations, opening an important factory at Craigavon which is still one of the largest in the Province. I was led to understand at the conclusion of these negotiations that if I ever decided to get out of politics the Chairman of Goodyear would have a job waiting for me. This was quite flattering but I made it clear that I had no intention of quitting politics.*

The long hush-hush negotiations with Rolls-Royce constituted one of the most dramatic episodes of my time at Commerce. Rolls-Royce insisted on the secrecy for their own reasons and we were not interested in quibbling if it was going to bring a major world firm to Northern Ireland. It was known in the Ministry only as 'Firm X' and its file was marked with this code.

Until I announced the successful conclusion of the negotiations at Stormont one Thursday afternoon no one in Northern Ireland, other than myself and three senior men at Commerce, knew the name of the firm with whom we were negotiating. It was a doubly memorable day for me because I was also, as Master of the Iveagh Hunt, parading the hounds at the Royal Agricultural Society's Annual Show in Belfast. Although Thursday was a Parliamentary day I had taken some trouble to ensure that no questions were put down to me, because it was an occasion which only came round to each Hunt every ninth year. The Nationalists had proved very understanding and agreed to co-operate. But when I returned to the collecting ring after parading the hounds I found a message from my Private Secretary saying that Rolls-Royce was ready to go public. I rushed back to Stormont in my riding gear, pulled on a jacket and tie and a pair of trousers over my breeches and boots, entered the House and, with the permission of the Speaker, intervened in the debate to announce our coup. All sides of the House were delighted at the news which seemed to augur well for the future. An aircraft engine parts factory subsequently opened at Dundonald, near Belfast, employing about a thousand men.

Before I became Minister of Commerce, most of our industrial drive had been directed towards Britain and the USA—we had an industrial development office in New York. I felt that Germany, a country where there were already around two million foreign workers and where industry was expanding very rapidly, was an obvious source for future investment. So I visited it regularly, meeting the Minister for Economics, and established an industrial development office with a

* After his retirement from active politics in 1976 Lord Faulkner became re-involved in industrial affairs and, among other things, was acting as European consultant for Goodyear International. It was around this time too that Goodyear announced they were making Northern Ireland the headquarters of their European operations.

Ministry of Commerce representative to spearhead our drive. It was a success resulting in the build-up of about twenty German firms in Ulster, employing thousands of people. I also visited ministers in Switzerland and the Benelux countries and generally got a European development programme going.

All these industrial promotion trips naturally involved me in a great deal of moving around; I was travelling all over the USA at least once every year, and visited industrialists and officials in Europe several times each year. I travelled over 150,000 miles in my first three years—the equivalent of six times around the globe—and became pretty accustomed to all shapes and sizes of aeroplanes in the process. On one occasion when Harry Jones, the Permanent Secretary, and I were returning from Frankfurt in Germany the plane suddenly dived down very steeply about ten minutes after taking off. We were disputing the name of the river we seemed to be heading towards when there was an announcement asking everyone to remove their shoes. Soon we saw Cologne airport below and we landed very fast, skidding to a halt as firetenders and police cars raced towards us. Only when the stewards were directing us out of the emergency exits did they tell us there was a bomb scare—intending, no doubt to speed up our departure. But Harry Jones objected strongly when he was told to throw out his shoes and brief-case before sliding down the emergency chute. He had a bottle of duty-free Scotch which he was reluctant to see smashed, bomb or no bomb! I hastily urged him to agree and the Scotch survived the fall. Three hours and much searching later it was declared a bomb hoax and we continued safely on our journey. I never discovered if the hoax was connected with our presence on the plane.

I have a day's diary entry here from one of our visits to Germany. Before breakfast—which is particularly unkind—I was phoned by BBC Northern Ireland for their current affairs programme for a progress report on the visit. Immediately after breakfast I went off to visit a manufacturing company situated some distance away, to inspect their plant and have a discussion with the Directors, who were interested in investing in Northern Ireland. I came back again for lunch with a representative group of businessmen from the Chamber of Commerce and Industry, bankers, planning consultants, and economic journalists, and afterwards gave a speech on Ulster's industrial incentives. Then there were interviews for German television and radio stations, an interview on Northern Ireland affairs for one of the American television networks and off I went to catch a flight for the next city on our itinerary. There we drove out to a firm I had previously visited, this time to sign the contract—it is now manufacturing machinery in Craigavon—and afterwards I had a series of interviews with the local press. Then dinner, with a group of journalists from the trade press, and before bed the only moments of relaxation in the day: fifteen minutes' walk round the deserted city centre at midnight for a breath of fresh air. It was hard going, but exhilarating and satisfying work.

I have always been anxious to get home, often taking a chance on being held up when the weather forecasts were not too good, rather than spending another night away and waiting for a plane next morning. Sometimes we were unlucky. One night, because of fog at Aldergrove, we were diverted to Dublin where the airport authorities, as always, went out of their way to facilitate me, and a car with a driver from the Garda Siocanna (the Irish police force) was organized to take us home. However, I thought this was an imposition on the driver, so I asked him to stop at the Garda station as we passed through one of the villages on the road north so that I could phone for an RUC car to meet us at the border. I got out of the car and knocked, and after a longish wait a large sergeant opened the door and said off-handedly, 'Yes?' I said: 'I'm Brian Faulkner, the Northern Ireland Minister of Commerce.' 'You are, are you!' said he, in obvious disbelief, then, peering closer at me in the darkness, 'By God, you are too! Come on in, sure isn't it great to see you!'

Often the investment decisions rested on a knife edge, with firms on the brink of establishing a factory somewhere else, so we were prepared to go fairly far to get them to Northern Ireland. It was a matter of stitching together a package most suited to the needs of a particular firm and our flexibility gave us an edge over most competitors. Small things, such as the speedy provision of houses for key workers could turn out to be extremely important and our closely knit administrative structure allowed us to react effectively. An elaborate computer game preceded the decision of one major European firm to come to Northern Ireland. Its corporate planning department had collected data on all the possible locations for new investment and over two nail-biting days this was all fed in to the firm's computer to see which location came out best. We were the only competitor with a Ministry of Commerce official on the spot monitoring the feed-in, and I was able to approve personally any modifications in the original package which seemed appropriate.

It was very satisfying to see so many well-known firms investing in Northern Ireland: Courtaulds and Rolls-Royce from Britain, Hoechst and Grundig from Germany, Goodyear and Ford from the USA. But it was equally satisfactory and at least as important to have attracted a greater number of smaller and less well-known firms from Europe and Britain. We needed to avoid simply transferring all our eggs from one basket to another, and these smaller firms were essential to a broadening of the industrial base.

This economic strategy was not without its critics, of course. Some people, such as the Northern Ireland Labour Party, wanted more strings attached to government aid, and pointed to cases of firms which had taken assistance and then failed completely or closed down after a few years. Naturally, these dangers concerned me greatly too, but I was taking calculated risks which were well worth while so long as the failure rate in new industries kept below five per cent, which it did consistently. A *Daily Express* article in February 1967 described me as a 'big spender' who had been touring the world in the past four years 'putting out money in the cause of posterity'. But, as I told the reporter who wrote the article, 'unless we take risks we won't get new industries. Other government departments are not taking the same sort of risks; we are, as it were, peering into the future.' If we were going to tie up assistance with all kinds of conditions we would be in danger of killing the goose that laid the golden egg; we had to avoid abuse of the generous assistance to industries while keeping the terms free enough to make our location attractive.

There were doctrinaire critics who objected to capitalists getting government money in the first place, and advocated as the panacea state-sponsored industries. The government attitude to this was very open-minded and absolutely non-doctrinaire; if it could be shown that there was a possibility of developing any resource and providing employment through state industry we would give it our backing. We did in fact hold extensive enquiries into the practicality of such projects for the sugar-beet industry and for peat production. Bord Na Mona, the Irish Turf Board from Dublin, lent us their expertise to look at the possibility of developing our peat resources, and it soon became clear that this would not be a viable project. Although we were keen to encourage local initiative we knew that it must be a slow process and that, though it should go ahead, we needed large investments quickly on a scale which local enterprise could not yet offer. We acted to preserve employment in the huge Belfast shipyard Harland and Wolff, which went through extensive re-equipping and modernization with the aid of government money. But it is worth noting that at this time public expenditure per head in Northern Ireland was lower than in both Wales and Scotland.

By 1966, our development programme was well under way and showing every sign of being a complete success. Our figures for new jobs promoted rose from 5,000 a year in 1963 to 8,000 in 1965, and there was good reason to believe that the five-year target of 30,000 jobs in manufacturing set out in the 1964 Development Plan by Professor Wilson of Glasgow University would be exceeded. In 1965 too unemployment dropped to $5\frac{1}{2}$ per cent, our lowest figure for many years. Unfortunately the economic problems which hit the United Kingdom in the late 1960s affected Northern Ireland and slowed our rate of expansion right down, while the American investment curb in 1968 reduced investment from there. Unemployment rose again to over 7 per cent and O'Neill and I had to go over to London to secure financial assistance from Callaghan. The political upheaval of 1968/9 coming on top of this was the last thing we needed when we were beginning to reverse the drop in new jobs once again.

In spite of all these difficulties we did reach a figure of 29,000 new jobs in manufacturing during the period of the Development Plan, a very real achievement. And, of course, these jobs generated new jobs in service industries. Thus even given the temporary economic problems we would have had good reason to look forward to the future with real optimism at the end of the 1960s. We had created a soundly based and diversified economy. The old declining industries were now relatively less important and could be expected to contract less in terms of employment. The training schemes were starting to pay off. As the economic consultants who prepared the 1970–5 Development Plan put it, 'If... Ulster had been able to maintain and consolidate a new reputation for political tranquillity in a world where there is so much disorder, her economic future would have begun to look vastly more promising.'

A speech at Ulster Week in Leeds in 1966 summed up my view of the Northern Ireland economy:

We want you to learn that here is a community proud to be British and leading a busy productive life. Our farms and factories are as much a part of the economic muscle of the country as the mills of Yorkshire. We export linen and whisky, ships and missiles, optical lenses and oil drills, playing a full part in the economic struggle for prosperity which is vital to every citizen in Britain.

5
Civil Rights

In the summer of 1964 the Prime Minister carried out a wide-ranging
Cabinet reshuffle and reorganization of departments. I was on a ten-
day holiday in Majorca at the time, blissfully ignorant of everything
that was happening in Ireland and, so I thought, out of reach of the
constant telephone calls which are an integral part of any Minister's
life. This rosy view of the situation was rudely shattered when an
attendant approached me on the beach one day to say that there was
a phone call at the beach kiosk. Fearing some catastrophe I hurried
to take it.

John Whitlaw, my Private Secretary, was on the line to say that
the Prime Minister had made sweeping changes but that my Ministry
did not appear to be much affected. The major change was the creation of a new Ministry of Development to modernize the approach
to environmental planning, urban development, and local government
(similar to the Department of the Environment later set up in Britain).
Bill Craig was to be put in charge of what was obviously a pretty high-
powered Ministry, and his role was heralded in the press as that of
a new 'supremo'. There did appear to be some suggestion that his role
in the new urban 'growth centres' might encroach on that of the
Ministry of Commerce—though this suggestion never materialized.
In addition, Jack Andrews, the Deputy Prime Minister, was being
made Leader of the Senate, a Cabinet post which carried little political
muscle. It meant he had to resign his seat in the Commons and be
elected to the Senate. I thought it was simply a manœuvre to demobil-
ize Jack Andrews politically and I was sorry he accepted it.

Conscious as I was of O'Neill's concern for his political position
I did my best several times to assure him that I wanted to work with
him rather than undermine his position. He always said that he
accepted this, but the temperature of our relationship varied greatly
and the favourable publicity I received as Minister of Commerce

seemed to worry him. Sometimes we seemed to be getting on very well and his attitude was friendly and helpful. Once at a Cabinet meeting shortly after his return from a trip to the USA he turned to me and said quietly, 'I saw this in New York and thought it might be useful to you.' It was a refill for a particular kind of ball-point pen which I had bought on a previous trip to New York, and he must have realized that I could not get one on this side of the Atlantic. That kind of small thoughtful gesture encouraged me to believe that our relationship was improving, but then he would take some high-handed action which created suspicion between us.

One day in January 1965 at about 1 p.m. I was sitting in my office at Stormont working when the telephone rang. It was Cecil Bateman, then Secretary to the Cabinet, and he said, 'The Prime Minister is at the moment having lunch with Sean Lemass in Stormont House. He would like you to come over at three o'clock and meet him.' I think I said, 'You must be joking!' He soon convinced me that he was quite serious, and I arrived at the appointed hour to have tea and buns with the Taoiseach. I had met him before during my visits to the Dublin Horse Show, but it was the first meeting for most of my colleagues and it was the first visit to Stormont by a Premier of the Republic.

I welcomed the fact that this meeting was taking place; in fact I had put before the Cabinet a few days previously a proposal that I should go to Dublin to meet the Minister responsible for tourism (at that time Erskine Childers, late President of the Republic) and discuss co-operation on tourism on an all-Ireland basis. The Cabinet had agreed to this visit, which took place shortly after the Lemass meeting and led to valuable agreements on tourism and an electricity grid link-up. But these practical achievements had already been overshadowed and, in retrospect, somewhat undermined by the political upheaval over the surprise visit of Lemass to Belfast.

I did object to the manner in which this visit was arranged, particularly the lack of trust in his colleagues which O'Neill's failure to consult them seemed to indicate. The cloak-and-dagger atmosphere fed inevitable popular suspicions of any dealings with the Republic and gave Reverend Ian Paisley, at this time emerging as a politico-religious demagogue, an easy issue to exploit. Lemass was a moderate man with whom we should have been able to strike up a mutually useful relationship which could end the Cold War between North and South initiated by de Valera, but the lack of consultation or public preparation made the whole affair seem furtive and suspect. I think it is probably true to say that it started the slide away of support for O'Neill within the Unionist community which ended with his resignation in 1969. He fought back by representing all his critics as shell-backed reactionaries, and the scene was set for the bitterly divisive and unproductive split in the Unionist Party during the last few years of the 1960s.

Terence spent a lot of his time manœuvring politically and one constantly felt the need to tread warily. Too many rows with his Ministers and his backbenchers seemed to come to a head when they might have been avoided. Early in April 1965 he asked the Parliamentary Party for a vote of confidence, which was given, though there was some straight talking at the meeting. I spoke in support of the motion, stressing my continuing loyalty to O'Neill and saying quite frankly that many of his problems arose from lack of consultation. Afterwards he thanked me for my support.

A few days later there was a clash between the Prime Minister and Ivan Neill, then Minister of Finance and Leader of the House, which resulted in the latter being sacked as Leader of the House. I was pressed to take on the job and, though I was reluctant to accept because my frequent trips abroad would make it difficult to attend the House regularly, I eventually did so. When Neill resigned as Minister of Finance the Prime Minister pressed me to take this post too. I told him I appreciated being offered what was technically the most senior Ministry and was normally run by the Deputy Prime Minister but that I was deeply involved in important negotiations at Commerce and felt that I would find the much less active ministerial role at Finance very frustrating. I said I would like to be his Deputy, but suggested that I could do this and still stay at Commerce. We agreed to think it over.

That evening I was having dinner with Roy Mason, then visiting the Province as President of the Board of Trade, and was interrupted by a phone call from Cecil Bateman. He tried to persuade me to accept O'Neill's offer but I told him I was very happy at Commerce. Next morning the Prime Minister phoned me and we agreed that I would stay at Commerce, but become Deputy Prime Minister.

In September 1966 there was a major leadership crisis which brought to the surface many of the tensions which had been simmering in the party since Lord Brookeborough's resignation. A group of backbenchers, led by Desmond Boal, MP for Shankill, moved to oust O'Neill from the Leadership. They asked me to resign and spearhead the move, but I refused. They then asked whether I would take on the leadership of the party if asked to do so. My reply was, 'Only if that is the wish of a majority of the Parliamentary Party.' They held various meetings before a group came down to see me at home one evening and tried to persuade me to resign and contest the leadership. Again I took the line that a change of leadership was a matter for the majority of the Parliamentary Party. I was supported in this by Harry West, who was visiting me with his wife. Harry argued strongly that O'Neill should be given a fair chance to prove himself. I think it was the next day that they showed me a list of names totalling one less than a majority of the party. If I resigned and opposed O'Neill there would be a majority against him, but I refused again. I had already notified the Chief Whip, James Chichester-Clark, that there were moves afoot to oust Terence, and he had simply thanked me and left it at that.

I left for the United States on a Ministry of Commerce visit, but the matter continued to develop in my absence and Terence held a Party Meeting at which he got majority support. Local journalists rang me in America when news of the crisis became public and asked if I supported the Prime Minister. I said I stood unequivocally behind the policies of the Prime Minister and the Government and was not interested in personalities. This was presented in the media as an ambiguous reply, and when I returned to Belfast, Terence told me he disapproved of it. He also said that he did not intend to stay on as Prime Minister indefinitely but only for a few years.

The aim of industrial development in Ulster was not only to create new jobs. We believed that by raising the general level of prosperity for everyone, by making it possible for all our citizens to have a secure job and thus a good house and a decent standard of living, the traditional divisions in our community would soften and become blurred. I believe that we almost succeeded. In fact we succeeded too well, for there were those who saw that with greater prosperity, and a greater gulf between living conditions north and south of the border, the United Ireland of their dreams was becoming more and more a mirage. In the 1960s there was greater interest in building a modern prosperous Northern Ireland, and more participation in that work by the minority community. People retained their basic constitutional outlook, pro- or anti-Union with Great Britain, but on both sides there was more and more willingness to get on with work for the welfare of the community at large.

Nationalists had traditionally shunned any part in the administration of Northern Ireland affairs. They boycotted all official functions and turned down appointments to public boards, or even as Resident Magistrates. Those who accepted such appointments were ostracized by the politically committed among their community. The Nationalist Party had refused to accept the title of 'Official Opposition' at Stormont and generally pursued the policy of obstruction outlined by its leader, Eddie McAteer, in a pamphlet called 'Irish Action' published in 1948. The religious element in the quarrel had been underlined by the refusal of the Catholic Church to appoint a chaplain to Stormont.

This sort of thing was beginning to break down in the 1960s, and after the Lemass visit in January 1965 the Nationalist Party took on the role of Official Opposition. O'Neill was making the main plank of his premiership the improvement of community relations, and I welcomed his efforts in this direction. But the methods he used were not always helpful to the cause. Flamboyant gestures were no substitute for real action and only raised hopes that were not being fulfilled. Eddie McAteer and I met for lunch after the Nationalists had become Official Opposition and he quizzed me as to whether or not Terence had any specific plans to give effect to the sentiments in his speeches. At a Unionist meeting in County Down in 1967 I made a speech referring to the 'change in the air', arguing that this could only 'strengthen the whole country, politically, socially and economically'. But I stressed that this should be 'a gradual process, developing deep roots, undisturbed by too much probing and not forced up by the spotlights'.

There was not only the danger of causing frustrations in the Nationalist community, there was the risk of provoking fears and a reaction against change among Unionists. The latter had long regarded the Nationalists as a wrecking fifth column in league with a neighbouring state which was trying to take over our territory, and some still believed they could not be trusted in positions of responsibility. Because of the overlap of political and religious differences, and because it was often more easy to identify someone's religion than his political views, this had led to some discrimination on a religious basis. Too much publicity about our wish to change this only fed the fears which Ian Paisley was beginning to exploit: fears that better North/South relations might undermine Ulster's position as part of the United Kingdom; fears that the South was only trying to find a new way of effecting its claim on our territory; fears aroused by the massive republican celebrations of the fiftieth anniversary of the 1916 Rising and the accompanying riots; and fears that the ecumenical movement was in Northern Ireland designed to reduce opposition to a takeover by the Catholic Irish Republic.

Paisley was busily building up his church by a blend of religious and political attacks on other church and political leaders in Ulster, and was stirring up old community antagonisms by a series of provocative marches and demonstrations. One of the most notorious of these took place outside the Presbyterian General Assembly in June 1968. The Governor, Lord Erskine, and his wife had been present, and when they and I were leaving together we found a mob jeering everyone emerging from the building, with Paisley calling on his followers (even then) to keep their loudest jeers for Brian Faulkner. All of us were infuriated and disgusted by this ugly display which was obviously designed to intimidate. I remember stopping in the street, folding my arms, and glaring angrily at the crowd. Lady Erskine subsequently took ill as a result of her experiences that evening.

As Minister of Commerce I got a two-fold view of these and similar events. As an Ulster politician I was well aware of the dangers of stirring up emotions and fears, dangers which were underlined by the murder of two Catholics in 1966 by a newly emerged band of thugs masquerading under the once honourable title of the Ulster Volunteer Force. But as a representative of the Province who travelled abroad seeking to attract industrialists to a modern go-ahead Ulster I was acutely aware of how badly these ugly events were affecting our image. Ian Paisley and I were basically in competition—he was travelling the world seeking (and gaining) notoriety for his anti-papist views, while I was seeking to highlight the increasingly forward-looking attitudes of most Ulstermen. He was an easy target for the media; he became for them the stage Ulsterman, but without the affectionate indulgence granted to his Southern counterpart. As I said in a speech at the time, 'The actions of so few can reflect ignominy and shame on so many...'

These tensions in a period of change were also seen in the Orange Order. Phelim O'Neill MP was expelled from the Order by a narrow majority because he had attended a Catholic funeral service. This was surprising since Orangemen in the country have always been in the habit of attending the funerals of their Catholic neighbours, as I do myself, and I had never known anyone to be expelled for it. The decision gave further ammunition to the critics of Unionism, as most leading Unionists were also Orangemen. On an Orange platform on the 'Twelfth'—the big annual celebration of the Battle of the Boyne by the Orange Order when some hundred thousand people marched in what had become Ulster's major folk festival—I said: 'It is up to all of us to say quite clearly to our fellow citizens that tolerance is one of the fundamental tenets of Orangeism', that the Battle of the Boyne was fought to ensure freedom throughout Europe, and that 'William of Orange was a liberal and enlightened monarch and this is what we mean by (the slogan) "Remember 1690".' I remember being very encouraged by the good reaction from the huge crowd listening to the speeches that day. It is hard for people outside Ulster to realize it now, but general relations between the communities had never been so good. On that particular day in my own constituency decorations put up by the Orangemen were left, by prior arrangement, for the Catholic community's celebrations a few weeks later.

The question of Catholics wishing to identify with support for the Union by joining the Unionist Party became an issue in the latter half of the 1960s. In 1959 and 1960 it had received an airing when a lot of publicity was given to a speech made by the Chairman of the Standing Committee, Sir Clarence Graham, and backed up by Brian Maginness MP. Violence-orientated Republican politicians (Sinn Feiners), who had won considerable Catholic support in the early 1950s, had by 1959, when the IRA campaign was in operation, lost most of that support to constitutional Nationalists. Some people were so euphoric about this that they seemed to think it meant the Catholic community were ready to vote solidly Unionist. I regarded it as a 'phony' issue and said so. It did not seem likely to help moderation among Nationalists if we suggested that opposing Sinn Fein was tantamount to being a Unionist. But as the 1960s went on it became clear this was something we ought to be thinking about. The evident economic progress of the Province, the benefits brought by the British link, and the healing properties of time itself were leading to a new willingness among many Catholics to consider voting Unionist. The figures in my own constituency in the 1965 election proved conclusively for the first time that there at least many had done so.

The 'troubles' came to Ulster at the end of two decades of accelerating prosperity. On almost every economic index our performance in the 1950s and 1960s was well in advance of that for the rest of the United Kingdom—gross domestic product, industrial production, productivity and real income were all rising rapidly. This prosperity was fully shared among all our citizens, Catholic and Protestant, Unionist and Nationalist. Throughout my six years at the Ministry of Commerce there never was a single industrial decision taken on political grounds; practicality and need were the decisive factors in our calculations. Allegations that Nationalist areas were deliberately neglected are totally without any foundation in fact. There was actually government bias towards these areas: more generous financial inducements were available to firms prepared to go to the predominantly Catholic border areas such as Newry, Strabane and Londonderry than were available elsewhere.

The case of the Michelin Tyre factory illustrates both the truth of this claim, and the limitations of what the Government could actually do. Michelin had built one factory at the county town of Antrim and then decided to build another one in the Province. We specifically offered them one million pounds extra government assistance if they went to Londonderry, in order to get more male employment there. In spite of this, Michelin decided that it was in their interests to site the factory elsewhere and built it at the predominantly Protestant town of Ballymena, in County Antrim. The Government was, of course, accused of not really trying to get the factory for Londonderry, a shallow political criticism which I deeply resented.

We were quite successful in our efforts on behalf of Londonderry and 'the West'. Between 1964 and 1969 over 7,000 new jobs negotiated by the Government were brought to County Londonderry. As early as 1966 we were anticipating full employment in the city of Londonderry within a few years through industries already established or in the pipeline. These hopes received a set-back in 1967 when the Monarch Electric factories closed down suddenly, throwing 1,400 men out of work. But we went ahead seeking to attract other new industries to the North-West, succeeding with firms such as Molins and Courtaulds. After looking at these and many other facts the economic consultants who drew up the 1970–5 Development Plan concluded that 'the main facts about the period since 1964 do not support the view that the West has been neglected in public expenditure'.

The Government's decisions on a new 'Growth Centre' policy were sometimes claimed to show bias against Nationalist areas, and in particular the establishment of the new city of Craigavon in the centre of the Province. There was a silly row about Bill Craig's choice of the name Craigavon in memory of Ulster's first Premier, but I took no interest in it. The Growth Centre policy was the result of joint memos from the Departments of Commerce and Development. It was very important to our industrial strategy because there was no more space for industries in Belfast unless we abandoned the green belts, and the 'Matthew Stopline' was established to prevent that happening. We needed an alternative urban centre and it was generally thought that a population of 60,000–80,000 was necessary to attract major industries. Craigavon, Londonderry, and Antrim/Ballymena were named as our major Growth Centres. Craigavon was as far west as was reasonable to expect the necessary movement of population which it was designed to attract from both Belfast and from the South and West of the Province. It was another example of a straightforward planning and business decision which displeased certain political interests and was therefore misrepresented as sectarian.

The roots of our upheaval do not lie in economic and social deprivation. They lie rather in the increasing prosperity and the social strains so brought about. The old ineffective Nationalist 'farmers party' was being replaced by a new breed of Catholic leaders—teachers, lecturers, accountants, solicitors and businessmen.

This does not imply any complacency about the continued existence in some areas—both Protestant and Catholic—of unemployment and bad housing. Continued effort was necessary to provide a job and a good home for every citizen of Northern Ireland. But to understand how much progress had been made it is important to remember the amount of leeway Northern Ireland Governments have had to make up since the war. The inter-war years were years of severe depression and the Government had to spend vast sums on unemployment relief. The inflexibility of the financial relationship with Westminster meant that other expenditure had to be cut and so house building and industrial development were seriously neglected. As a result, post-war Unionist governments had to start from a much lower base-level than most other parts of the United Kingdom. It is this factor which largely explains the existence of an extremely high house-building rate (50 per cent of the population lives in post-war housing) alongside a comparatively high proportion of old and unfit housing, and the existence of high unemployment in spite of rapid industrial growth.

Prosperity is a relative thing, defined by experience or knowledge. So I return to the point that in the late 1960s people in Ulster, Protestant and Catholic, were more prosperous than ever before; they were all certainly much better off than any of them would have been in a united Ireland. A new Ulster of which we were immensely proud was emerging with the expansion of education, social services, housing and employment. Tourism was bringing increasing numbers of visitors to our shores. A first-class network of roads was opening up all parts of the Province to speedy travel. And the development of Growth

Centres was building up new communities and new traditions. We little thought that it was all going to blow up in our faces.

The year 1968 is usually seen as the beginning of the present 'troubles'. And the particular incident which marks off that tragic era is the Civil Rights Association (CRA) march in Londonderry on 5 October which attracted world-wide publicity. From that march and its violent confrontations followed marches and counter-marches, riots and counter-riots, bombings and counter-bombings, killings and counter-killings which have spread a tragic stain of blood across the face of Ulster society.

The Civil Rights Association began as an ostensibly non-sectarian body seeking to have rectified certain alleged grievances, but with no overall political views on the Ulster situation. It called for fair local government boundaries, abolition of the ratepayers franchise and company votes in local government, fair allocation of houses by local authorities, measures to prevent discrimination in employment, abolition of the Special Powers Act and disbandment of the Ulster Special Constabulary. And there were clearly some legitimate grievances. The local government boundaries were out of date in several areas, those in Londonderry being the most obvious example. Government spokesmen were often left to defend the indefensible here. But a complete review of local government had been announced in 1966 and was under way, a fact not mentioned in the leaflets emanating from the CRA. In none of these areas was there any grievance which could have been held to justify the death of one single Ulsterman.

It is a job for historians to decide at what stage the IRA took over the Civil Rights Movement; but it is quite clear, and it seemed quite clear to me at the time, that irrespective of the ideals of those who started it off, subversive elements were quick to realize the opportunities for exploitation and to jump on the band wagon. As I said in a speech on the day that the Londonderry march was taking place, civil rights was 'a very convenient banner for a republican to hoist aloft'. Reading it now, in retrospect, this speech sums up so much of how I and others like me regarded the CRA of those days that I quote it here:

I know there are people dedicated to the precepts of civil rights and who are acting according to the dictates of their conscience and who have no aim or desire to cause provocation or civil strife. These people have my sincere respect, and I respect equally the political ambitions of the Nationalist Party, openly and sincerely avowed. Liberty of conscience, liberty of speech, liberty of assembly are rights fundamental to every democratic community. Criticism is the very life-blood of the democratic process, and a government which stifles criticism becomes a dictatorship. But no government worth its salt will allow deliberate provocation to cause civil strife among the people it is elected to protect. As every Ulsterman knows only too well we live in a country in which political murder and retaliation are not very long buried in the past. Community relations is an overworked catch phrase these days. But if we are to be able to live together in mutual respect there is no place for humbug or hypocrisy.

The support which was given to the CRA was not dependent on its specific aims or grievances; it became for Nationalists and Republicans a new way of getting at the Unionists and discrediting the Stormont Government in the eyes of the outside world. The fact that 'One man one vote' became the banner under which the CRA marches took place was, I believe, no coincidence. It sounded, to a world attuned to such protests, a positive humanitarian cry from an oppressed people. It also seemed to involve a very basic right—not many people would stop to ask, on seeing such a slogan, if it referred to the important elections for the parliaments at Westminster and Stormont where in fact one man one vote was as much a part of the electoral system as elsewhere in the United Kingdom, or to local council elections where there was still a ratepayers franchise. Many well-meaning but ill-informed people, even in Britain, were under the impression that the 'evil Unionist government' had made it illegal for Catholics to vote in elections. From such initial misconceptions much of Westminster's subsequent mishandling of the situation arose.

The march on 5 October 1968 received world-wide publicity—carefully organized by instigators of the march, who were wilfully breaking the law. It was difficult for the Minister of Home Affairs, then William Craig, to decide whether to ban the march or allow it to go ahead, as either decision was likely to arouse considerable opposition. I think he was right to prescribe a restricted route and the Cabinet unanimously supported him. But the tactics used by the RUC in enforcing the ban left something to be desired, and TV cameras were ready and waiting to make the most of the event. The selective screening of certain shots in which marchers were being beaten by policemen had a very adverse effect on public opinion in Britain and left the incident judged in advance of anything the Northern Ireland Government might say or do.

The subsequent rash of rioting and marches brought about a very tense atmosphere in the Province. Comment was made at Westminster on these events and at the beginning of November, Terence O'Neill, Bill Craig and I went to London to see the Prime Minister Harold Wilson. The meeting was not very momentous—it revolved mainly around discussion of housing and local government, which were not within my brief. I think we realized clearly after that meeting that the British Government was anxious to see reforms being made to conciliate the Nationalist minority. Harold Wilson made some remarks in the Commons next day which were not very helpful to easing tension in Northern Ireland. He adopted a vaguely threatening posture and talked of a 'reappraisal' if things did not improve. But the waving of the big stick from Westminster only made it more difficult to bring people in Northern Ireland along with change.

A few weeks later, on 22 November, the Government announced a five-point reform package involving a points system for housing allocation, an Ombudsman, abolition of the company vote in local elections, a review of the Special Powers Act, and the replacement of the old Londonderry Corporation by a Development Commission. These proposals were welcomed by the Opposition, and were accepted by the Unionist Standing Committee, the governing body of the Unionist Party, on the understanding that no further concessions to the agitation were contemplated. It was becoming obvious even then that 'one man one vote' was being allowed to build up into a sort of sacred cow for both sections of the community—for the Unionists a concession which they must not make, and for the civil rights agitators the most crucial gain to be wrested from the Government. The whole thing was getting totally out of proportion.

However, the situation did appear to calm down for a few weeks towards the end of the year. Terence went on television and made his famous 'Crossroads' speech, so-called because he began it with the words 'Ulster is at the crossroads'. As so often he said all the right things, and I fully supported the sentiments he expressed. It was on the question of how all the words were to be given effect that we eventually parted company. There was much public support for the ideas in the broadcast, and the CRA agreed to suspend marches temporarily to give the Government a chance to effect reforms in a less tense atmosphere. But the next day William Craig made the second of two speeches clearly critical of government policy and he was asked to resign by the Prime Minister. There was clearly no other action Terence could take in view of the way Craig was putting himself out on a limb, and I supported him. It was a great pity to see someone who had started off as such a forward-looking politician, as Craig had, becoming bitter and resentful. O'Neill's premiership must have brought high hopes to Bill Craig; he started off as Minister of Home Affairs and confidante of the Prime Minister, and was subsequently promoted to Development, a post which he clearly enjoyed. But after the leadership crisis in 1966, in which he supported O'Neill, he was put back into Home Affairs (then a smaller Ministry) and that move seemed to bring about a change in him. I think it left him with a certain sense of grievance which coloured his political attitude. When Terence O'Neill asked for his resignation he was convinced, as I was not at that time, that Craig had ideas of independence for Northern Ireland. Subsequent events have shown that O'Neill was right and I was wrong.

The pause in violence and confrontation was broken in the first four days of 1969 by the deliberately provocative 'People's Democracy' march from Belfast to Londonderry. Young people, many of them students, were cynically used as bait in a hoped-for and expected attack which could be used to arouse community antagonisms. In the aftermath of this march there was serious rioting in Londonderry for several days putting the RUC under impossible pressure and resulting in breaches of discipline which further alienated the Catholic community. O'Neill felt that a new initiative was required and on 15 January secured the agreement of the Cabinet to the appointment of a Commission (subsequently known as the Cameron Commission) 'to inquire into and report upon the violence and civil disturbance in Northern Ireland since October 5th 1968', and to investigate the background of these disturbances.

I opposed this decision and regarded it as a major blunder by the Government. It was an initiative to avoid initiatives, a backdoor method of abolishing the ratepayers' franchise. It was obvious that the Commission would report that 'one man one vote' was the foremost demand of the protesters and would recommend that it be met. The Cabinet actually prepared for this by agreeing that if the Commission did recommend it they would introduce the appropriate legislation. But at the same time the Prime Minister was proposing to say that there was no change in government policy and that the question of the local franchise could only be considered after the completion of the reshaping of local government, expected in two years' time. This was not only dishonest, it was a disastrous political tactic which could only damage trust between people and government and consequently reduce the capacity of the Government to give any real lead to the community. It was building up a belief among Unionists that 'one man one vote' was an important issue which must not be conceded, and making it more difficult to secure agreement when the time came.

I had of course previously defended government policy on this as on most other issues, as I was frequently cast in the role of television spokesman. But I had already made my willingness to consider change clear in a speech to Unionists in County Armagh on 4 January, when I pointed out that this was a matter of policy with pros and cons like any other matter of government policy. It was not some great deprivation of civil rights, nor was it a major bulwark of the constitutional position of Northern Ireland for which Unionists should fight at all costs.

In the Cabinet I opposed the setting up of the Commission as an abdication of government responsibility which would place the Government in the position of appearing to be forced against its will to grant reforms. I proposed two alternatives: the Government should either decide to resist the pressures being brought to bear on it, or decide that there were other changes (including reform of the local government franchise) which were desirable and necessary and put that view with honesty and determination to the people. I favoured the latter alternative. When this was rejected I knew I could have no heart in being part of a government which was increasingly refusing to face realities and was losing control of the situation.

I went home and spent several days thinking over my position and discussing it with my wife, as I have done most of the important decisions of my life. When I finally decided on 23 January that I must resign only one other person, Harry Jones, a civil servant whose friendship and loyalty had meant a great deal to me, was aware of my decision. I had consulted no one else, political or otherwise, and having made up my mind I told no one else outside the family until my resignation was in the hands of the Prime Minister. It was a very personal decision, and it was a heart-breaking one. I was leaving a Ministry of which I was intensely proud. I have formed from experience the highest possible regard for the professionalism and integrity of the Northern Ireland Civil Service. In Commerce the personnel were quite unparalleled in their enthusiasm and initiative and I look back on my work there as the most satisfying and rewarding period of my entire political career.

I delivered my resignation to the Prime Minister by hand in

Stormont House and said to him that if he and I firmly put it to the party that 'one man one vote' must be agreed we could succeed. But he was quite convinced that the findings of the Commission would be necessary to combine with the Westminster stick in order to beat his party into acceptance.

My letter of resignation was published and I was surprised by the depth of personal bitterness revealed in O'Neill's published reply. It seemed that the full weight of the government publicity machine was utilized to fix on me, quite unjustly, the image of a scheming, disloyal and ambitious colleague for whom this resignation was merely another stage in a devious political game. Terence was presented as the 'beleaguered moderate' and I as the leader of a 'black reactionary group' (so described by Harold Wilson in his memoirs) who were trying to unseat him. So successful were Terence's personal attacks on me at this time that for many years it was widely believed that I had been spending most of the previous six years plotting against him. The fact that my resignation was exploited by those opposed to O'Neill's policies lent credibility to these accusations. Yet I can truthfully say that neither in 1969, 1966, nor at any other time during O'Neill's Premiership did I initiate or was I involved in any plots to oust and replace him. Political intrigue was not something for which I had much taste, nor was I very good at it. Had I been making a move for the leadership I would at least have sounded out political colleagues before resigning. Terence's fertile imagination sometimes created plots where none existed, and commentators were too ready to attribute cynical motives when criticisms of naïvety might have been more appropriate. Some forgot rather quickly my previous support for government policies. For example the *Belfast Telegraph*, in 1969 a strong supporter of O'Neill, had in 1967 referred to a speech I made as showing 'a commitment voiced in language which appeared more forthright than that heard in any open declaration of support for the Premier by his other Cabinet colleagues'. I simply replied to O'Neill's attack by saying, 'I would prefer not to indulge in recriminations.'

The reaction to my resignation and the way it was exploited by opponents of the Prime Minister surprised me. Two other members of the Government resigned shortly after, saying they thought too many concessions were being made. A group of backbenchers came out openly against O'Neill and so he decided to call an election to secure popular endorsement of his policies. The election, held on 24 February 1969, was a particularly unpleasant one, with all the Unionist candidates neatly divided by the media into 'pro' and 'anti-O'Neill', and the latter represented as reactionaries, bigots and hard-liners. The Prime Minister himself canvassed against some of the officially selected candidates of his party, which seriously weakened his position. The election results were a grave disappointment to him since they failed to provide the decisive popular mandate he needed, and there had been less support than expected from Catholic voters. From then on it was only a matter of time until his resignation. Although he received the ritual votes of confidence from the Parliamentary Party and from the Unionist Standing Committee, the situation on the streets continued to deteriorate. Belatedly O'Neill decided to ask the Parliamentary Party to support 'one man one vote' and the issue went to a vote. I voted in favour, but it was carried by only two votes, and O'Neill's position looked weaker than ever. He announced his resignation on 28 April 1969.

Terence O'Neill was a hard-working Prime Minister who had much to contribute to Northern Ireland. He had a certain flair for publicity and for saying the right things. Had we been able to work together better I think we would have made a strong team for the good of Northern Ireland. But I do not think he ever felt really at home in Ulster politics. His personal remoteness made it difficult for him to lead his party along new and difficult paths at a very crucial period in the Province's history. And in so far as some of the mud he threw in my direction stuck he made it more difficult for his successors to carry through further political changes. He was worthy of a better legacy. If there had been less talk and more action Northern Ireland might now be a peaceful and pleasant place in which to live.

6
Reforms

Major James Chichester-Clark, Minister of Agriculture, resigned from O'Neill's Government on 23 April 1969, the day after O'Neill's decision to introduce 'one man one vote' in local elections. 'It was too soon for such a move,' he said. On the surface this seemed to precipitate O'Neill's resignation. But there were many, like myself, who thought it was a scheme arranged between them to ensure that power was kept in the hands of the 'Big House'. Chichester-Clark had strong social and personal ties with O'Neill (both were Eton and the Guards), though he was politically unknown and inexperienced. His resignation placed him in the public eye at a time when we were daily expecting O'Neill's resignation. When O'Neill resigned five days later and held a farewell tea party for his political friends at Stormont Castle to which the Major was invited it was clear who O'Neill was backing to succeed him.

The 'Pro-O'Neill' faction took up the Major as their candidate. Everyone at that time was labelled as either 'moderate' or 'extremist', 'progressive' or 'reactionary'. It was a destructive and blinkered practice which did little justice to the complexity of people and their political opinions. Chichester-Clark, who had resigned in opposition to universal franchise in local elections, was labelled a 'moderate' while I, who had resigned in favour of universal franchise three months earlier, was labelled a 'reactionary'. My convictions were expressed in a speech to East Down Constituency Association that month when I said that 'the present policies of reform must be implemented to the full, in the spirit as well as the letter. Let it be absolutely clear, by actions as well as words, that sectarianism is not equated with Unionism ... and that as a party we are quite aware that justice has to be seen to be done.'

On 1 May the election for Leader of the Unionist Party was held (the old consultative system had been quickly done away with after

1963). This election was the only occasion on which I actively campaigned to become Leader. I could not believe that the party would
elect someone with no apparent popular influence at such a crucial
time for Ulster, but it soon became obvious that it would be a close
contest. Chichester-Clark had virtually formed his Cabinet 'designate'
before the voting took place! We both addressed the gathering of
Unionist MPs in Committee Room 17 at Stormont, Chichester-Clark
emphasizing the need for determined enforcement of the law while
I emphasized the need for a decisive and positive approach to the
building up of a patently fair system of government. Chichester-Clark
won by one vote—'the safer choice' said *The Times*. It was the *Irish
Times* which neatly summed up the difficulty of fitting me into a category by coining the phrase, 'the soft-hardliner'. My daughter Claire
wrote to me from school in England saying 'Thank goodness that one
man didn't vote the other way! Even if the country does go to ruin
... we'll still have our ol' Da!' As always my family were a great source
of strength to me at a difficult time.

A few hours after the election Chichester-Clark asked me to take
on the job of Development. I would have much preferred to go back
to the Ministry of Commerce, but he made it clear that Roy Bradford
had already filled that post, and Herbie Kirk had been asked to take
on Finance. He said I could have Education if I wanted. I felt that,
having come to power by only one vote, he had a duty to try to unite
the party and give fair representation within the Cabinet to all sections
of opinion. So I put it to him that I would not be prepared to join
the Cabinet as the sole representative of the section of the Parliamentary Party which had voted against him as Leader. He seemed to
accept this point, and offered posts to Brooke, Dobson and Taylor,
all of whom had supported me. The Ministry of Development had
so many intractable and urgent problems to be solved that it seemed
likely the Department might provide a convenient political burial
ground for me. But after thinking it over for forty-eight hours, I decided to accept the post. It was a crisis situation requiring everyone
to pull together.

I was soon glad I had accepted. Development became a challenging
and interesting post at the very centre of the reform programme.
House building, the introduction of a points system to ensure fair
allocation of houses, the reorganization of local government—all
these things and many others fell to the Ministry of Development.
It was a real bed of thorns, but I looked forward to the fight with
a certain amount of relish. As I said in a speech soon after taking

up the post, 'there are occasions when I feel like the ram caught up in the thicket, but let me assure you, I shall not be led meekly to the slaughter. I shall fight every inch of the way... I will not undertake to please any section of the population of Northern Ireland.' I found Chichester-Clark a loyal and helpful colleague with whom to work; he was honest and direct and I gained a new respect for him during the period that he was carrying the burden of the Premiership.

The new Government pushed forward rapidly with reforms. Within two weeks decisions to go ahead with 'one man one vote', to grant an amnesty to all those involved in the riots, and to set up a local government ombudsman had been announced, and the new Prime Minister had gained the unanimous backing of the Unionist Standing Committee. The local government ombudsman, known as the Commissioner for Complaints, was an innovation in the United Kingdom and has provided a deterrent both to abuse of their powers by local authorities and appointed bodies and to the making of extravagant and unsubstantiated allegations of bias against them. The Prime Minister and I also visited Downing Street and Wilson declared himself 'happy' with our proposals.

The city of Londonderry, heart of the civil rights agitation, was one of our most urgent problems. Already the corporation had been dissolved and replaced by a Development Commission responsible to my Ministry. My first appointment at 9.30 a.m. on a Monday morning was a meeting, at my request, with the Chairman of the Commission, Sir (then Mr) Brian Morton. He was already becoming a respected administrator in that predominantly Nationalist town, and had earned a great deal of goodwill from all sides—goodwill which he later showed to be amply justified. I followed up this meeting with a visit to Londonderry a few weeks later during which I walked around the Catholic Bogside and the Protestant Fountain Street areas of the city. The visit to the Bogside was a particularly noteworthy event for a Unionist Minister and I got a good reception. I remember standing talking to a crowd of people when one woman said, 'Everyone seems to think we are different here from people anywhere else.' I replied that as far as I was concerned the people of the Bogside were as much citizens of Northern Ireland as the people of the Shankill Road, or the Falls Road, or Fountain Street or anywhere else in the Province and the crowd all cheered.

I found the Ministry of Development raring to go on reorganization of local government. The existing system was basically that provided by Westminster in 1898 with 73 authorities (by 1969 reduced to 67) involving 1,400 local councillors and divided into rural and urban councils at the bottom tier, with county and county borough councils as a second tier, and then, since 1921, the two-Chamber Stormont Regional Parliament at the top. Naturally this system had been showing signs of strain in meeting the industrial and social needs of the new Ulster. In a province with a population of $1\frac{1}{2}$ million and a total rateable value of £14 million, and with urgent social and economic problems, the pointlessness of the duplications and delays produced by so many authorities had become very obvious. This was no reflection on the local councillors, many of whom had given unstintingly of their time and talents in the service of local communities; the system had simply outlived its usefulness.

The Stormont Government had begun in 1966 a review of local government with a view to the complete reshaping of the whole system. A Statement of Aims was published in 1967 and when I took over Development in 1969 it was time to put forward definite proposals. I stress here the background to these proposals for two reasons. First, although the publication of our proposals in the summer of 1969 followed several months of upheaval in Northern Ireland during which allegations against local government emerged as a major point of grievance, the proposed reshaping was not conceived solely as a 'reform' to placate the critics; it was also an administrative and political modernization—admittedly overdue—but begun over three years previously to meet the needs of a developing society. Secondly, the centralization of functions which took place after the inter-governmental talks of September and October 1969 was not some new conception dreamed up by the Westminster Government and visited upon an unwilling Stormont Government. It was the development of a line of thought which we had been increasingly favouring, namely that considerable economies of scale were necessary to produce efficiency in local government.

A lot of midnight oil was burned in my first few months at Development as I swotted up the background to my new job, collated the views of numerous bodies on local government changes, and prepared to announce firm decisions. I amassed so many opinions that I felt like a Gallup pollster who had telescoped a year's work into one month, but soon we were getting things moving. By 14 June we had finished collating the views of local councils on a points scheme for the allocation of houses, published our own model scheme and sent it out to the local authorities with a 31 August deadline for its adoption. On

20 June we published the Greater Belfast Urban Area Plan, for the rebuilding of one-third of the city by 1990, together with proposals for the protection of people affected by re-development. On 2 July, we published our White Paper on Local Government Reshaping, proposing seventeen single-tier authorities elected on universal adult franchise from electoral areas to be drawn up by an independent statutory commission, and a tight time-scale leading to elections under the new system in the autumn of 1971. In this and subsequent work at Development, I was ably assisted by a hard-working team of civil servants, and in particular by Bill Stout, the Permanent Secretary, with whom I had previously worked very closely at Home Affairs, and by John Oliver, who helped spearhead the local government drive. These two men were industrious and very efficient. It was pleasant to be part of such a team.

Serious political problems confronted the Government. On the one hand the CRA, which had called a temporary halt to marches a week before O'Neill resigned, appeared to be anxious to get back on to the streets and into the limelight again. In March, four members of their Executive, including one well-known Communist, had resigned because of 'extremist infiltration' of the organization, and it was now clearly under the control of IRA sympathizers. The vice-chairman, who was later tried for possession of arms in the Republic, called for organized breaking of the law and the setting up of a league table for fines achieved. After the new government had been in office less than three weeks the CRA announced plans for a campaign of civil disobedience which they threatened would be put into effect if a time-table of reforms were not published within six weeks. They must have known that a new round of protests and marches would stir up sectarian tensions and violence, and of course the presentation of such an ultimatum angered Unionists and made it more difficult for the Government to make conciliatory gestures. As I said at the time, 'We are not interested in decibel democracy . . . There is a general weariness with threats, demands and ultimata.' If a slackening of tension were to be achieved 'it would help if spokesmen of the minority parties were to call a cease-fire to the barrage of ludicrous anti-Unionist propaganda, the tales of Fascism and ghettos, so obviously untrue that Ulster men and women cannot believe that other people take them seriously'.

A parliamentary time-table of proposed government measures was in fact put to the Opposition at Stormont and publicly endorsed by them as 'reasonable'. But the CRA had grown greedy on success and on media attention and was soon back on the streets. Its attitude was irresponsible and indeed subversive, attempting to goad on the Nationalist section of the population to new levels of street militancy. The words 'civil rights', which once had some dignity and meaning, have long since become in Northern Ireland part of a shabby political con-game directed at well-meaning but gullible liberals in Britain and abroad.

On the other side of the political spectrum William Craig was travelling the Province addressing Unionist meetings and, on several occasions, making speeches which bordered on open incitement to rebel against the United Kingdom Government. This kind of talk, coming from a Privy Councillor and former Cabinet Minister increased the general air of crisis and made the Government's task more difficult. It led many Unionists to believe that violence might soon be necessary to protect their rights and thus contributed to the widespread willingness to interpret the events of August 1969 as an uprising which must be suppressed by whatever means possible.

Craig was still a member of the Parliamentary Unionist Party, and he was doing his best at meetings to make life difficult for the Government when it was attempting to persuade backbenchers of the necessity of proposed reforms. Harry West, who had always felt a keen sense of injustice over his dismissal as Minister of Agriculture by O'Neill in 1967, was also determined to make his presence felt, and, living as he did in County Fermanagh, he was particularly aware of the apprehension felt by Unionists in the west of the Province where they were in the minority. He was soon to form the West Ulster Unionist Council, a dissident body to campaign against the Government's policy of 'appeasement' and organize opposition within the party. Many of the Parliamentary Party meetings were lengthy and strongly argued but Craig and West always found themselves in a small minority.

Splits and rumours of splits in the Unionist Party and in the Cabinet had become the main scoring point of the elected Nationalist leaders, while in the media the game of 'spot the liberals' continued. 'We know you are really planning to welsh on the reforms behind closed doors,' ran the story. Yet nothing could have been further from the truth. The Cabinet had decided from the first that its approach should be one of taking the steam out of the civil rights agitation by a programme of far-reaching reforms combined with firm and impartial enforcement of the law. Major Chichester-Clark, Robert Porter, the Home Affairs Minister, and I were carrying the main burden of Cabinet work, but the Cabinet was meeting frequently and often for long periods to thrash out effective policies. Sometimes we would be in virtually continuous session over a weekend to meet some crisis—usually a demonstration or riot—or to prepare for a major initiative. Naturally there was discussion, sometimes argument, with Porter and I continually hogging the floor. In general the members of the Government worked well together, and I think a look at our record will show that a large number of major changes were pushed through Stormont at very great speed.

The security situation was not improving. Robert Porter was still struggling to control the series of marches and riots and to rehabilitate the RUC, whose morale was very low, with the Catholic minority. They had been much criticized for their handling of earlier riots and a massive propaganda campaign against them had brought relations with the minority to an all-time low. Little account was taken by their critics of the fact there were only 3,000 full-time RUC men in the whole Province and that when widespread trouble broke out they were hopelessly stretched. They could not control crowds by weight of numbers, such as has been done in demonstrations in Trafalgar Square by up to ten thousand policemen on occasions. It is ironic that in a State attacked as a police state by its enemies we suffered from a shortage of policemen.

The only back-up force at our disposal was the part-time Special Constabulary, 8,500 strong. It was a para-military force recruited and organized locally throughout the Province and designed to combat terrorism. It had played an honourable role in defeating previous IRA campaigns and in helping to establish law and order in a State which was only fifty years old. But it was now almost entirely Protestant and its uniforms and weapons were increasingly out of date. It was represented by civil rights activists as an anti-Catholic force and in the British media frequently described as 'the hated B Specials'. It was part of the programme of the CRA that it should be abolished. Because of the deep emotions concerning the force, and because it had no professional training in riot or crowd control, we were very reluctant to call it up to assist the overworked RUC. But it was becoming increasingly obvious that they would need assistance from some source if the situation deteriorated.

The widespread violence which flared up in the summer of 1969 brought things to a head. Several people died and hundreds were injured, a high proportion of them policemen, in riots during July and

August. The causes of this violence have already been thoroughly discussed in the Report of the Tribunal of Inquiry headed by Lord Justice
Scarman, and it is unnecessary to go over them again here. In July
there was serious rioting after the traditional Orange parades, and in
Londonderry this persisted for three days with looting and burning
of shops. On 12 August it flared up again in Londonderry where it
developed into a major confrontation between over a thousand in-
habitants of the Bogside and several hundred RUC men, with baton
charges and later CS gas used by the police, and barricades, stones
and petrol bombs used by the rioters. The same evening RUC stations
in Coalisland, Strabane and Newry were attacked by crowds of 'civil
rights' supporters, and the next day stations in Catholic areas of Belfast were also attacked. This tied down our limited police reserves and
prevented adequate reinforcements being sent to Londonderry where
the situation was getting out of control. Engraved on my mind, as
on the minds of so many Ulster people, are the TV films of those
August days in Londonderry with the men of the RUC sitting or lying
on the pavements in attitudes of total exhaustion after days of continuous duty and harassment from the Bogside. Something of what the
RUC suffered at this time can be understood from the fact that in 1969
over 1,700 members of the force received injuries requiring hospital
treatment.

The July 1969 riots had forced the Northern Ireland Cabinet to prepare for a time when the RUC would have to be reinforced. Unlike
the Metropolitan Police in London, or the British county constabu-
laries, we could not call in reinforcements from a neighbouring force
to meet a major crisis, and we were therefore faced with a choice
between calling out the 'B' Specials or seeking assistance from the
Army which maintained a permanent garrison of some 3,000 men at
military bases in the Province.

Early in August there were exchanges with the British Government
concerning the constitutional implications of such a request for assistance. The Northern Ireland Government was, under the Government of
Ireland Act 1920, responsible for the 'Peace, order and good government' of the Province, including policing and internal security, but the
Army was under the control of the Ministry of Defence at Westminster.
We were told that assistance would be forthcoming if requested, but
that we should think long and deeply before requesting it, as the relationship between Stormont and Westminster would be fundamentally changed. This caused concern to the Cabinet and the view was
strongly expressed to the Home Secretary, James Callaghan, that there

should be no question of extracting a political price for carrying out the common law duty of upholding the authority of a democratically constituted civil power in a climate of serious communal disorder. But it was soon clear that Callaghan was determined to use any military involvement to allow him to intervene decisively in the political situation, though he did not put to us anything he thought we ought to be doing but were failing to do.

Because Westminster insisted that all the resources of the civil power should be utilized before troops were called in, the Northern Ireland Government was forced to mobilize the 'B' Specials for riot duty in Belfast and other urban areas, a task for which they were never intended and for which they were not trained. The unrest in Belfast increased and the security forces at times overreacted to what looked like a full-scale uprising. There was widespread shooting and sniping and five people died. We had to delay our formal request for military assistance until 14 August, after things were clearly out of control. This was morally and tactically wrong. In effect the threat of civil disorder was being used to undermine the Stormont Government; come on your knees or do not come at all was the message. A democratic government was being put in a corner, and not the law-breakers and rioters. Faith in democracy has never quite recovered in Northern Ireland.

The Army, when it moved on to the streets of Londonderry and Belfast on 14 and 15 August, proceeded to implement the spirit of the Westminster policy. Their arrival was greeted with cheers by the rioters who, feeling the withdrawal of the police was an admission of defeat, set up what they called 'liberated' areas. The Army proceeded to stabilize and even to formalize this arrangement. Instead of moving in to support the civil power they dug in as a sort of peace-keeping force on the fringe of the barricaded areas and tacitly accepted the right of various Republicans and known IRA men to rule and speak for these areas. In Londonderry they even went so far as to draw a white line across the road, on one side of which lay 'Free Derry' and on the other side of which lay Her Majesty's territory. The desire to approach this situation cautiously can be fully appreciated, but it was a grave misjudgement of the kind of men with whom the Army was dealing. What chance did the many law-abiding Catholics who did not support Republican organizations have of asserting themselves in this situation? The RUC had operated normally in Nationalist areas before 1969. It is hard to believe now, but policemen walked the beat on the Falls Road, and there was a policeman regularly on traffic duty at the junction of the Springfield and Grosvenor Roads. It was during the months of 'No Go' areas that the IRA, especially in Belfast, built itself up from an organization with few troops to a closely knit and powerfully armed subversive force.

The whole crisis had already been seriously exacerbated by an incredibly irresponsible intervention by the Dublin Premier, Jack Lynch, on the evening of 13 August when the rioting was at its worst. He demanded that a UN peace-keeping force be sent to Northern Ireland and announced that units of the Irish Army were being moved to the border to set up 'field hospitals'. Little imagination is required to envisage the effect of this statement on the thousands of rioters whom an exhausted and numerically weak RUC was struggling to control. 'Lynch is sending up the army boys' must have been a heartening cry behind the barricades. No doubt Lynch had problems with his own extremists (as the gun-running trial in Dublin a few months later showed) but this intervention, coming on top of Lynch's attempt to use the 1968 riots as a means of re-opening with London the whole question of Northern Ireland's position within the United Kingdom, was naturally seen by us as an example of treacherous back stabbing.

No wonder Ulster Unionists felt isolated and besieged. Across at Westminster was a Labour Government holding back on providing assistance, clearly disposed to accept much of the prejudice and scorn which had been poured out in liberal media against Stormont since 1968, and under pressure from its foreign embassies over the bad press Ulster was getting it. And to the South was a government apparently determined to portray the situation as a popular uprising in favour of Irish unity, and which was using its embassies to spread anti-Unionist propaganda throughout the world. The Stormont Government, struggling to maintain order, under pressure politically, with limited resources, and consisting largely of men more experienced in administration than in publicity, had little chance of making its voice heard above the chorus of comment.

7
Big Brother

On 19 August 1969 Major Chichester-Clark, the Prime Minister, Jack Andrews, the Deputy Prime Minister, Robert Porter, the Minister of Home Affairs, and I, went to Downing Street for discussions. We were very aware of the changed relationship which existed following the involvement of the Army and expected a thorough discussion of the security position and the security forces.

I was surprised when, on arrival at Downing Street, Chichester-Clark turned to me in our ante-room off the Cabinet Room just as we were preparing to go in and said, 'By the way I will be recommending that the Army GOC should be the Supreme Security Commander for Northern Ireland. I have agreed this with the RUC Inspector-General.' That may have been the right decision to make, but it was not the right way to go about it. I think the Prime Minister may have finally made up his mind on the way across; certainly Jack Andrews knew nothing about it. James Callaghan has since indicated that he was surprised and pleased by this proposal, which was Chichester-Clark's opening gambit at the meeting.

The Westminster representatives were Harold Wilson, James Callaghan, Denis Healey, the Defence Minister, Michael Stewart, Foreign Secretary, and Lord Stonham of the Home Office, with the Chief of the General Staff, General Sir Geoffrey Baker, and two senior Whitehall civil servants in attendance. We had with us Sir Harold Black, Secretary to the Cabinet, Ken Bloomfield, Deputy Secretary to the Cabinet and the Prime Minister's Private Secretary. The atmosphere of the meeting was serious but friendly, with Harold Wilson puffing at his pipe and generally orchestrating the discussion rather than dominating it. He usually seemed to come to meetings undecided about which pipe he was going to smoke, for he set a rack holding three or four pipes in front of him and selected from them at the beginning of the meeting.

Chichester-Clark and Porter did most of the talking for our side, explaining the security situation and answering points put forward by Wilson and Callaghan. My main contribution was to outline our plans on local government and housing. Chichester-Clark's proposal that the GOC should have overall control of security led on to a discussion on the role of the 'B' Specials. It was agreed that their use to deal with urban riots was unsatisfactory and Chichester-Clark made it clear that we would not wish to do this again. Callaghan and Healey pushed the matter further, urging that if the GOC was to take responsibility there should be central control over the 'B' Specials' arms. Chichester-Clark pointed out the dangers for men who lived in isolated rural areas, especially near the border, and it was generally agreed that bearing these problems in mind the matter would be left to the discretion of the GOC. There was no suggestion whatever that the Specials should be disbanded, and the agreed position at the end of the meeting was precisely as stated in the communiqué:

> With the increased deployment of the Army and the assumption by the GOC of operational control of all security forces, it will be possible for the Special Constabulary to be progressively and rapidly relieved of these temporary duties (riot and crowd control) at his discretion, starting in the cities.

It seemed quite clear to the Northern Ireland delegates that this statement implied simply a return to the pre-August role of guarding local security installations, in addition to a stricter central control of arms under the GOC.

It was also agreed that an inquiry into the whole policing policy should be set up in view of the fact that the forces at the disposal of Stormont had not proved adequate to deal with the disorders and some modernization was obviously required. Announcement of this decision was however to be postponed for two days to give Chichester-Clark time to consult with Peacocke, Inspector-General of the RUC.

Discussions then ranged over other issues, including a proposal that two senior civil servants from London should be temporarily stationed with the Northern Ireland Government in Belfast to represent the increased concern which the United Kingdom Government had acquired in Northern Ireland affairs through the commitment of the Armed Forces. We accepted this proposal with some reluctance; I felt sure that it would merely undermine the authority of the Government and provide a channel of complaints by Nationalists which would circumvent the need for Ulstermen to face up to each other in honest political debate. (So in fact it turned out; the practice of hurrying to the representatives of 'Big Brother'—first at the Conway Hotel and later at 'Laneside', Craigavad, outside Belfast, where the Westminster men established a base—became a substitute for attempting to reach a *modus vivendi* in Ulster. There also seems to have been an almost total failure to use this channel to keep in touch with the views of anti-government forces on the right—men such as Craig and Paisley—and therefore a considerable imbalance in the assessment being fed back to London.) The whole meeting lasted from 2 p.m. to 11 p.m., and the standards of Downing Street hospitality were not up to scratch on this occasion: Harold said there was no food available. The Northern Ireland representatives' last meal had been breakfast that morning. I was very grateful to Denis Healey, the decent man who shared his sandwiches with me.

When the main points of the now famous 'Downing Street Communiqué' had been agreed, Wilson and Chichester-Clark went off to appear on TV. The rest of us watched the broadcast in a small room off the Cabinet Room. There was consternation all round when Wilson, in answer to a question about the 'B' Specials, said that they would be 'phased out'. Callaghan exclaimed in an exasperated voice: 'I told him not to say that.' We knew that Wilson's words were not a fair representation of what had been discussed, and could do immense damage in the highly emotive atmosphere then existing in Northern Ireland. The 'B' Specials were highly thought of among Unionists because of their effectiveness during previous IRA campaigns and were regarded as the main guarantee against forcible incorporation into an Irish Republic. The apparent suggestion that we had agreed to their disbandment (or that the Westminster Government had even put such a proposal to us) increased the fears of Unionists and seriously undermined our position.

When we returned to Belfast I attempted to retrieve the situation by holding a press conference on behalf of the Government and explaining that 'There is absolutely no suggestion that the USC should be disbanded.' But much of the damage had been done, and it was easy for Craig and Paisley to represent my statement as a dishonest cover-up of 'doing the dirty' on the Specials. For years afterwards when government spokesmen attended Unionist meetings throughout the Province there were people at the back of the halls shouting 'What about the Specials?' which always raised a cheer.

After this meeting Callaghan very quickly became 'Big Brother'.

There was no formal diminution in the powers of the Northern Ireland Government, but there were a lot of quiet pressures being applied. Of course we still carried the can publicly for any decisions made and suffered politically for mistakes. People have often said to me since about many of the events of these years, 'Why did you not do this or that?' 'Why did you not put your foot down?' I think it is very difficult for people to believe, especially with all the modern cynicism about politicians, that many public leaders feel a great deal of responsibility towards the people they try to lead. An atmosphere of violence and fear such as then existed in Northern Ireland makes one particularly reluctant to do anything which might worsen the situation or undermine confidence in the fragile social structures still operating. We had been forced as a government to show that with the resources at our disposal we simply had not been able to govern; the community had walked to the edge of civil war. Faced with that kind of dilemma I knew that I wanted to be on the side of construction rather than destruction, and that if a senior minister such as I began to rock the boat it would be another step towards social disintegration. I had the opportunity and the responsibility of trying to rebuild what we could of the old hopeful spirit of the 1960s, even when that meant staying in a government I thought was making mistakes. Anyone who had sat with me round the Cabinet table in Stormont and seen the faces of those patently decent men determined to do what was best would have understood my anger at the easy sneers and the condescension of so many of the experts who flew in looking for a quick phrase with which to sum up our problems.

James Chichester-Clark was a big man with a big heart. He was perhaps too trusting of Jim Callaghan, who, in his own 'Uncle Jim' sort of way, was not above a bit of bullying if he thought it might work. Throughout the months of September and October 1969, I increasingly felt that he was pressurizing and bullying Chichester-Clark and Porter into taking hasty decisions.

Callaghan followed up the Downing Street meeting with a three-day visit to Northern Ireland beginning on 27 August. It was, as he himself has since very aptly termed it, a 'cocked hat affair'. He was very conscious of the impression he was creating both in the minds of the Northern Ireland people and with the scores of pressmen from all over the world then in the Province. In the aftermath of the terrible events of that month he arrived like some Kissinger-before-his-time breathing goodwill and understanding. To give him his due he did handle both his press conferences with a great deal of skill and made a considerable impression on the public. The Unionist population were just as ready to hope that he would be able to help the situation as were the Nationalists, though one particular episode during the visit caused uncertainty and suspicion. While in the Bogside Callaghan was filmed by TV cameras leaning out of a first-floor window in a house addressing a large crowd through a loud-hailer, and in the section of his speech shown on thousands of screens in Northern Ireland he was saying: 'We are on your side.' It may be that quoted out of context the phrase is misleading but I know it stuck in the minds of many who suspected that the Home Secretary was really 'agin the Unionists' all along.

Callaghan attended two meetings of the Cabinet during these three days. We had interesting and lengthy discussions but nothing of very great significance or novelty emerged from them. Certainly there was no opposition to his proposals for joint working parties on housing, fair employment, and economic matters sufficient to justify the subsequent building up of the melodrama of a 'dramatic watershed' in Stormont/Westminster relations such as Callaghan later described in his book. The Downing Street meeting had been much more significant. Callaghan's role at this time was, to use his own words again, 'to give the impression that things were being taken in hand' and he did it very well. Pending the report of the inquiry into policing, by now established under the chairmanship of Lord Hunt and including Sir Robert Mark of the Metropolitan Police, there were few new reforms of substance which could be proposed, and we wanted to see what practical and useful ideas could come out of the Whitehall machine. One point raised was the appointment of a Minister of Community Relations in the Cabinet. This was Callaghan's idea; ours had been the creation of an independent Community Relations Commission with a Catholic chairman. Eventually we decided to set up both.

The Home Secretary's second visit, five weeks later, coincided with important developments in the Province. The Hunt Report on policing was published and the Government accepted its conclusions. Proposals to centralize housing functions, formerly the responsibility of local authorities, in a Central Housing Executive and to set up a new Local Government Review Body, were also announced after completion of the studies of the joint working parties.

The Hunt Report had first come into the hands of the Cabinet on 8 October and thus we had one day to consider it before meeting Callaghan on 9 October. He was piling on the pressure for immediate publication and acceptance; he seemed to think there would be no question but that we should acquiesce to the proposals *in toto*. The recommendations of Hunt were, in brief, that the RUC should cease to have any para-military role and should normally be unarmed, that a representative police authority should be constituted to administer the RUC in order to prevent accusations of a 'political police', that there should be closer association between the RUC and police forces in Britain, that an independent Director of Public Prosecutions should be appointed and the 'B' Specials should be replaced by two new forces, an unarmed RUC Reserve and a locally recruited part-time military force under the command of the GOC (later known as the Ulster Defence Regiment).

The question of a 'normally unarmed' police force was difficult. The RUC itself was anxious that it should have a less para-military role, as the Police Federation emphasized, but although the ideal of an unarmed force was one to which we were all ready to subscribe we were less than confident that the facts of law enforcement in Ulster would permit the full implementation of this essentially 'British Bobby' concept. But we agreed, for the sake of community relations, to give it a try.

The 'B' Specials were an even more thorny problem. The attacks on them by the Nationalists and by the British media as a 'sectarian' and biased force had merely magnified in the minds of Unionists their importance as an indispensable part of the defences of the Province. We were surprised by the proposal that they should be disbanded, having expected a continuation of their rural anti-terrorist function. But the recognition that they would be replaced by a local defence force with the most modern equipment and training and with a chance of gaining Catholic recruits, we found reassuring. After long discussion and with much reluctance we agreed to accept. In retrospect the way in which the changeover from the old to the new force took place left a lot to be desired, and we should have pressed these points more strongly. The Specials were off duty long before the new Ulster Defence Regiment (UDR) was capable of effectively dealing with the terrorists. Thus the IRA were able to use the gap to move arms and explosives around the country unhindered and built up their strength.

We demanded more time to study the Report, and the publication was held over from 9 to 10 October (a Friday), though we argued that it should not be published until after the weekend. Callaghan was in too much of a hurry to make things seem to happen while he was in the Province and would not agree to wait. Widespread rioting took place in some Protestant areas of Belfast immediately after publication. Several people died on the Shankill Road, including the first RUC man to be killed, and civilians shot in exchanges of fire with the Army, which was brought in to back up the RUC. We had expected an outraged reaction and a massive political attack on the Government, but nothing like this. I suppose it was something which had been building up over several months: the feeling that Republicans and troublemakers were being given a credence they did not deserve, that Ulster was being pilloried unjustly, and that an insidious attack against the State was under way yet no one seemed to recognize it. And now here the defences of the Province were to be taken away; self-help was the only answer. The events of that weekend were a cry for attention from those who felt neglected and ignored while their enemies were the darlings of the world. They were understandable, but they were certainly not excusable.

Chichester-Clark's broadcast to the Province on the Sunday in an attempt to steady the situation was an example of the way Callaghan was pushing him around at this time. He was persuaded by Callaghan against his better judgement that he should go on the screen with only prompt notes rather than a script; as a result he appeared weak and at a loss for something to say when, above all, an impression of strength and resolution was required. It was a complete disaster for the reputation of the Government.

The decision to appoint Sir Arthur Young, Commissioner of the City of London police, as Inspector-General (later called the Chief Constable) of the RUC was also a mistake. There were too many snap decisions being taken at that time by the Cabinet after prior consultation between Callaghan, Chichester-Clark and, sometimes, Porter. At a Cabinet meeting held to consider the question of a new Inspector-General (Peacocke, the then Inspector-General had decided to resign, presumably after pressure had been put on him; he was the scapegoat for the police mistakes in August) we found Chichester-Clark and Porter had already been firmly recommended by Callaghan to appoint Sir Arthur Young. Callaghan said he was the best policeman in Britain. This was really just a piece of blarney to get his own man in and we subsequently realized that the major factor governing Callaghan's view on this was the pliability of Sir Arthur and his willingness to report directly to Westminster. It was very obvious after a certain amount of debate in the Cabinet that Porter and Chichester-Clark had decided that they would have to accept Callaghan's proposal and it was pushed through. I thought it was a mistake for two reasons.

First, there was no adequate consideration of other possibilities and the decision was pushed through hurriedly. Secondly, Sir Arthur, with respect, was simply not the kind of policeman we needed. His approach was 'colonial' and he never really won the trust of his men. And of course he took a lot of stick as the man who had to implement Westminster's 'Softly, softly' approach to getting down the barricades in republican areas.

The Stormont Government pushed ahead over succeeding months with the implementation of the decisions announced. I had a huge job on my hands seeing through the establishment of the Central Housing Executive and yet another complete review of local government. The thinking behind this new review was largely political. We had previously proposed at Development that there should be a streamlining of local government and some centralization of functions, but we had not envisaged taking major functions, such as housing, completely away from local authorities. There was, however, a need for a crash programme in housing which could best be co-ordinated by one authority, and because most of the accusations of discrimination, particularly in allocation and building of houses, had been made against local authorities I thought it was best for community relations if these matters were taken out of their hands. They would still be subject to democratic scrutiny by the Stormont Parliament.

The decision to set up the Central Housing Executive raised new questions on the functions of local authorities in relation to planning, roads, the provision of water and sewerage and so on, and all of this needed to be examined. If this was not to mean putting back the next local government elections for several years (with consequent accusations of trying to keep the old councils in power) I knew we would have to move with incredible speed. We debated the new approach at Stormont in October and November and in December I appointed the Review Body under the Chairmanship of Mr (now Sir) Patrick Macrory. I thought myself very lucky to get him. He was a man with a knowledge of Northern Ireland and with a very business-like approach. I had to go and see the Chairman of Unilever, where Sir Patrick was a Director, and persuade him that Ulster's need was greater than his at that time. Fortunately he was very co-operative. The other members of the Body were widely representative of business and trade union interests, both Protestant and Catholic, and together they made up a very talented and knowledgeable group of men. They pushed ahead rapidly, working very hard, seeing hundreds of people and producing a Report by June 1970.

Throughout the latter half of 1970 the bulk of Cabinet work concerned consideration of the Macrory Report and assessment of comments on it. We had a two-day debate in Stormont and on 17 December the Government announced firm decisions of principle. We accepted the Report: a new single-tier system of twenty-six district councils would be set up and area boards appointed by the Stormont Government, but with up to 40 per cent of district council representatives, would administer Education and Health and Social Services. We planned to have the new authorities operating by the autumn of 1972—an incredibly fast time-scale for a complete review of local government, the redrawing of boundaries by an Independent Commission, the framing and passing of numerous pieces of legislation, and the holding of elections. But we kept right on schedule for as long as the Government was in Unionist hands.

Almost before we had begun to implement these measures, political opposition began to build up among Unionists. Craig and West both denounced our plans and called for a system of four or five larger councils—presumably the largest number one could safely have while hoping to keep Unionist control of all of them. My reaction was to say that 'if people are going to demand a 1969 gerrymander in favour of Unionism, I am not going to father any such schemes. I will resist pressure from groups to change the plan...to the point of resignation.' Local councillors were also aggrieved at the apparent downgrading of their role.

'You can take a horse to water', they say: one of my tasks was to try to persuade Unionists that these changes were practical and beneficial, and not just a sop to Westminster and appeasement to the agitators. Night after night, when the desk in my office was cleared, I had a quick meal and went off to Unionist meetings throughout the six counties, making speeches, answering questions, explaining and persuading, speaking to two hundred people in a hall in a county town, or fifty crowded into a small Orange hall somewhere in the country, in places with names like Ballymacaramary or Ballymageogh. They all had one thing in common: a large proportion of the audience was hostile, in varying degrees. Many were local councillors who felt that their years of service to the community were being shabbily rewarded, others were suspicious and hostile to change. At any time to sell radical changes in the structure of government, especially as it closely affects the daily life of a community, is a difficult task. To persuade people that such changes were necessary against a background of civil unrest and fears of a constitutional sell-out was a mammoth undertaking. There were occasions when the heckling was such that it seemed I would not be allowed to speak at all. These were nights when my early political experiences stood me in good stead, when I used to speak from a lorry on the corner of a Belfast city street to a crowd which often contained more hecklers than supporters. But as always, if one is prepared to face up to the heckling and abuse, the Ulster crowd will give a speaker credit and respect for having the courage of his convictions and a fair hearing, with more heated discussions afterwards over tea and the home-baked cakes at which the Ulster woman excels.

By being the chief protagonist for unpopular government policies in those days, I built up a lot of personal enmity in the Unionist community from the hundreds who felt that their services in local government had been slighted, and from the vast numbers of Protestants in rural areas who had looked on the 'B' Specials as their first line of defence against their traditional enemies, the IRA.

We jumped the usual hurdles of meetings of the Unionist Council and the Unionist Standing Committee successfully in spite of a campaign against us. The West Ulster Unionist Council produced a leaflet entitled 'Faulkner's Fiddle' denouncing the Macrory Report as an attempt to ensure 'Republican rule immediately in some areas of Northern Ireland, leading ultimately to control of local and central government and the overthrow of the Constitution'. But throughout 1970 our position was being eroded as the campaign against us gained momentum and, most important, as an IRA campaign of shooting and bombing was beginning. It would have helped us if the minority leaders had, at this time, recognized the efforts of the Government to conciliate them and made a positive response, but having come to prominence themselves as street leaders they were, I think, having difficulty translating their new position as elected representatives into a positive political lead for the minority. They were caught in the position of continually having to try not to be left behind by militants on their side. Their constant pose of reluctant citizen did not make our task any easier. The one positive response we got was from the Catholic Church. I had a private meeting with Cardinal Conway and in recognition of our local government reforms he appointed a chaplain to Stormont for the first time.

By the time the Conservative Government came into office after a General Election in June 1970 the IRA campaign was well under way. The fear generated by events in the summer of 1969 and the subsequent credibility given to leaders at the barricades of 'No Go' areas had provided the IRA with the ideal opportunity to organize its forces and draw in young people. It was helped in this by funds from the Irish Republic, as became obvious when Lynch sacked two of his senior Ministers in May 1970 for suspected gun running to Northern Ireland (it has subsequently been announced by an investigating committee in the Dail that thousands of pounds of government funds cannot be accounted for in relation to 'Northern relief'). The old guerrilla campaign was on again, and at a time when the security forces of Northern Ireland were in the process of a complete reorganization including the establishment of an unarmed police force. By June 1970 there had been fifty explosions and by the end of the year twenty-five people had died.

Chichester-Clark was running out of enthusiasm for the whole thing; despite his best efforts the situation seemed to be collapsing around his ears, and he did not feel that the security policy of Westminster was sufficiently resolute to deal with the escalating violence. We tried not to make a public issue of our disagreements with Army policy and had frequent discussions with Maudling, the new Conservative Home Secretary, to get action to clamp down on riots. Graham Shillington, who had succeeded Sir Arthur Young as Chief Constable of the RUC, was warning us that the situation on the streets was being allowed to drift, but because of the repercussions from a search operation in July 1970 which had gone wrong we found Westminster very apprehensive about any further searches. At a meeting in London on 18 January 1971 it was agreed by Maudling and Lord Carrington, the Minister of Defence, that the Army must make arrests and not simply confine rioting to an area. I noted in my diary when I got home: 'The atmosphere of the talks was warm. There was a readiness to help. But they are scared about arms searches.'

On Friday 26 February two RUC men were shot dead in Belfast at 11.30 p.m. At 1 a.m. Shillington rang me at home to say he was withdrawing all unarmed patrols in Belfast and was issuing revolvers to any RUC men going out on duty. It was the effective end of hopes that the RUC could operate as an unarmed 'English Bobby' style police force.

On 10 March 1971 a horrifying incident took place. Three teenage Scottish soldiers were lured from a pub and brutally murdered on a country road outside Belfast. I think that the shock waves this sent through the whole community made Chichester-Clark decide that unless the Army could take decisive action he would resign. The Cabinet met in yet another emergency session on Sunday the 14th and the Prime Minister said he was going over to London to see Maudling again and request five more battalions of troops. I advised against this on the grounds that if he came back empty-handed the situation would be worse, but I was in a minority of one and Chichester-Clark was determined to go. He said Maudling and his colleagues were 'caving in' and would give him the extra troops. The next day he went to London but returned virtually empty-handed—he was promised 1,300 troops. His statement was badly received by the party and there was widespread talk of his resignation.

The following Saturday Carrington and the Chief of the General Staff visited Belfast and underlined to the Cabinet that they could not provide the troops we were asking for. The Prime Minister wrote out his resignation at the end of the Cabinet meeting and made it public at 10 p.m. He left a job in which he had done his duty as an officer and a gentleman, but which I doubt if he ever really wanted.

8
Premiership

In March 1971 the Premiership of Northern Ireland was not a political prize to be coveted. Two Prime Ministers had fallen in two years, not because of electoral defeat but because of loss of authority in a deteriorating political and security situation. Conflicting political pressures, the apparent disintegration of the Unionist Party, and escalating terrorist violence had all created an atmosphere of fear and confusion in which demagogues could attract support and the voice of reason was difficult to make heard. There were some ready to predict that the sixth Prime Minister of the Stormont Parliament and Government would be the last.

It was a daunting prospect, but it was also a challenge and an opportunity, a challenge which almost inevitably fell to me. My name had been linked to the Premiership since it was learned that I was one of the three considered for the post in 1963, I was the most experienced Minister in the Government, and I had been the most publicly active member of the Chichester-Clark Government. Many liberal Unionists, who had once accepted O'Neill's version of my politics, were now convinced that I was genuinely committed to the cause of progress and fair government. It was generally expected that I would succeed Chichester-Clark, and even before he resigned I could see this assumption being made. At the end of the rather unproductive all-day meeting of the Cabinet on 20 March attended by Lord Carrington and General Baker, Chief of the General Staff, the two London visitors took their leave by shaking hands with everyone. When he came to me Carrington added to the usual formalities the words 'and good luck'.

Few people are, or should be, in politics who do not believe that they have some contribution to make to the life of their country. I certainly hoped that I had such a contribution to make by taking up the challenge which now faced me. I saw it as an opportunity to bring a new style of government to Northern Ireland, to try to clear out some of the cobwebs of old-style Unionism and restore momentum to the political life of the Province.

Shortly after the announcement of Major Chichester-Clark's resignation two Cabinet colleagues, Herbert Kirk, the Minister of Finance, and Nat Minford, Minister of State at Development and later Speaker of the short-lived Northern Ireland Assembly, came to me and said, 'The party is virtually unanimous that you should become the new Leader.' I agreed to put my name forward and it went to the Chief Whip proposed by Herbert Kirk, well known as a moderate, and seconded by Joe Burns, a traditional tough-minded Unionist from the west of the Province. It had become clear in previous months that unless a real effort was made to heal old wounds and create unity of purpose in the party, it was heading for a decisive split. The readiness of both sides in the former 'pro' and 'anti-O'Neill' struggle to support me seemed to augur well for the future, and I was determined to do what I could to cement that unity without sharpening fears and divisions in the community at large.

It was agreed therefore that the party Whip should be restored to four Unionist MPs who had been expelled from the Parliamentary Party a year earlier for refusing to support the Government on a confidence motion—Craig, West, Boal (a political loner who later held office briefly as Chairman of Ian Paisley's Democratic Unionist Party), and McQuade, a tough docker from West Belfast (who also later joined Ian Paisley). It was known that Bill Craig intended to put his name forward for the Leadership and since his support was obviously minimal, bringing him back into the Parliamentary Party would give him the opportunity to be soundly beaten, and, hopefully, oblige him to accept the democratic verdict of the party. Harry West, I believed, could be won round and this later proved to be the case.

On the morning of Tuesday 23 March the members of the Unionist Parliamentary Party, MPs and Senators, gathered in Committee Room 17 of Parliament Buildings at 11.30 a.m. to elect a new Leader and, in effect, a new Prime Minister of Northern Ireland. The meeting took only fifty minutes and the result was even more decisive than I had hoped: Bill Craig received four votes and I received twenty six. I despatched a message by hand to the Governor, Lord Grey, informing him of my election, rang my wife to tell her the news, and then went down to the Great Hall of Stormont to meet the press.

As I walked down the white marble staircase, dominated by the statue of Lord Craigavon, I could see below me scores of cameramen and journalists from all over the world, Europe, America, Africa,

Australasia—you name it, they were there. As the television arc lights went on and the camera bulbs started to flash I realized that what I, the Premier-elect of a mere Provincial Parliament governing 1½ million people, was about to say would be broadcast or telephoned all over the world that day, and it was violence which had made the occasion so newsworthy. It was an intimidating thought, but I had little time to get nervous. John Dobson, the Chief Whip, had already announced the vote, so I launched straight into a statement outlining my general ideas for the new government. I had written down some points on the back of an envelope the previous night before I went to bed and, working from that, I addressed the assembled representatives of the media. I was determined to get my premiership off to a good start and, feeling more at ease with my own notes than I would have done with a prepared script, I was reasonably happy with the result. Knowing how often the press make judgements from quick personal impressions it was important to create an atmosphere of confidence and action, so that they would go away with less gloomy predictions about the future.

The following are extracts from the Civil Service note of what I said:

My most important single aim is to restore confidence throughout the entire community. Without that all else would be futile. Obviously the kernel of our immediate problem is the law and order situation. Let me say right away that I am convinced that what we need on this front are not new principles, but practical results on the ground in the elimination not only of terrorism, but of riots and disorder. The basic principle must clearly be that the rule of law shall operate in all parts of Northern Ireland, so that the security which goes with the rule of law can be enjoyed by all our citizens...I will not expect harsh or repressive measures—no law-abiding citizen will have anything whatever to fear from my administration—but I will be looking for effective measures...I shall endeavour above all else to make people think clearly about our situation—there are far too many at the moment, on all sides, involved in blinkered dashes towards impossible or unworthy goals...

I fully realise that I am taking on a tough job. I would not be doing so if I did not myself have a deep confidence in the future of NI and in our present constitutional position. We are profoundly grateful for all the help we have received from the United Kingdom Government, but I think that all agree that our problems can only satisfactorily be solved by Ulster's own people. As an Ulsterman,

I can only promise to do my best for this Province and I appeal to all my countrymen to help me.

After this necessarily generalized statement of intent I answered a few questions and went off to the Governor's residence at Hillsborough to complete the formalities of my appointment.

Lord Grey asked if I was confident that I could form a government; I replied that I was, and then received letters of Appointment from Her Majesty the Queen. Lord Grey of Naunton had already in the three years since his appointment, shown himself to be a new kind of governor. He clearly did not regard himself as a mere rubber stamp and figure-head to be rolled out on State occasions. He took an interest in every aspect of life in the Province, and was anxious at every available opportunity to discuss public affairs with members of the Government. For example, two days after my election, the new Cabinet went to Government House at 10 p.m. for a meeting of the Northern Ireland Privy Council, a body which usually met about six times a year, presided over by the Governor as the Queen's Representative, to approve certain Government Orders and Regulations (known as SR and Os). Two new members of the Cabinet had first to be sworn in as Privy Councillors, with a lengthy oath of loyalty and secrecy administered by Sir Harold Black as Clerk of the Privy Council. Then all the 'Right Honourable' Gentlemen gathered in the Governor's large study to receive a homily on the need to create unity and harmony in Northern Ireland. Lord Grey was a talented and witty speaker and his advice, put forward on a political-philosophical rather than a party political level, was sound. But I must say that, almost alone among my colleagues, I regarded the office of Governor as rather archaic and colonial in a province of the United Kingdom and, although Lord Grey rapidly won the personal affection and respect of people of all political views, I did not see that the post fulfilled any indispensable constitutional function. Sometimes when Harold Wilson, as Leader of the Opposition at Westminster and a member of the United Kingdom Privy Council, wished to meet me for private discussions he would ask to see me on Privy Council terms, which meant terms of absolutely binding secrecy. But other less archaic means could have been found to serve that purpose.

There was much to be done in preparing to set up the new administration, and after my appointment I immediately got down to an examination of the problems facing us so that I could plan how to make the best use of the political and civil service talent available. Initial press reaction had been good and, though the *Daily Mirror* underlined the crisis which we faced with the headline 'The Man with the Worst Job in the World', the two most influential Belfast dailies, the *Telegraph* and the *Newsletter*, covered the election with editorials headlined 'The Best Man Won' and 'The Man For The Hour' respectively. If I was to have any chance of living up to the hopes and confidence being expressed there was no time to be wasted. I would have to build a Cabinet showing the qualities of dynamism and purposefulness for which the previous Cabinet had not always been noted during the two years of crises.

My first appointment after election was with General Tuzo, the current GOC in Northern Ireland, whom I asked to come and explain the security position to me. We held a very long discussion in the Prime Minister's room at Stormont, and it soon became clear that he and I viewed the situation in similar terms. We both knew it was important that some means be found of stopping the escalation in terrorism if the explosive tensions in the community were to be reduced and public confidence restored. General Tuzo was a humane and broad-minded man, but he did not enjoy exposing his men in a semi-passive role where the initiative lay almost entirely with the terrorists. Many members of the public were convinced that the security forces were operating under severe political restraints which were preventing them taking actions which they knew to be necessary to achieve success, so this was the first point which I sought to clear up. It was obvious to me that, by the very nature of democratic government, there must be policy guidelines within which the Army and the police operated, even in a crisis. General Tuzo pointed out that the practice of 'minimum force' was not a 'policy', in the normal sense of the word, which could be changed the next day, but rather was the obligation of uniformed men as of civilians under the law of the United Kingdom. On the other hand this did not mean simply containment, and I pressed on him my view that it was a mistake for the Army to be seen as a mere 'peace-keeping' force, a sort of UN role which imposed no obligation to seek out and destroy the terrorist. Tuzo accepted this and we got down to discussing in some detail specific ways in which the security forces might seize the initiative and put pressure on the terrorists. He showed me the general orders under which the Army operated and suggested various new measures. By the end of our discussion I was convinced that really effective progress could be made in hindering the movement of terrorists, cutting their supply lines, and getting more information on their activities and personnel.

The role of the Royal Ulster Constabulary was also crucial. The effects of the reorganization following the Hunt Report in 1969 had been disappointing. Recruitment had certainly stepped up considerably in 1970 in both Protestant and Catholic sections of the population—some 20 per cent of recruits during that year were Catholics, as compared to 10 per cent in the pre-Hunt period. But a serious mistake had been made in not putting the new civilianized force immediately into the former 'No Go' areas, with the result that for the population of these areas there was little effective change on the ground. The Chichester-Clark security reforms simply passed them by leaving them with the same grudges against the system, and increasingly in the intimidating grip of thugs and gunmen. The IRA campaign had escalated and Catholic recruitment to the RUC was drying up as the murder of policemen and soldiers became more common, with particular viciousness being directed at Catholic members. It was an important aim of the IRA to prevent cross-sectarian security forces emerging, since this would have destroyed their own pose as defenders of the minority, and they were prepared to commit some of the most gruesome murders to secure it. Yet if any return to normality was to be achieved—and no one wanted the Army to remain for ever on the streets of the Province—the RUC would have to take over the weight of law enforcement, and preparations for that could not start too soon.

So I invited Sir Graham Shillington to come and see me also. In the two days between Chichester-Clark's resignation and my appointment speculation about impending changes in security policy, and in particular the role of the police, had been rife. One London daily reported that I was likely to 'review the Hunt report' and create an armed riot police; another suggested that Chichester-Clark had resigned because he wanted internment, and that a new Prime Minister was likely to introduce it. Edward Heath was moved by these reports to declare in the Commons on Monday 22 March 1971 that there would be no general rearming of the RUC, no reviving of the 'B' Specials, and no formation of riot police. While the specific issue on which Chichester-Clark's general dissatisfaction had eventually come to a head was his request for more troops and the refusal of the Ministry of Defence to meet it in a manner which he regarded as showing adequate appreciation of the urgency of the matter, there were also broader issues involved. When he said in his resignation statement 'I can see no other way of bringing home to all concerned the realities of the present constitutional, political and security situation' the phrase 'all concerned' was carefully chosen. He had found himself under pressure in his own party to adopt a tough law and order policy and go back on the Hunt Report, with little apparent recognition of the fact that Stormont was not a sovereign parliament; under pressure from Nationalist politicans, who persisted in accusations of 'repression' and refused to accept his good faith in attempting to conciliate them with a programme of reforms pushed through against opposition in his own party; and under pressure from Westminster, which wanted liberal public relations exercises and was not taking enough account of his need to secure his own party base. He was the man-in-the-middle, trying to reconcile all these pressures and taking the blame for everything that went wrong; the tensions were enormous, nor could they be reconciled unless people on all sides started being more realistic.

It was to pre-empt any further speculation that my election meant a decisive policy switch towards any one of these pressures that I said in my first statement that what we needed were 'not new principles, but practical results'. And it was with a view to finding ways of achieving these results that I was now holding detailed discussions with the GOC and the Chief Constable.

I ended the discussions with the clear conviction that a more effective enforcement of existing policies was possible, and that the Army in particular was ready and willing to carry it through. Naturally the heavily armed troops, rather than the civilianized police, would have to carry the burden of the campaign against a ruthless and dangerous terrorist enemy. The police needed to settle down after the massive reorganization, to build up their morale, and to widen public support and co-operation with them as a police service offering the protection of the law to all.

There remained the question of how the Government would administer its security responsibilities. I decided that, since the success of any government was going to hinge on its success in reducing violence, I would hold the portfolio of Home Affairs myself, concentrating on security and devolving most of the other business of the Ministry to a Minister of State. I believed that influence on and knowledge of security matters had been slipping away from Stormont and towards Whitehall in recent years. This had led sometimes to local insensitivity in operations, and had rendered Stormont increasingly impotent in a major field of policy, undermining its authority. More expert advice was necessary if we were to be authoritative and well informed in our discussions with Westminster and the Security Chiefs.

So I decided to set up a small high-powered branch in the Cabinet Offices for the co-ordination of security policy and the servicing of the Joint Security Committee (a committee of Police, Army and Government which met regularly). I appointed a senior civil servant as security adviser and he played an invaluable role as link-man, attending each of the weekly briefing sessions given by the GOC at Lisburn Army HQ, and acting as special adviser to the Cabinet.

The next priority was to build my Cabinet. For many of the appointments there were obvious choices, where experienced Ministers were holding posts in which they were performing well: Sir John Andrews, son of the second Prime Minister of Northern Ireland, an honourable and loyal man who had been Deputy Prime Minister and leader of the Senate under Chichester-Clark and was highly thought of among all sections of the Unionist Party as an elder states-man who had no taste for the party in-fighting which had marred recent years; Billy Fitzimmons, a compassionate man who was deeply committed to the welfare state, at Health and Social Services; Herbie Kirk, an accountant by profession, with six years experience in the senior Ministry of Finance; and William Long, a Minister with a quick mind and an ability to get on with people, at Education. But I was determined not to produce simply the 'mixture as before', so I set three objectives in seeking to draw up a balanced Cabinet. First, it would have to put the best men in the most suitable jobs, thus producing a government marked by efficiency, by being on top of its job. Secondly, it should be as broadly based as possible, breaking through party political divisions to create the idea of community rather than simply party government. And thirdly, it should help to produce greater unity among members of my own party, the Unionist Party.

I knew there was one man trusted and respected by many grass-roots Unionists alarmed by the rapid political changes, and whom I could hope to persuade to join the Cabinet—Harry West, the Minister of Agriculture dismissed by O'Neill in 1967 and now President of the rebel West Ulster Unionist Council. He and I had been personal friends and I had first persuaded Lord Brookeborough, when I was Chief Whip, to bring West in to the Government as Parliamentary Secretary at the Ministry of Agriculture. When O'Neill dismissed him after a dispute on the purchase of land near his home in County Fermanagh West felt he had been victimized. I thought he had been ill-advised in his handling of the affair and that O'Neill's motives in hounding him out of office were entirely political. Subsequently an east–west tension had become obvious in the party with West, appropriately enough, becoming the spokesman for Unionists in the more conservative and rural western area where the local government changes in particular had caused alarm. But I believed that he had greater sympathy for the position of the Government than many of the right-wingers with whom he associated and that he could be won over. It took me nearly forty-eight hours to get his agreement after much discussion and argument. It was a difficult political step for him and he had to be given time to consult his friends and to weigh the alternatives. He put considerable pressure on me to agree to various policy changes to appease the right wing of the party, but I told him that I was inviting him to join the Government on the basis of existing policies, including a full commitment to the reform programme.

He then urged me to offer a post to Bill Craig as well, saying this would bring about complete Unionist solidarity. But I was quite adamant about that; there was little possibility of Bill Craig and I agreeing on policy as his stance over the previous few years had been increasingly extreme and his speeches inflammatory. His inclusion in the Cabinet would have put great strain on our relationship with Westminster and demolished the prospects of good community relations in Ulster. He had already taken his defeat quite badly and told the press within hours of my election that if government policies were not reversed I would only last a couple of months after which there would have to be a general election. Eventually, however, West accepted my offer on the basis of what I was able to tell him about the more effective lines of action I intended to see pursued by the security forces.

My next task was to get someone from outside the ranks of the Unionist Party to accept office. I had already decided that the man I wanted was David Bleakley, former Chairman of the Northern Ireland Labour Party and its best known politician. Until recently one of Labour's small band of Stormont MP's, he had done much valuable work in peace groups in East Belfast when there was serious rioting in that area. The Government of Ireland Act provided for appointment to the Cabinet for a maximum of six months of a person who was not a member of either House, and David Bleakley seemed an appropriate Minister of Community Relations. After some thought he accepted my offer. This was the first time that a non-Unionist Minister had been appointed to a Stormont Government, and I regarded it as a significant step in the direction of creating a broader-based Government. It also helped our relations with the Labour Opposition at Westminster at that time, as Callaghan was a firm advocate of links between the Northern Ireland Labour Party and the British Labour Party.

The rest was quite straightforward; I brought in Robin Bailie, a young and able solicitor from the moderate wing of the party, as Minister of Commerce, a post he was clearly pleased to be offered. Roy Bradford, who had been at Commerce, agreed—after much grumbling—to take on Development. He did not appear to recognize that it was one of the most important posts in the Government. And finally, John Brooke, son of Lord Brookeborough and an enthusiastic and sociable politician, came in as Chief Whip.

It was, I believed, a Cabinet more widely representative of the population of Ulster than any previous Stormont Government. It had given recognition to ability and to experience. If this Government could work together in harmony, in spite of the diversity of political and social background, then I believed we had a good chance of grappling with, and overcoming, the divisions and tensions in the community at large.

The top civil servants in the Cabinet Secretariat were a talented group and I decided to make no major changes. Sir Harold Black, the *eminence grise* of the Stormont Civil Service was an efficient administrator, meticulous, and with a memory like a filing cabinet. Ken Bloomfield, the Deputy Permanent Secretary, was a thinker of the highest order with an unequalled talent for a very important government activity—drafting statements summing up decisions made—as Harold Wilson himself recognized at Downing Street on a later occasion: 'the quickest drafter of good statements I have seen,' he said. In addition to these two I decided to bring in two members of the staff at Development whom I had learned to work with easily; Jack McNally became my Press Officer, and Robert Ramsay became my Private Secretary.

Robert Ramsay was young for such an important post, but his sense of humour and his general unflappability made him the ideal aide in a crisis. I like to think it meant there were always two of us keeping calm. Robert had been with me at Commerce, so there was a considerable amount of continuity in the civil service teams with whom I worked during my Ministerial career.

There is a real danger for all Ministers that they may be absorbed into the civil service structure and become totally dependent on it for advice. The top civil servant is trained and tuned to meet his Minister's every need—and to anticipate it if possible. It would be very easy to become too administration-minded and lose touch with the man in the street, and the danger of this increases the longer one has been in office. I had been conscious of it for some time, and it was one of the reasons I was anxious to build up the research and policy section of the Unionist Party. But no individual Minister has the resources at his disposal to challenge the conclusions and detailed facts presented by the civil service, and simply has to rely on his own judgement and experience in selecting from the alternatives put to him. As Prime Minister I was going from one meeting to another, switching rapidly between quite different subjects, with only limited time to master the various briefs presented to me beforehand. I had long since discovered that one of the secrets of ministerial efficiency was the ability to master a brief quickly. Every Minister has found himself at some time faced with an unexpected item on the floor of the House and with perhaps two minutes to grasp the main points of a civil service brief before making a convincing answer. Fortunately I seemed to have the knack of doing this and was not often caught out.

I can remember one of the occasions I faced at Stormont without a brief, when Bill Craig was Minister of Development. An important Bill on transport came up in the Commons earlier one day than had been expected. Craig was in his office, and so if no one moved the Second Reading of the Bill it would fall by default. I was the only Minister on the government benches and so I got up and moved the Bill, urging the House to recognize all its good points and generally flanneling until Bill Craig could reach the Chamber and give the official supporting speech. It was one occasion when I was delighted to see him arrive.

During Sean Lemass's famous visit to Stormont in 1965 I was interested to discover during conversations how highly he rated the ability to master briefs. I happened to mention my surprise at his recent appointment of Charles Haughey as Minister for Agriculture in Dublin. 'I have known him for some years in the hunting world,' I said, 'but I never thought he had much interest in Agriculture.' 'Ah well, that's as may be,' said Lemass, 'but Charles has a great ability to master a brief, and he is managing the briefs in Agriculture as well as he ever managed the briefs at the Department of Justice.' (Charles Haughey was dismissed from the Dublin Cabinet in 1970 by Lynch for suspected involvement in gun-running, but reinstated as a Front Bench Fianna Fail spokesman in 1975—this time for Health and Welfare!)

Inevitably, in this kind of operation the civil service has a potential for influence probably not realized by most members of the public. Some Ministers scarcely wrote a single one of their own speeches and, although I tried to keep my hand in as much as possible, at least half of the time I had to work from scripts drafted by the civil service.

The announcement of the various decisions and of the composition of the Cabinet on Thursday 25 March 1971 made an immediate impact. 'Shock' and 'Sensation' screamed the headlines. 'Mr Brian Faulkner has formed a government that could only have been formed by Brian Faulkner,' said the editorial in the *Belfast Telegraph*; had it not been for the next sentence which referred to 'boldness, imagination, and agility' I would never have been sure that it was not a carefully phrased insult! A press statement outlined the basis of the Cabinet:

My object in forming this administration has simply been to find the men best qualified, in my view, to hold the various offices. I have also sought to create a broadly-based government but I want to make it absolutely clear that every member of it has fully endorsed the principles of policy which I outlined on taking office.

Naturally I did not please everyone—those with experience of Ulster politics will testify to the impossibility of doing that. From Republican sources there came criticism of West's appointment, on the grounds that he was a right-winger who would wish to go back on reforms; some liberal Unionists were also apprehensive about the consequences of his entry into the Government. But West issued a statement the same day explaining his position: 'I have accepted', he said, 'that the decisions which have been taken cannot be altered, and that what we must all now do is to ensure that the campaign against terrorism, within the framework of accepted policy, is pursued with the utmost vigour and effectiveness.' On the other hand some of Craig's supporters on the right wing of the party criticized Bleakley's inclusion on the grounds that he was not an elected representative and it was therefore undemocratic. But in general reaction was good and people accepted the need to bind the community together in government.

In keeping with my hope to broaden support for the Government I spoke to Jack Lynch on the phone about my hopes for my Premiership. I noted in my diary afterwards that he was 'pleased and congratulatory'. It seemed possible that we could have a good working relationship.

Within six days I had to face two major meetings of the Unionist Party organization. The governing body of the party, the Standing Committee, met on Friday 26 March and three days later the Annual General Meeting of the Ulster Unionist Council was held in Wellington Hall in Belfast.

I think there must be few Prime Ministers or party leaders in western democracies who found their parties as difficult to handle as Unionist Prime Ministers did, nor was this only due to the crisis situation in the Province. The Unionist Party had started off as a vehicle for the mobilization of the entire spectrum of pro-Union opinion in Ulster and its structure reflected that fact. There had always been extremist groups to the right which operated outside the party—Paisley's Protestant Unionist Party being the latest—but within it there was a remarkable range of social and political attitudes. Landlords and peers, businessmen and professional men, farmers, labourers and industrial workers all sat together in the associations and central organs of the party. Almost every town, village and hamlet had its Unionist branch and its right to be heard at party meetings. The central party headquarters in Belfast had little control over associations and had been neglected by leaders because the party had never been in opposition. All of this meant that a relatively small number of dissidents could perpetually harass and embarrass the Government by calling a series of meetings of the most important bodies of the party to discuss motions of no confidence or criticisms of our policy, as they had done to my predecessor. On one occasion during his Premiership Chichester-Clark suffered the embarrassment of being removed from the vice-chairmanship of his local branch. None of this made an already difficult task any easier.

These two meetings were, however, quite satisfactory from my point of view. I received 3 to 1 votes of confidence from both the 300-strong Standing Committee and the 900-strong Ulster Unionist Council, the party's supreme body, and standing ovations after my speeches. Bill Craig lost his position as one of the Vice-Presidents, and was isolated as spokesman for the troublemakers. I appealed in my speech for party members to 'throw away their labels', and made it clear that, although I wanted party cohesion, I was not prepared to pursue it at the expense of the community at large.

> The desire for party unity is there, and my administration will certainly respond to it, [I said] but at the same time I want to lay it plainly on the line that there can be no desertion of the principles of our policies, which are aimed not only at achieving economic and social progress, but at assuring British standards in every sphere of life for all our people. I make no apologies for these policies. I will not backtrack on their fundamental principles. Let that be clearly understood.

9

A Meeting of Minds

I made my first speech to the Stormont House of Commons as Prime Minister the next day, when the Government sought a vote of confidence. I had spoken there so many times before, but this was for me an historic occasion.

The Stormont Commons was very much like a smaller version of the Westminster Commons. It had long blue leather benches for Government and for Opposition (green, as at Westminster, had been thought an unduly Nationalist colour), a Speaker's Table with Despatch Boxes for Front Benchers on either side, a silver mace on one end, and an elaborate Speaker's Chair at the other. On our benches sat the thirty-eight Unionist MPs, flanked by Ian Paisley at one side, and across the floor sat the six Social Democratic and Labour Party MPs, led by Gerry Fitt, the remnant of the old rural Nationalist Party, and the one Labour Party representative, Vivian Simpson. It was interesting to see Gerry Fitt and Paddy Devlin, the two proletarian Nationalists from Belfast, sitting side by side as members of the SDLP. They had been members of different parties—the Republican Labour Party and the Northern Ireland Labour Party respectively—until the formation of the Social Democratic Labour Party (SDLP) a year earlier had brought together some of the more energetic anti-partitionists and civil rights activists in a new-look party to replace the Nationalists. Many of us could remember the famous occasion in the Commons when Fitt and Devlin had come to blows behind the Speaker's chair after a speech by Fitt, and had to be separated by attendants! At least the old rivalry would now take place inside the one party, and Gerry, as Leader, clearly had the upper hand.

I began my speech by concentrating on the economic issues, too often neglected, relating them to the security and political situation, and pointing out our common interests:

In our discussions here over recent months, the economic issues have been overshadowed. But . . . the recurrence of redundancy, and the marked absence of major new industrial projects serve to remind us— and by us I mean all Ulster people—that our bread and butter is at stake here. . . . Without order and stability we will fail to create new jobs . . .

I pointed out the commitment of the Government to the reform programme:

I contest most strongly the suggestion that what has been done is a matter of mere form and nothing more. Consider the massive housing development in Londonderry; the fact that all over the country public authority housing is being let on a points basis; and the clear evidence that the Parliamentary Commissioner and the Commissioner for Complaints are doing very thoroughly the job they were appointed to do . . . I stand ready to have discussions without delay with the Hon. Member for Dock (Gerry Fitt), as Leader of the largest single Opposition party, to whom I am anxious to extend all courtesies in terms of consultation and otherwise, which are appropriate to his position.

This last statement was more than an empty promise. I had some very definite proposals in mind for involving the Opposition in the life of Parliament and the work of government in a way which went far beyond any proposals already made. With hindsight I regret not having put them forward in this first debate, but I had not discussed them with the new Cabinet and anticipated some argument before I could bring everyone with me. At the end of the debate we received a decisive vote of confidence, in spite of bitter opposition from some members of the SDLP.

On Thursday 1 April I went to London to meet the British Prime Minister, Ted Heath. He was a politician with whom I had not had very frequent contact during my time in politics, as he had never shown any special interest in Irish affairs. I was his host during his first visit to Ulster in 1959 (as I pointed out earlier) and I had met him occasionally since then. After his dramatic election victory in June 1970 Heath had left Ulster affairs in the hands of the Home Secretary, Reggie Maudling. The latter had not, however, made a very good public impact in the Province, largely because the flamboyant style of Callaghan had led people to expect frequent public relations exercises demonstrating concern and activity and assuring them that Westminster would see them through. Maudling did not have the style nor the inclination to set up these rather superficial circuses and messianic visits, and the one occasion on which he tried to do so proved that he was better off sticking to his own style of quietly efficient politics. On 4 March he visited Stormont and addressed a joint meeting of both Houses of the Northern Ireland Parliament in the Great Hall. It was a very dramatic setting for such an unusual meeting and naturally the press gave it a great build-up beforehand. Everyone was speculating on the important things he must wish to say in asking for such a meeting to be arranged. So when he addressed the assembled politicians in a very ordinary speech it was a considerable anticlimax and damaged his standing in the Province. It seemed also to damage his standing in the Cabinet and, in particular, in the eyes of Ted Heath.

The resignation of Major Chichester-Clark had shaken Westminster—as he had intended it should—and, although Maudling was insisting there had been no real disagreement on policy, Robin Chichester-Clark MP, brother of the outgoing Premier, knew otherwise and, backed by his seven Ulster Unionist colleagues, was putting on pressure at Westminster for a more decisive approach. The Conservative backbenchers were angry and worried about the line being pursued by their Ministers and were supporting the Unionist criticisms. I knew that these pressures would strengthen my hand in this crucial first meeting as Prime Minister with Heath. It was very important that we understand each other's mind if there was to be a re-establishment of confidence in Stormont–Westminster relationships and if the Army—which was of course under Westminster control—was to be able to carry out an effective security policy. I was firmly convinced after the meeting that Heath and I viewed the Ulster situation in very similar terms.

Black, Stout, Bloomfield, Ramsay, and I flew over to Heathrow on a commercial flight without police escorts, as was usual until August 1971. We were met by Scotland Yard detectives and a government limousine, which carried us swiftly on to the motorway for London and then broke down, much to the embarrassment of the driver. It took forty-five minutes for a replacement car to reach us after a radio call, and the result was some dislocation of our schedule of meetings.

Maudling was waiting at the Home Office with Sir Phillip Allen, the Permanent Under-Secretary, and after an abbreviated discussion we walked across Treasury Yard into Downing Street to meet the Prime Minister. Heath, accompanied by Lord Carrington, and Sir Alec Douglas-Home, Foreign Secretary, greeted us cordially. I was soon to regard these three—Maudling, Carrington, and Home—as Heath's regular advisers on Ulster matters. There was never any doubt who was in charge; Heath dominated his colleagues totally at all meetings I attended during his Premiership. Carrington, who was the least vocal of the triumvirate at meetings, seemed to have a good personal relationship with Heath; one felt that his opinions were made clear privately before and after meetings. Sir Alec was courteous and sociable; he was very much a Unionist, in the traditional sense of favouring the Union. Maudling, relaxed and easy-going, did not fit in too easily with Heath's brusque and business-like style and after some months I began to feel that Maudling was losing influence and being left out of decisions. There seemed to be an element of personal coldness involved which put this relationship in a different category from the general problem of communication with Heath experienced by several of his ministers. Willie Whitelaw later told me that when they wanted to find out what was being said in the constant private contacts which developed between Heath and myself they had to 'pump it out of him'. For my part I liked Heath's action-orientated approach. We were joined by the new Chief of the General Staff, General Sir Michael Carver, whose first day it was in office, and by General Tuzo. Five of Whitehall's most eminent civil servants—Sir Burke Trend, Secretary to the Cabinet, Neil Cairncross of the Cabinet Office, Robert Armstrong, Heath's Private Secretary, Donald Maitland, Heath's Chief PRO (later ambassador to the UNO and then the EEC) and Howard Smith completed the gathering. It was quite an audience for our first joint performance.

The discussion proceeded smoothly, covering security, the economy, and community relations. Heath showed considerable interest in the details and took quite a tough line. He said that the position of Ulster within the United Kingdom was inviolate for as long as that was the democratically expressed will of the people of the Province, and emphasized that his administration would not wish to play the role of 'Big Brother' pushing the Stormont administration around in public; he wanted rather a two-way relationship between the Stormont and Westminster governments, so that the former would have adequate authority and resources to carry out its responsibilities while paying attention to the London perspective. He was particularly emphatic that the IRA must be beaten, and asked detailed questions on security tactics, pressing the possibility of more border security by such measures as the blocking of minor cross-border roads. The question of internment arose; General Tuzo said plans were ready for its implementation if necessary, and Carrington said prisoners could be accommodated in the Maidstone prison ship in Belfast Lough and in temporary camps.

I explained the economic situation in the Province, stressing the diffi-

culties of achieving the targets set in 1969 for our Five Year Development Plan in spite of the remarkable resilience of industry. It was agreed
that everything possible should be done to maintain employment, and
a Northern Ireland civil servant would be attached to all our official
teams at the EEC to safeguard Provincial interests.

Heath expressed approval of the appointment of David Bleakley to
the Cabinet; it was a step forward, he said. I commented that I would
like to widen the base of government as much as possible, but that the
SDLP had recently made a clear statement that they would not take
part in the government, even if asked.

The meeting ended around 1 p.m. and, after a private half hour with
Heath when I told him of my talk with Lynch, our party went off to the
Ulster Office in Berkeley Street for lunch. A press conference with
some seventy journalists followed almost immediately and, boosted by
the morning's successful meetings, I quite enjoyed it. The press reports
were pleasantly complimentary. A rapid succession of interviews for
radio and television filled the rest of the day before we retired to our
hotel, the Sonesta Tower (later the Carlton Tower), recommended to
us by the Special Branch because its design facilitated security. On this
as on later occasions, our bodyguards were based in the next room.

The reason for the overnight stay was a lunch which I had arranged
to give at Claridges the next day for editors. About fourteen turned up
for this informal occasion, including the editors of the *Daily Telegraph*,
Mirror, *Daily Express*, *Spectator*, and *Economist*. It was a useful public
relations exercise for us, and enabled me to improve my personal contacts. Press and politicians need each other and it is best if they operate
on a basis of mutual respect.

I flew back to Ulster that afternoon, more optimistic than I had been
for some time. Everything seemed to be going even better than I had
hoped—and I have often been called an incurable optimist ('Look-on-
the-bright-side Brian' a member of my family called me). There was no
doubt that the new administration was off to a good start. There had
been a lull in violence and the Army, after its early blunders in what was
inevitably strange territory, seemed to be getting a firm grasp of the
situation. I had secured the broad-based Cabinet for which I had hoped
and firm backing from my party. Without Harry West the rebel West
Ulster Unionist Council was collapsing and Craig was isolated. The
SDLP were taking a guarded but less hostile approach. And now I had
found in the British Prime Minister an ally who clearly could be relied
upon in the crises that would inevitably occur. My aides were enthusiastic about my meeting with Heath. They felt it contrasted favourably

with previous Prime Ministerial meetings and that Heath and I, as hard-headed and practical men, would have a special relationship. The phrase 'a meeting of minds' seemed to sum it up.

Becoming Prime Minister of Northern Ireland did not dramatically alter my lifestyle, though the pressures and tensions notably increased. Since the beginning of what had been an almost continuous crisis, or series of crises, at the end of 1968 it had been difficult to take any holidays with members of my family, and naturally my period as Prime Minister did not provide any additional leisure to do so. I soon discovered that a Prime Minister's time, even in a small place like Northern Ireland, is not his own, that his private life is cut to a minimum, and that he is always on duty at all hours of the day or night, whether awake or asleep.

There had since the War been no official residence for the Prime Minister, perhaps a reflection on the fact that my predecessors had ancestral seats in the country. There was an elegant and spacious Speaker's House in the grounds of Stormont Castle which had been vacated by the Speaker during the Premiership of Brookeborough and O'Neill to ease the travelling problems of these two. But at the end of O'Neill's Premiership the new Speaker, Ivan Neill, laid claim to the house, as he was legally entitled to do, and Chichester-Clark had to arrange for the furnishing of a small flat in Stormont Castle to provide accommodation in emergencies.

My own home is a comfortable house in eight acres of land some thirty miles from Belfast at Seaforde, County Down, and I continued to travel from there to work on most days. A scrambler telephone line had to be installed, and it was a common occurrence to receive a call at 2 or 3 a.m. as some crisis or incident developed. I remember Major-General Farrar-Hockley, a soldier whom I deeply respected, ringing me once in the middle of the night after one of his men had been killed in the Markets area of Belfast. He was the kind of man who felt deeply about such things.

There was never a day during my time as Prime Minister on which I was not in contact with both the Secretary to the Cabinet and the Security Adviser; even on Christmas Day there were decisions to be taken and things to be attended to.

On an average day I would get up before 7.30 a.m., have breakfast, attend to the horses, and leave for the office about 9 a.m., giving the Private Office time to open the mail before I arrived. My arrival home varied considerably, from around 7 p.m. some days to midnight on others. The following is taken at random from my diary of that time:

9.30 a.m.	Briefing on overnight security incidents and morning newspapers.
9.50 a.m.	Clear mail and official papers.
10.15 a.m.	Chair Cabinet meeting.
11.30 a.m.	Finalize text of speech for Parliament and for evening party speaking engagement. Discussion with advisers.
12.15 a.m.	Receive deputation brought by MP about problems caused to traders by security measures in small Ulster town.
12.45 a.m.	Finalize answers to Parliamentary Questions.
1.00 p.m.	Leave for official lunch (speech to be made) at nearby hotel.
2.30 p.m.	House of Commons, Question time.
3.15 p.m.	At PM's room, Stormont; interview with overseas journalist.
3.30 p.m.	Talk to some backbenchers about government policy, backed up by Chief Whip.
4.00 p.m.	Clear afternoon official papers; dictate some letters.
5.30 p.m.	Speak in adjournment debate.
6.30 p.m.	Eat, then sign letters.
7.00 p.m.	Leave for party meeting in the country. Speech followed by question and answer session.
11.30 p.m.	Home; telephone messages.
12.30 p.m.	Bed.

Family life I have always regarded as very important, and I have tried to minimize the extent to which my political career interfered with it. From my happy family circle I have drawn much strength and I have the greatest of respect for those bachelors who have achieved high office without such inspiration. I have been fortunate in having a wife with a history degree from Trinity College, Dublin, and experience of journalism in Belfast, who had also been for a time Personal Secretary to the third Prime Minister of Northern Ireland, Sir Basil Brooke. She acted for me as manager, secretary, adviser, groom, helper, cook, and was often the first sounding board for my ideas. My whole family took a great interest in politics and the 'Seaforde Cabinet' was always abreast of developments.

All this was in private of course, as I tried to keep my public life and my family life as separate as possible. I remembered as a young man taking a poor view of politicians who projected their families for political advantage and brought their wives on to the platforms at potentially difficult election and party meetings, apparently in the hope that this would ward off strong criticisms. I did not wish to take such shelter from the rough and tumble of blunt debate and so I often tried, not always successfully, to dissuade my family from attending meetings. The first family pictures circulated in the media were taken after my appointment as Prime Minister when the press descended on my home obviously determined to get some background material, and we did not encourage later efforts to do the same.

There were other, more sombre, reasons for keeping publicity about one's private life to a minimum. Politics can be a dangerous profession in Ireland, and I got used to living with death threats and security guards as early as 1959 when I became Minister of Home Affairs during the previous IRA campaign. As Prime Minister I was given a permanent guard of seven plain clothes policemen and arrangements were made for the security of my family. On the daily journey to and from the office I was 'topped and tailed' as the police called it; we travelled fast in three cars over a variable route. Threats, phoned and written, reached my office, my home and various associates in increased numbers, the majority purporting to come from Republican sources but some also from extreme loyalists who had dubbed me a 'traitor'.

On more than one occasion when my elder son David was studying at Aberdeen University we received a threat against him from someone who clearly knew his whereabouts and his place of residence. There were bomb scares at his halls of residence, which caused inconvenience to the authorities and embarrassment to him and we received telephone threats—one which caused us a nasty afternoon before we could contact him said he had already been 'dealt with' by the IRA. Thankfully none of these threats came to anything.

Sometimes the Special Branch would intercept a threat or intelligence reports of a threat and tell me about it fi they thought it sufficiently important. It was a strange thing to be told that there was a threat to kill me the next day, but I never let it interfere with my plans or my work. We were careful, but we did not live in fear, and in the beautiful countryside of County Down it was sometimes difficult to believe that such dangers existed. There was the lighter side too, when I went hunting, as I still tried to do on most Saturdays. None of my bodyguards was a horseman and as the hunt galloped across the fields they would dash around the side roads in cars trying to keep near us, which I know they did not find as amusing as I did.

Hunting hounds is a way of clearing one's mind and getting away from the civil service briefs and political problems by doing something which requires total concentration.

In the early 1960s I became Joint-Master of the Iveagh Harriers with Albert Uprichard of Gilford, whose family were hunting men for three generations, and who taught me all I ever learned about hounds. After a few years I became Master, carrying the horn myself. We were officially a Harrier pack, but in recent years, with an intake of foxhound blood in the pack and foxes becoming much more numerous, we have been hunting foxes.

I have heard it said that the man who carries the horn is like the conductor of an orchestra, he has to bring out the best in each performer, and mould them all together to form a perfect whole. A huntsman must know each of his hounds as an individual so through the summer I visit the kennels and take my hounds out for road exercise on foot. There are few greater pleasures than to be greeted by their joyful clamour when they recognize my car driving into the yard. To watch the pack working on a stale scent and assist them with a successful cast that sets them on the line again, and then to be with them on a good horse as they go streaming away across the County Down countryside—as 'Snaffles' puts it in the caption under a famous hunting picture, 'If there is Paradise on Earth it is this, it is this, it is this!'

It is important for huntsmen to know the country they hunt over, and the farmers who live there. I have kept diaries over the past twenty years in which after supper on a hunting day, I write up that day's sport: the coverts we draw, the hounds that work best, the townlands we hunt over, and the names of the people who were out with us. It was the hunting background and the country humour of *Experiences of an Irish RM* by Somerville and Ross that made it my favourite literary companion over many years.

I have always thought that a twenty-four-hour day seven days a week sustained over a period could only reduce one's efficiency, energy, and capacity to deal with crises. Hunting is not politically and socially useful in the same way as, for example, golf might be, since few of my political colleagues or of the media pundits have done more than ride a donkey at the seaside as children. But in a way that has been a bonus since it has made the break from politics more complete.

At the end of two months in office things seemed to be keeping more or less on course. The political atmosphere was distinctly better all round, there had been few major incidents on the security front and though sporadic bombings continued at a level which could never be acceptable, it seemed that army tactics might begin to pay off; rioting had almost disappeared, and the capacity of the IRA to muster active support in Catholic areas seemed greatly reduced. We knew there was going to be no overnight resolution of the situation, but I was convinced that the steady and consistent application of clearly stated and widely accepted policies in the political and security fields would gradually give us the upper hand with the terrorists, and produce an atmosphere of hope and confidence in which political reconciliation could be achieved. The only option for the terrorists was to attempt to inflame public opinion and provoke reprisals by committing atrocities. It was a war of nerves and none of the political interests—the Westminster Government, the SDLP, or the Unionist Party—could afford to lose that war. If they did democratic politics would be discredited and violence could spread like a disease.

10
Lost Opportunity

The year 1971 was the fiftieth anniversary of Northern Ireland and its government. Plans for celebrations to mark the occasion had been in hand for several years and, in spite of the unhappy circumstances now surrounding its arrival, we had decided to go ahead. The people of Ulster had much to celebrate. Fifty years earlier it was thought that economically and politically the Province had no chance of survival. Yet it had survived the hungry 1930s, played a vital strategic role in the Allied victory of World War II, and had established thriving new industries which gave all its people a standard of living which their neighbours in the Irish Republic did not enjoy. This celebration was therefore an opportunity to restore a battered morale, to demonstrate resilience in the face of renewed attack by traditional enemies, and to direct public attention to a more hopeful and light-hearted side of life.

Yet even here politics and community divisions intruded. Nationalist leaders felt less inclined to celebrate the survival of Northern Ireland. In deference to the feelings of the minority plans for a parallel celebration of fifty years of the Stormont Parliament's existence were played down and the community festival side made the central theme.

One sunny May morning the 'Ulster '71' exhibition in Belfast's Botanic Gardens was officially opened by Sir Peter Studd, Lord Mayor of London, followed by a light-hearted tussle in the dodgem cars between the members of the press and the Stormont Cabinet, with my car receiving special attention! The centrepiece of 'Ulster 71' was a large exhibition hall—created out of the newly constructed Queen's University gymnasium and sports centre—featuring every aspect of life in Ulster: scientific work, such as the pioneering in cardiac care at the Royal Victoria Hospital; development plans for new towns and redevelopment of some older ones; and the traditions, culture and history of the province. There was also an exhibit portraying many of the famous personalities of Ulster descent or birth—ten American

Presidents, British soldiers such as Alexander, Templer, Montgomery, and Alanbrooke, and personalities in cultural and sporting life such as St John Ervine, Louis MacNeice, Mike Gibson, Mary Peters, Paddy Hopkirk, and many others. The whole thing was brought up to date with 'a tunnel of love and hate', carrying the appropriate graffiti and accompanied by the sadly familiar recorded sounds of riots and violence. Outside the hall were other exhibits and an open-air arena for concerts and special sporting events.

Pride in one's history should never become a substitute for pride in the present, but these celebrations came at an opportune time for those of us who were trying to restore some normality and confidence to the community. I was certainly pleased to see that they gave a great deal of enjoyment to many thousands of people who had become accustomed to living almost in a state of siege.

Towards the end of May, however, security started to deteriorate. The IRA had been apprehensive about the increased Army activity of the previous two months, but had grown used to it, and were becoming bolder again. Explosions in business premises and government offices started to escalate, and there were riots in several parts of Belfast. On 19 May there was a chilling exhibition of IRA confidence and support in the Falls Road area of Belfast when Republicans gave a military-style funeral to one of their members who had been killed while trying to shoot soldiers. Over a thousand IRA supporters marched in military formation wearing the Republican 'uniform' of a black beret and dark glasses. They paraded openly, conveying to the world a horrifying message: 'We support the IRA and their killing of policemen, soldiers and civilians, their bombing of offices, businesses, and public buildings; we support the declaration of war on our fellow-citizens.' The spectacle of this force on the march in a Catholic area inflamed highly dangerous tensions and community animosities which are still being played out today.

A few days later, on the evening of 25 May, a suitcase packed with explosives was thrown through the door of Springfield Road RUC station, landing in a reception area crowded with civilians, most of them Catholics from the surrounding area. There was panic among the men, women and children present and a virtual massacre would almost certainly have occurred were it not for the quick thinking and outstanding bravery of two men, Sergeant Willetts of the Parachute Regiment, and Inspector Nurse of the RUC. Sergeant Willetts, who was posthumously awarded the George Cross, helped usher civilians to safety before placing his body over the bomb, thus muffling the explosion, which of course killed him almost instantly. Inspector Nurse was seriously injured while shielding some children from the blast (he was later awarded the George Medal). Altogether twenty-two people were injured, including a two-year-old baby which suffered a fractured skull. The callous brutality of the IRA fanatics responsible brought expressions of revulsion from all sides of the community.

The events of these days dealt a blow to the new optimism and public confidence which the Government had been trying to build up, and led to renewed speculation and uncertainty—the life-blood of terrorism —which I had hoped would be halted by a display of resolution on the part of the Westminster and Stormont governments. Perhaps I had not warned people enough about the long haul that a war of attrition against the terrorists would involve; too many were expecting quick successes and were thus shaken by any set-backs. It was a knife-edge situation, and there were disturbing signs that some people who should have known better were beginning to throw their weight against stability. In Dublin Jack Lynch recommenced stirring the pot, and John Whale of the *Sunday Times* leapt in with a demand for a new 'political solution'; it was time, he said, to 'think the unthinkable in Ireland' and hold a constitutional conference to prepare for 'reunification'. The sheer idiocy of such a policy in Ulster in 1971 might be easily explained coming from a junior reporter making his first despatch about Irish affairs; what made it disturbing was that it came from a senior journalist on one of the major opinion-forming papers of Britain, a paper which had always taken the stance of 'objective liberal commentator' rather than 'convinced protagonist of united Ireland'. The political motivation suggested at this time was later underwritten by the whole *Sunday Times* Insight Team when in their book on Ulster they described the State of Northern Ireland as an 'immoral concept'. Most modern journalists would feel justified in helping to destroy what they regarded as an immoral concept.

Talk of 'political solutions', once started, spreads very easily among media men, and so I tried to stamp on the idea immediately. On 4 June 1971 I spoke to a meeting of the Foreign Press Gallery in the Dorchester Hotel in London, pointing out that civil rights were no longer an issue in Ulster and that the fact of a terrorist campaign having developed from a protest movement should not be allowed to disguise the present attempts of a small group of violent men to overthrow the democratic system by violence. Their aim was to 'create a situation of such violence and despair that a "solution" to the problem will be sought in terms of establishing an all-Ireland Republic... It is always attractive, when faced with grave difficulties, to speculate about change, in the hope that change will somehow by itself effect an improvement in the situation.'

I thought some of the media men took the point, but I was aware, however, as I flew back to Ulster, that only by keeping democratic politics firmly in the centre of the arena of action could I prevent the IRA from regaining the initiative. I was regretting not having introduced my committee proposals at the beginning of my Premiership; there was a danger that introduced at this time they were going to look like new concessions to new violence. But they were virtually ready and agreed, and the sooner they were put forward and, hopefully, operated by Opposition and Government the sooner I believed the politicians could be seen to regain some initiative. Tuesday 22 June was the fiftieth anniversary of the Stormont Parliament and would provide a suitable opportunity.

Meanwhile, another crisis arose. Orangemen in County Londonderry were planning to hold a march into Dungiven, a predominantly Nationalist town, on 13 June and the RUC knew that if it was allowed to go ahead conflict between the two sides was likely, given the tensions and feelings in the Province. I issued an order banning the march but the organizers decided to defy the ban, claiming that it was an infringement of their liberties. The march was stopped outside the town and, after some stoning, troops dispersed the crowd with rubber bullets and CS gas. The disgraceful scenes which occurred brought great discredit on those who had irresponsibly led these men into a position of confrontation with the security forces in the name of loyalty to the constitution, and were widely condemned. It was yet another example of the wild men on all sides being listened to far too easily, but in a way I did feel afterwards that it had brought home to some of the Unionist population the foolishness and danger of always trying to push 'rights' to the limit in a time of violence.

On Tuesday 22 June members of both Houses of the Northern Ireland Parliament gathered in the Great Hall at Stormont for the formal opening of the new session of Parliament by the Governor, on behalf of the Queen:

On this, the fiftieth anniversary of the opening of your first Parliament by my grandfather, King George V, I take great pleasure in sending my cordial greetings and good wishes to the people of Northern Ireland. It is my hope that in the years to come the Province will develop in confidence and harmony, and that the happiness, contentment and prosperity of all its people will be assured.

They were innocuous enough sentiments with which we all could agree, but unfortunately the SDLP and Nationalist Parliamentarians absented themselves from the formal proceedings, as they had done habitually in all previous Parliaments. They did this I think to demonstrate both their disapproval of British royalty or its representatives, and their general view that the survival of the Stormont Parliament for fifty years was something to be mourned, not celebrated. It was a bit sad, but we all treated it as a ritual gesture towards Nationalist theology, since they turned up in the Commons immediately afterwards to debate the Queen's Speech. I had prepared what I hoped would be a major speech which could set the political wheels in motion again and get the Opposition constructively involved in the work of Parliament and Government. I spoke for fifty minutes outlining my plans and hopes:

> I see it as our duty to give a real lead; to be ready to propose quite exceptional measures to break out of the mould of fear and mutual suspicion.
>
> Today is the fiftieth anniversary of the opening of our first Parliament, and we rightly remember and honour all who have contributed to the achievements of this Parliament over the past half-century. But all these achievements will be set at naught if we cannot today on all sides—and I emphasize 'on all sides'—summon up new reserves of generosity and imagination. This must not be allowed to happen, for, in our Parliament, if we use it aright, we have an institution which can be the means to progress for all our people...
>
> This is our potential, but we are falling short of it. We in this House, who have it in our power to give a lead to the whole community in our capacity for working together, have on the contrary rather been reflecting more and more the tensions and distrust which exist outside this House. Our exchanges have become increasingly bitter and sterile. If that trend, with all its disastrous implications for the future of this community, is to be reversed, all Hon. Members have a contribution to make. But I acknowledge the special responsibility of my colleagues and myself as the majority here to give a lead in that direction.

I explained that I was proposing three new functional committees which, taken with the existing Public Accounts Committee, would cover the whole field of government activity, and that the Opposition should always hold at least two of the four salaried chairmanships. These committees would be involved in policy-making at the formative stage, in reviewing and probing the performance of the Executive, and in giving expert consideration to certain legislation. They would have power to send for persons and papers and to require the attendance of Ministers and civil servants. I stressed however, that, though these committees and their chairmen would have real status, ultimate executive responsibility must be placed in the hands of those whom the majority elected to represent them, as was the custom in a democracy:

But we are a free society as well as a democratic one, and this means we must aim to govern with the consent and acceptance of a far wider majority than is constituted by those who elect the governing party ... we must try to provide the means for all responsible elements in our community to play a constructive part in its institutions ... If for decades past, representatives of the minority have not played a proportionate part in various aspects of our life, that has surely stemmed quite as much from lack of inclination as from the lack of opportunity. It would be encouraging to have occasionally a more frank acknowledgement that there have in the past been failures of vision and imagination on both sides.

I went on to outline the Government's response to terrorism and the need for a united repudiation of such methods by all elected representatives, listed the anti-discrimination measures we were taking, and reviewed our common economic problems. I ended by renewing the offer made in my first speech as Prime Minister but not yet taken up: I was willing and anxious to have private talks with the Opposition at any time they wanted to see me.

The Opposition response was at first cautious, but Gerry Fitt promised that the SDLP would study my speech and bring forward a considered response later in the three-day debate. Craig and Paisley were, of course, noisily critical, the former taking the line that the reformation of the 'B' Specials would solve all our problems. John Hume, the Deputy Leader of the SDLP, also took a cautious line in a speech on the second day, though he made a spirited denunciation of terrorism and sounded generally hopeful:

It should be made clear to all people today who say that no change has taken place that this is simply not true. There have been changes in this community and there must be more changes, but it takes time before legislative changes become reality in the lives of the people and, if people interfere in the progress of that change by violence then they can only increase the frustration ... progress is not in a straight line but progress is taking place ... the choice we face today is a very

serious one and it can be expressed very simply—chaos or community.

Although he went on to talk of the failure of partition, I was generally
pleased with this response from a person regarded at that time by
Unionists as one of the most intransigent and bitter opponents of the
State. In the meantime the press had given an enthusiastic reception to
my proposals and there was a general expectation in the community
that the politicians could use them as a basis for reaching some agreement. By the third day of the debate the SDLP had decided on the position they should take up, and Austin Currie proposed an Amendment
on their behalf. Again it was cautiously worded and carefully refrained
from expressing overall approval. Indeed in some other Parliaments it
might have been taken as a raspberry directed from the Opposition to
the Government; but it began with a welcome and it was a long time
since the anti-partitionists in Stormont had given a welcome to anything
done by the Government. The amendment said:

> ... and while welcoming the expressed wish of the Prime Minister to
> ensure in the future genuine and constructive participation in the
> work of Parliament by all its members and to initiate consultations
> with members of Opposition parties, [the Opposition] humbly regrets
> that the Government's proposals represent only a tinkering with the
> system in Northern Ireland and calls for the setting up of a Select
> Committee representative of the House, which would have available
> to it the necessary expertise and secretariat, for the purpose of recom-
> mending the necessary institutional and procedural changes.

It was a carefully phrased guarding of the flank against hard-line Republicans, but reading between the lines it was clear to me and to most
commentators that the SDLP were very pleasantly surprised and knew
that I had gone a very considerable distance to meet them. Paddy Devlin,
the heavyweight representative for the Falls Area, best expressed the
feelings of SDLP members when he spoke towards the end of the debate
in his inimitable blunt and homely fashion. He said that he was surprised by my proposals, as he had thought that 'like other people' I was
discouraged. But he was pleased to welcome the proposals, which
showed plenty of imagination, and it was my 'best hour' since he had
been elected to Stormont:

> I feel that the Prime Minister is right in his approach. He realizes
> the nonsense of trying to attract that lot on his back-benches ... if we
> get over the next three or four months without trouble from marches

we will be over the crest of the hill and we may well have gone a million light years in making this a more settled community than it has been over the past two years.

In summing up the debate I asked the SDLP not to press their amendment and the Queen's Speech was then approved without a division. It seemed clear that I would be able to do business with the SDLP, and I immediately set about arranging the private talks we had proposed during the debate. Hope was in the air as July approached and there was much speculation on the practical details of how the committees would work and how much power they would give to the Opposition.

On 29 June we held talks with leaders of the Orange Order and the Black Preceptory (a senior branch of the Orangemen) to try to persuade them to curtail the number of marches that summer in the interests of public order. We had some success in doing so, as there was no answer to our argument that every soldier and policeman tied down supervising and guarding parades was being diverted from the more important task of pursuing the terrorists. There was criticism of this meeting from Nationalist quarters, where it was hailed as evidence of the frequently alleged Orange influence on the Government. I thought such criticisms silly and short-sighted; it would have been reckless and irresponsible for the Government not to have taken every step to secure co-operation from the widest possible section of the community. In my experience the influence of the Orange Order on decisions by Stormont Governments has been minimal.

Eight days later the private talks between the Ulster Unionists, the Northern Ireland Labour Party, the Nationalist Party, and the S D L P began. They were frank and good-humoured, and served a useful purpose in getting a real dialogue going away from the glare of the press. Such direct exchange of views between Ulstermen had been all too rare a feature of Stormont in the previous two years, as the SDLP and Nationalists had tended to direct their propaganda effort almost entirely at British Governments and media to get them to 'make' the Unionists do various things, rather than taking the more fruitful and intelligent course of trying themselves to persuade their fellow Ulstermen.

At the end of the meeting we all agreed to a joint statement:

We have had today the first meetings of representatives of various parties and interests in the House of Commons. Nothing of this sort—involving private and completely frank exchanges—has been attempted before. It is not to be expected that anything in the nature of concrete decisions or proposals could emerge from the first such meeting. What is important is that the meeting has been approached by everyone in a helpful and constructive spirit and as a result the position on a number of issues has been clarified. We all think it worthwhile to continue with this experiment in patient discussions and intend to meet again for further talks.

Two days later there was an explosion of violence in Londonderry and the SDLP gave an instant reaction which led over the next few weeks to a complete dissipation of all the hopes and goodwill we had been so carefully nurturing. Throughout the first week of July violence had been simmering in Londonderry as gangs of violent youths from the Bogside smashed up the city centre and stoned the troops. Behind them the IRA were fostering their aggressions and using them as a cover for shooting and nail-bomb attacks on the troops. (A nail bomb was a particularly vicious weapon constructed quite simply by surrounding an explosive charge with nails and pieces of metal which sprayed the surrounding area on detonation, often causing the most horrific injuries.) It had been announced repeatedly that persons seen throwing or about to throw these or the many other lethal weapons used by rioters could be shot without warning. On the night of Thursday 8 July, less than forty-eight hours after our discussions at Stormont, serious rioting again broke out in Londonderry. The troops, who had been under continuous nightly attack all week, suffering more than two dozen casualties while pursuing the policy of minimum force reaction, decided this time that firmer action was required. In the early hours of the 9th two of the rioters—Seamus Cusack and Desmond Beattie—were shot by the Army. The troops were convinced that both men had been armed, one with a rifle and the other with a petrol bomb, at the time of the shooting. But some local people claimed that they were innocent by-standers who had been brutally murdered by the British forces. Cusack might in fact have lived had not his companions, with obviously criminal mentalities, driven him several miles across the border to Letterkenny Hospital instead of to the nearby Altnagelvin Hospital in Londonderry.

In view of this background I was astonished and saddened by the reaction of the SDLP. John Hume demanded an official inquiry by the Westminster Government into the shooting immediately, and the following Monday he announced that unless an official inquiry was agreed to within four days the SDLP would withdraw from Stormont and set up its own alternative assembly. Many theories have been put forward as to why this sudden change of heart in the SDLP occurred; some have said that the party never really intended to make the committee system work, others that they got themselves on a political hook without intending to, believing that the Government would agree to the inquiry. My own view, which is inevitably based on informed guesswork, is that the SDLP was genuinely representing the Catholic community in welcoming the committee proposals, but that the position of the Londonderry members of the party—Hume and Cooper—was more susceptible to extremist pressure. Since the events of 1969 and the emotions whipped up as a result of them there had been a general air of lawlessness in the city, and political representatives on the minority side were finding it difficult to keep control of public opinion. Law and order were dirty words, and many Bogsiders who would have thought of themselves as 'non-violent' nonetheless saw the rioters as 'our lads', and were more disposed to stick up for them than for the British Army. Thus emotion was easily exploited after the shootings of the 9th, and the whole of the Bogside was soon complaining angrily. Public representatives were reduced to dragging along on the coat-tails of the IRA.

The trend of events was shown by a blood-chilling call from Mrs Maire Drumm, a Provisional leader, speaking at a meeting in the Bogside on Sunday 11th: '... the only way you can avenge these deaths is by being organized,' she said to the emotional crowd, 'until you can chase that accursed Army away. I would personally prefer to see all the British Army going back dead... You should not just shout "Up the IRA". You should join the IRA.' She was followed by another Provisional spokesman who declared: 'Victory is within our grasp... we are going to finish it this time. We are on the highroad to freedom and what we need to do is to rock Stormont and keep it rocking until it comes down.' Mrs Drumm later received a six-month prison sentence for her speech at this meeting.

All this was bad enough, but on the same Sunday as the IRA meeting, Jack Lynch, speaking at the 'Garden of Remembrance' ceremony in Dublin for the Republican heroes of 1916 called on the British Government to declare itself in favour of a united Ireland. It was an extraordinary time for him to make such a statement, and considering how sensitive Dublin always is to events in the Catholic areas of Northern Ireland it is difficult to believe that it was simply tailored to the Dublin audience and coincided unintentionally with violence in the Bogside. I issued a statement pointing out the irresponsibility of doing anything which could 'encourage the terrorists in our midst to believe that their objectives can be attained'. Three days later in another statement I warned

Lynch that he had a choice to make: 'He can develop with us a relationship of mutual respect in which, while acknowledging our fundamental differences, we can do business on practical issues; or he can switch to a hard-line anti-partition stance, addressing himself to London rather as if this Government and the people who elected it do not exist.' I was not clear what, if any, strategy the Dublin Government was pursuing. But I was reaching the end of the road in tolerating their provocative statements at crucially violent moments.

Hume's demand for an inquiry was of course refused by the Westminster Government; they could not allow themselves to appear to lend credence to the Republican version of the deaths or hold an inquiry every time someone died, however much they might have wanted to give the SDLP a way of remaining in Stormont. But I found it difficult to believe that all the hopes and opportunities of recent weeks would be thrown away because of this one incident, especially as it concerned the Army which was under the control of Westminster and not of Stormont. It was Westminster which had the power to set up an inquiry, and it would have made more sense if the SDLP had threatened to withdraw their representative, Gerry Fitt, from there rather than pulling out of Stormont. I issued an appeal to the SDLP on the day their ultimatum expired pointing out that only weeks ago they had been welcoming the opportunity to participate more fully in the affairs of Parliament, but were now threatening a total boycott of Stormont and the setting up of an alternative assembly:

It is not for me to tell the Opposition how to conduct their affairs. I will just say this. They, too, have a choice. They can have real and effective participation in our affairs, a chance to do genuine constructive work together; or they can have the instant politics of exploiting every issue as it arises without consideration of the long-term effects. They cannot have both . . . I had hoped—indeed I still hope—for the advice of all parties and interests as we move forward. But move forward we will, together—if people choose to be responsible and constructive—but alone, if that is what others force us to do . . .

It was to no avail. At a press conference on the morning of Friday 16 July the SDLP announced their withdrawal from Stormont and their determination to set up an alternative assembly. The Nationalist Party and the one Republican Labour representative indicated that they would follow suit. At the press conference rather tortuous arguments were used to justify the withdrawal; the deaths in Londonderry were described as the 'last straw', and the SDLP said that they had found themselves faced with a choice 'either to continue to give credibility to a system which is in itself basically unstable . . . or to take a stand in order to bring home to those in authority the need for strong political action to solve our problems and to prevent any further tragic loss of life . . .'. They added that there could be no solutions 'until the right wing is confronted', an argument to which we shall return.

It was a serious blow to political progress in Ulster and a sad day for democracy. Since the formation of the SDLP in 1970 the party had always taken the approach then outlined by its leader Gerry Fitt: 'We believe that Stormont is the only institution through which reform can come,' he said, and the SDLP had worked hard since, criticizing, pushing, making life difficult, but always on the basis that reforms must be made more quickly or more extensively. Only two weeks before they had welcomed new proposals for reform, and John Hume himself had pointed out the problems of making legislative change effective. But now, after a brief period during which no action had been taken by the Stormont Government which anyone pretended could justify such a changed attitude, they were withdrawing with a denunciation of the whole system. They no longer sought reform, they were supporting a revolutionary change, and resorting to the old dead-end Irish tactics of boycott and abstention to achieve it. They were abdicating leadership of the Catholic community at a time when firm and moderate leadership was most needed and when men of violence were most anxious and able to fill the vacuum and direct emotions in more militant and dangerous channels. No doubt there were pressures which it would have taken a very great deal of courage to stand up against, but many people were to die as a result of failure to grasp this opportunity.

Where, then, did reform go wrong? Ever since the O'Neill Cabinet announced the first programme of reforms in 1968 successive Unionist Governments had been engaged in sweeping programmes of legislative and administrative change designed to meet the alleged shortcomings of the State. Had this programme been totally inadequate to allow the Opposition parties to work within the democratic system? It is worth recapping on the position in the summer of 1971 to see if this was the case. It was a time for stock-taking, for examining just where all the months of argument and violence had brought us to. The Government published a White Paper entitled *A Record of Constructive Change* outlining all the commitments of 1969 and the extent to which they had been implemented, and reaffirming the principle that 'every citizen of Northern Ireland is entitled to the same equality of treatment and

freedom from discrimination as obtains in the rest of the United Kingdom irrespective of political views or religion'. At around the same
time a pamphlet on the reform programme was published by the New
Ulster Movement (NUM), a liberal centrist group which had in the
past been generally critical of Unionist Governments; their view was
that it was 'foolish, irresponsible, and a continuing threat to peace to
refuse to acknowledge that the Government was now trying to implement the reforms' and that it was 'also hypocritical to refuse to co-
operate in the promotion of such reforms', since they provided a
framework in which 'there could be equality of citizenship and an
opportunity to participate in the running of the community by all
groups including minorities'.

The facts speak for themselves. There had been allegations that local
government boundaries had been unfair to Nationalists. I have already
explained in a previous chapter the complete reorganization of local
government, including drawing of boundaries by an impartial commission, which was being pushed ahead at top speed. Londonderry, the seat
of many protests, was being administered by a Commission which had
won praise from virtually all sections of the community there. There had
been allegations that local authorities had discriminated in the allocation of houses; control of housing had been centralized in a Housing
Executive, and allocations were taking place on a points system that
ensured fairness. There had been allegations that job discrimination
against the minority was widespread in private employment, in local
authority appointments, and in government appointments, and that
not enough members of the minority were nominated to public bodies.
The Government had set up a Local Government Staff Commission,
taken steps to secure declarations of equality of employment opportunity from all public bodies or organizations carrying out Government
contracts, required all public bodies in the Province to adopt an
approved code of employment procedure, and had set up the independent offices of Parliamentary Commissioner and Commissioner of
Complaints to police the operation of these arrangements. There had
been allegations that Unionist Governments had not done enough to
foster good relations between different sections of the community but a
Ministry of Community Relations had been set up, and I had appointed
a member of an opposition party to run it, and an independent Community Relations Commission had also been set up under the chairmanship of a prominent Catholic, Dr Maurice Hayes. There had been
allegations that the RUC was under the control of the Unionist Party,
and so a Police Authority representative of the community had been set

up. There had been allegations of bias in the incidence of prosecutions in the courts, and so an independent office of Director of Public Prosecutions was being set up. There had been allegations that the Ulster Special Constabulary (the 'B' Specials) were a partisan Protestant force; they had been disbanded and the Ulster Defence Regiment under the control of the Army had been set up. There had been allegations that the RUC was a para-military force with too many arms: all its para-military functions had been abandoned; a decision had been taken that the force would be normally unarmed; there had been a complete organizational overhaul supervised by the nominee of a Labour Government, and strenuous efforts were being made to increase recruitment from the Catholic section of the community.

The only matter in which the 1968 programme of 'demands' of the CRA had not been met by 1971 was the abolition of the Special Powers Act. Harold Wilson himself had said in Parliament in May 1969 that 'no government in the world would have gone on with what was proposed (dispensing with these powers) until they were assured that there would be a period of law, order, peace, calm and quiet'. Not only was there little peace and quiet, there was a determined terrorist campaign which was escalating and emergency powers were essential to deal with it, as all governments since have recognized.

But if these reforms had been dealt with why did the political bitterness continue, why was violence escalating, and why were divisions in the community becoming greater? The major reason was bitter intransigent republicanism, which had stirred up emotions, exaggerated fears, manipulated the natural aggressions of young people to create riots, and with outside assistance had mounted a campaign of terrorism against the State. Its proponents had first discredited the RUC, and then by effective propaganda—aided by the unsuitability of soldiers for the task of policing—gradually turned many of the Catholic population against the Army, which had virtually replaced the RUC in their areas. The IRA objective was not a fair deal for Catholics within Northern Ireland; it was the overthrow of the State by whatever means possible in order to bring about its amalgamation into a 32-county Irish Republic. They had been able to gain support because of the unattractive face presented to the world by some of the more extreme Unionists, because the Northern Ireland Government had not itself been clearly seen to have taken the initiative in reforms, because of the guilty conscience of many British liberals about Ireland, and because of the latent and sometimes overt sympathy for their cause among many in the Irish Republic. The wholesale rioting of 1969 had produced an atmosphere of community distrust in which the I R A could thrive, posing as the last line of defence for the Catholic community. And now they had been able to apply such pressure to Catholic political leaders that the latter had opted out. It remained to be seen if the other two sides in the equation, the Stormont Government and the Westminster Government, could carry on and survive the crisis. If they did not, there was no doubt in my mind that it would be because violent, ruthless and very determined men had tested the nerve of the oldest democracy in the world, and found it wanting.

11
Internment

On Christmas morning 1971 I received a somewhat macabre present—
a black coffin. It was delivered to my home at Seaforde as part of what
had been planned as a province-wide protest against internment. In the
event, a wet morning and the counter-attractions of the season whittled
it down, but a small group marched to our gates to deliver my Christmas
box, a rousing Republican speech was made, and they dispersed after
wishing each other and the RUC men on duty the compliments of the
season.

   This was the year of the internees' Christmas cards. My mail, like that
of most other political figures, was full of cards, sometimes signed and
sometimes anonymous, sometimes pathetic and sometimes obscene,
produced in aid of 'the boys behind the wire'. As the Minister responsible for security it was my job (as later it became the task of successive
Secretaries of State) to sign individually every detention order on prisoners at Long Kesh, or 'the Maze', as it was re-named after direct rule.
It was not an enviable responsibility, and as well as the damage of public
criticism it brought with it a daily quota of private abuse in the mail and
on the telephone to my home. Throughout our troubles I have been on
the receiving end of more unpleasant calls than most people, because
it seems to me to be a derogation of one's responsibilities as a public
representative to have an ex-directory telephone number. But at two
periods the pressures on my family became almost unbearable, with
threats and abuse from anonymous telephone callers. One was during
the first few weeks of internment. And the other was almost three years
later from supporters of the Ulster Workers Council strike.

The decision to intern terrorist suspects was one which virtually forced
itself upon us. The IRA campaign of terrorism had reached an unprecedented level of ferocity in the summer of 1971. In July there were few
if any days when there was not serious violence at one or more of the

1 At the Belfast Collar Company at the beginning of the war with
(*from left*) Sir Basil Brooke, Mr Faulkner senior, and the Duke and
Duchess of Abercorn. The Duke was Governor of Northern
Ireland from 1921 until 1945.

2 Inspecting members of the Ulster Special Constabulary before a
church service in Belfast in 1960 with R. F. R. (Bob) Bunbar,
Permanent Secretary at Home Affairs (later Head of the NI Civil
Service), Captain McClughan, District Commandant, and Sir
Richard Pim, Inspector-General of the RUC.

3 At Goodyear headquarters in Ohio, USA, in 1966 with (*from left*) Alistair Maitland, British Consul-General, Russel De Yong, President of Goodyear, Jack Quinn, of the NI Ministry of Commerce, and Chuck Pilliard, President of Goodyear International. In front is a model of the large factory Goodyear opened shortly afterwards at Graigavon, Co. Armagh.

4 Entering Unionist headquarters at Glengall Street, Belfast, for a party meeting shortly before O'Neill's resignation.

5 A family picture at Seaforde soon after appointment as Prime Minister.

6 At Stormont Castle with James Callaghan, then Shadow Home Secretary, and Vivian Simpson, Labour MP at Stormont for Oldpark, March 1971.

7 At Chequers, September 1971, with Jack Lynch and Edward Heath for the first meeting of the three Prime Ministers since 1925.

8 On the balcony at Stormont speaking to the huge crowd
protesting against the suspension of Stormont with members of the
Cabinet and (*right*) William Craig.

9 The last photograph of the Northern Ireland Government taken
at the Governor's residence at Hillsborough, on the occasion of the
last meeting of the Northern Ireland Privy Council on 29 March
1972 (see Appendix III).

10 Observed by Ted Heath and Willie Whitelaw, Brian Faulkner is
shown as he received a standing ovation by the delegates for the
only speech he ever made at a Conservative Party Conference
(12 October 1973).

11 The first official meeting of the power-sharing Executive at
Stormont: (*left to right*) Paddy Devlin, Oliver Napier, Brian
Faulkner, John Hume, Basil McIvor, (P. A. Sythes and Ken
Bloomfield, Secretaries) John Baxter, Austin Currie, Herbie Kirk,
Gerry Fitt, Roy Bradford, and Leslie Morrell (see Appendix IV).

12 Representatives of the Dublin Government and the Northern
Executive at Hillsborough, 1 February 1974: (*left to right, front*)
Brendan Corish, Gerry Fitt, Liam Cosgrave, Brian Faulkner, John
Hume; (*second row*) Herbie Kirk, Richie Ryan, Garret Fitzgerald,
Roy Bradford; (*third row*) Paddy Devlin, Conor Cruse O'Brien,
Paddy Cooney, Oliver Napier, Declan Costello, Leslie Morrell,
Charles Tully.

13 Setting off with the hounds, 1968.

trouble spots in Belfast, Londonderry, Lurgan or Newry. There was rioting, shops were looted and wrecked, police stations, Army posts and members of the security forces on patrol were attacked with stones, petrol bombs and nail bombs, and crowds of rioting youths were often used as cover for snipers. There were more explosions, more shooting incidents, more injuries to civilians, policemen and soldiers than in any previous month of the crisis. The IRA had committed itself to total war against the State, and was demonstrating a capacity to carry it out on a more widespread and organized scale than ever before.

Cold statistics can never convey the depth of outrage felt by the Ulster people at what was being done to them; indeed, in view of the horrors which were to come later it would be easy to underestimate the impact of events in the summer of 1971 by relying on figures alone. It is a sad fact that people do get hardened to violence as the mind becomes numbed and unable to grasp the sheer volume of suffering being inflicted. In 1971 Ulster people were not hardened to violence, or resigned to accepting it as a background to daily life; they were demanding that the Government do something to stop it, and stop it quickly.

The statistics, however, were bad enough. By July 55 people had died violently; in the first seven months of 1971 there were over 300 explosions and 320 shooting incidents, and over 600 people received hospital treatment for injuries. All of this was happening in a small province of only $1\frac{1}{2}$ million people. Perhaps it can be better grasped by translating it into proportionate figures for the whole of the United Kingdom. Thus it would have meant over 2,000 dead, and in seven months 11,000 bombings, 11,600 shootings and 22,000 people injured. In view of later reaction to the Birmingham bombings in Britain it is worth bearing these figures in mind when assessing the reaction of the Ulster Government in 1971 and the extent of the restraint among ordinary people in the face of a ruthless assault on their society.

Not only was the increased volume of violence causing alarm, but also the sheer audacity and provocative nature of many of the attacks, and the way in which they were preventing any kind of normal life in the Province. Simple things, like catching a bus or driving through the city to see a friend or going to the cinema, were becoming increasingly hazardous. Pedestrians and shoppers were being injured by wild gunfire, and by sudden explosions in shops, offices and business premises. Hotels, including the prestige Europa Hotel in Belfast city centre, were being attacked; telephone exchanges, power stations and post offices were being blown up; buses were being hijacked and burned. In one spectacular explosion the *Daily Mirror* printing plant on the outskirts of Belfast was completely destroyed, at an estimated cost of £10 million. The 'commercial targets' of the IRA apparently included the Youth Employment Service, whose task was to find jobs for young people, and the Housing Executive, struggling to build houses for the homeless; both suffered extensively from bombing.

The many attempts to stir up sectarian animosity were quite undisguised. In July several Orange Halls were damaged by arsonists, and on the morning of 12 July 1971 there were ten explosions in Belfast over the route of the traditional Orange parade, injuring nine pedestrians and seriously damaging some of the city's largest stores. Fortunately, in spite of this provocation, the parades passed off peacefully. I spent much of that particular 'Twelfth' in a helicopter with General Tuzo observing the parades from the air. After watching the Belfast parades and satisfying ourselves that no serious trouble was likely we flew to Londonderry. There we also found peaceful parades, but when passing over the Bogside I saw for the first time a hijacking actually taking place. A crowd of youths stopped a lorry and pulled the driver out before driving it off, presumably to help build some barricade, but almost immediately crashed off the road. Neither Tuzo nor I enjoyed watching helplessly while this kind of lawlessness flourished in a part of the State we were supposedly governing.

The escalation of terrorism was obvious to everyone, and it was inadequate for us to issue bland assurances that this was a temporary difficulty which 'restraint and goodwill' on all sides would overcome. For several years I had been making appeals in speeches for restraint, for people to avoid retaliation at all costs and leave the job to the professionals. The response had been remarkable. Since the street fighting of 1969 the public had, with few exceptions, endured the terrorism with remarkable courage and restraint. After bombs or incendiary devices in businesses or offices, managers and workers would turn up together in overalls to clear up the damage, and it was commonplace to see 'Business as Usual' notices up within twenty-four hours. Instances of the increasing resentment spilling over into retaliation were rare. But it was becoming obvious that action was needed now, and it was action which the public was demanding.

I was holding long discussions with the GOC, the Chief Constable, and my security advisers to see if we could improve our tactics in any way. But the message was beginning to come through that there was only one major unused weapon in the government's anti-terrorist arsenal—internment.

The internment or preventive detention of suspected terrorists in an emergency situation has been employed by many Western democracies in the twentieth century. But it has probably been used most frequently in Ireland, North and South, against the IRA. It was used by the Irish Government during the Civil War, used again during World War II, and by de Valera during the IRA campaign of 1956–62 when it was introduced simultaneously in the North. It had generally been very successful, helping to demoralize the terrorists, break up their organization, exhaust their finances, and improve police intelligence. The fact that it was operated on an all-Ireland basis was of course an important element in its success.

During the Chichester-Clark Government the possibility of internment was discussed a few times in the Cabinet. I generally argued against, and I can recall at least two occasions on which the Prime Minister appeared in favour and I attempted to dissuade him, backed up by the other members of the Security Committee. I had already operated internment as Minister of Home Affairs during the last three years of the previous IRA campaign, but I regarded it as a weapon only to be used in extremity by a democratic government, and was concerned lest the 'No Go' areas of 1969–70 had undermined the RUC intelligence on which any successful internment operation must depend. Nor was the position in 1971 similar to that in 1960, when the IRA campaign had been largely confined to the rural and border areas; the urban guerrilla now posed a more difficult problem. It was simply too easy and superficial to say 'internment solved the problem before, and it will do it again'.

There was, of course, no shortage of people prepared to offer just such advice. In the last months of his Premiership Chichester-Clark had been pressurized from several sources to introduce internment. Various Unionist backbenchers were in favour. In March several thousand shipyard workers and shop stewards marched to the Unionist Party Offices to hand in a resolution demanding immediate internment of all known IRA leaders. In April several senior Army officers (not including the GOC) were also arguing for internment. A list of potential internees had been drawn up by the RUC Special Branch and Military Intelligence early in the year at Chichester-Clark's request.

My Cabinet discussed the issue several times in April and May 1971. West, Baillie and Bradford were the most hard-line on security, while Bleakley, the Labour Minister of Community Relations, was less so. I was still hopeful that the new Army tactics, combined with effective political action, would pay off and make internment unnecessary. By July it was becoming obvious that these hopes were not being realized, and the matter was again seriously considered in the Cabinet. It was made clear that, if I exercised the powers vested in me as Minister of Home Affairs under the Special Powers Act, I would have the firm backing of my Cabinet colleagues. The decision and the timing were left to myself and the security chiefs, but there was a general acceptance that unless the situation improved it would soon become necessary.

Pressures were also being exerted from less expected quarters for dramatic action to break the grip of the IRA on Catholic areas. Secret representations from responsible members of the Catholic community prominent in politics urged me to 'lock up' these men who were making life intolerable for ordinary Catholics through intimidation and violence. My personal mailbag confirmed the intense desire for a return to some form of law and order; I received many letters from housewives in places such as Andersonstown in West Belfast, urging me to 'get these terrorists off our backs'. Thus, while recognizing the dangers of misrepresentation, I believed there would be very many Catholics willing to tolerate internment in order to break the IRA, and I hoped that these people would be given a lead by moderate politicians.

A contingency decision had already been taken to build a new temporary prison for high-risk prisoners. The old prison on the Crumlin Road in Belfast was declared insecure by an investigating committee headed by Sir Charles Cunningham, and it was clear that we needed a top-security prison for convicted prisoners even if internment was not introduced. The Ministry of Defence and the Home Office undertook to design and build the temporary prison while I set in hand at the Stormont Ministry of Home Affairs plans for a new permanent prison (which under a later administration were inexplicably put into cold storage). Unfortunately, because of the speed with which the new structure at Long Kesh, a few miles outside Belfast, was erected, and because of its temporary nature, it came to look like the pictures of prisoner-of-war camps with which the post-war generation were all too familiar. In the autumn it became the main detention centre for terrorist suspects and the IRA propaganda machine sent pictures of the watch towers, patrolling soldiers and wire fences around the world to reinforce their claims that an oppressive military regime was being operated in Ulster.

By the middle of July a consensus was developing among my security advisers on the need for internment. The process was such a gradual one that looking back a few years later it is difficult to pick out a decisive point in our discussions. And because of the intense secrecy surrounding the matter and our reluctance to commit anything concerning it to paper there are few records which can be consulted, even in Cabinet documents. Neither General Tuzo, Graham Shillington, nor I were very anxious to introduce internment, but we were rapidly running out of arguments against it. The widespread violence and intimidation made it impossible to get witnesses, especially from Nationalist areas, who would testify in open court against the terrorists. We had examined all sorts of alternatives, such as special courts, but came to the conclusion that a court was no longer a court in any real sense if the accused and the accuser were not brought face to face.

The city bombings of mid-July tipped the scales and I took the decision that we must operate internment. No one objected, and we started to discuss the mechanics of the operation.

We discussed the relative merits of spreading our net wide in the initial swoop, or simply confining ourselves to the leaders and organizers of the IRA, both Official and Provisional. The former would involve perhaps five hundred arrests, the latter around a hundred. I was also conscious of the problem of not appearing to be victimizing Catholics, as the main objective of the operation would be to destroy the operational capacity of the IRA which consisted almost entirely of self-styled 'Catholics'. Maudling was later to underline this point by saying to me, 'Lift some Protestants if you can'; he was equally concerned that the operation should appear impartial.

On both these matters I relied entirely on the advice of the security forces. The Army and the police proposed a wide sweep involving the arrest of over five hundred, in order to strike a crippling blow at the terrorist organization and we agreed to this. With hindsight it can be argued that a more selective sweep as in previous RUC operations would have been more effective. The security forces were also adamant that there was no evidence of organized terrorism by 'Protestants' which would justify detention of persons other than IRA members. I have no doubt that this was an accurate conclusion at that time. The idea of arresting anyone as an exercise in political cosmetics was repugnant to me.

On 4 August I rang Maudling and said that I wished to speak to himself and the Prime Minister 'on a grave security matter'. He knew immediately what I meant and the meeting was arranged for the following day at Downing Street. Tuzo, Shillington and I, together with our respective security advisers, flew over secretly from RAF Aldergrove in an Andover early the next morning on what we fully realized was one of the most awesome missions on which we had yet gone to Downing Street. It was a decision which, once acted upon, would mark a whole new phase in our approach to the problem. It would mark an end to the attempts to secure parallel political and security progress, to achieve far-reaching constitutional changes in the midst of violence and instability; it would mean a frontal determined attack on the IRA which would call for qualities of steadiness and consistency over a period of many months.

Heath, Maudling, Home and Carrington were all at Downing Street to meet us, together with the Chief of the General Staff, Sir Michael Carver. The security chiefs waited in an ante-room while the rest of us discussed the situation. I outlined the possibilities as I saw them, explained how I had come to a decision, and asked for their support. Then Graham Shillington, Sir Michael Carver and General Tuzo were asked in to give their views. The Chief Constable said that in his opinion the time for internment had now arrived. General Tuzo said that internment was not absolutely essential in purely military terms, but whether the time-scale involved in defeating the terrorists by other means would be acceptable was not for him to determine. There was some more discussion and then Heath formally announced to me that it was the firm decision of the United Kingdom Government that if I, as the responsible Minister, decided to invoke the power of internment they would concur and ensure the necessary Army support. He said that this support was, however, conditional upon our agreeing to a ban on all parades, a condition which we readily accepted and imposed for six months.

It was decided to introduce internment in a dawn swoop on Tuesday 10 August (though contrary to some reports we did not adopt any generally used code-name for the operation; the number of persons involved in discussions was so limited that such an arrangement was unnecessary). But during the weekend serious rioting and shooting broke out in the Catholic Springfield Road area after a soldier mistakenly shot a motorist whose car back-fired, and so we decided to move internment forward twenty-four hours. Only Shillington, Tuzo and I knew of the change of plan until a short time before the arrests took place.

At 4.15 a.m. that Monday morning three thousand troops moved in simultaneously all over the Province to arrest the IRA suspects. The operation was carried through remarkably smoothly and within a few hours 70 per cent of the wanted men had been picked up. There were a few cases of mistaken identity where we had not been able to obtain photographs, and some who had been living in hiding for weeks because of the danger of internment escaped capture.

I was awakened shortly after 5 a.m. by phone calls on the scrambler line from the GOC and the Chief Constable to tell me how the operation had gone; they were both in good heart and pleased with its success. By 8 a.m. I was in the office and after hearing the latest reports I rang Maudling and Callaghan. Maudling offered his congratulations on the operation and asked me to pass on his personal congratulations to the Chief Constable. Callaghan expressed neither enthusiasm nor opposition but made it clear that he recognized we had no alternative and would go along with us. I met General Tuzo and he expressed considerable optimism: 'My Divisional Commanders are in better shape than I have seen them since I came to Northern Ireland, for we believe that at last we have taken decisive action,' he said.

At around 11 a.m. I went to meet the world's press, reading a prepared statement to camera and then answering questions. I explained that political progress was simply not possible in a climate of terrorism and violence, and that every means had been tried to make the terrorists amenable to the law.

> But the campaign continues at an unacceptable level, and I have had to conclude that the ordinary law cannot deal comprehensively or quickly enough with such ruthless viciousness. I have therefore decided, after weighing all the relevant considerations, including the views of the security authorities, and after consultation with Her Majesty's Government ... to exercise where necessary the powers of detention and internment vested in me as Minister of Home Affairs.

I pointed out that I would personally review the evidence on every case before signing a preliminary detention order and that an Advisory Committee would be set up to hear appeals. I was particularly anxious to get through to the responsible members of the Catholic community and I directed much of what I said to them.

> I have taken this step solely for the protection of life and the security of property. At all times I have consistently emphasized that it was not a step towards which I would be moved by any political clamour. Equally I cannot now allow the prospect of any misrepresentation to deflect me from my duty to act ... I ask those who will quite sincerely consider the use of internment powers as evil to answer honestly this question; is it more of an evil than to allow the perpetrators of these outrages to remain at liberty?

By that time of the day it was becoming very clear that such appeals for calm and rational judgement were necessary. Almost immediately after the first arrests well-orchestrated rioting broke out across the Province. As the army Land-Rovers and lorries rolled into the streets of Belfast and made their arrests the Republican tom-toms began to sound across the houses; the bin-lid bashers, women and young children, sent their tribal message across the city, rising to a crescendo of sound frightening in its intensity and its bitter message of revolt. The terrorists clearly had contingency plans of their own for internment, as the long public discussions by politicians and commentators on the subject had made them well aware of its possible introduction. Although we arrested many of the men we wanted there were also new activists who had not come to the attention of the security forces, due to the extreme difficulty of gathering intelligence in Republican areas over the previous few years. Those who escaped were determined to extract every ounce of propaganda advantage and immediately set out trying to whip up hysteria. Barricades went up in the areas dominated by the IRA and every available gun was brought out to take on the security forces in pitched battles. If they could raise the level of violence and arouse emotional opposition they hoped to reap long-term benefits in recruitment and international sympathy. 'This is a grossly repressive measure directed entirely towards you,' they were telling the Catholic community, and unfortunately there was no alternative moderate voice there to tell them the truth—that it was a measure taken as a last resort against a specific terrorist organization.

The terrorists went to extreme lengths to secure propaganda advantages: they organized the evacuation of over a thousand women and children who travelled south in trains under the label of 'refugees', an insult to those throughout the world really in need of protection and refuge from governments or natural disasters. The publicity was of course priceless for the IRA, but before long the 'refugees' got tired of the green fields of freedom and returned to their homes in Ulster and all the benefits of the British welfare state (this time without the glare of media attention—they had served their purpose).

In the two days after the internment operation seventeen people died violently, some of them IRA men, some innocent civilians caught in the crossfire, and two soldiers. The Army's superior firepower and training inevitably told and those terrorists foolish enough to take them on in gun-battles received a bloody nose, but the manipulated hysteria became self-generating and the result was rubble, burned out vehicles, injuries and general chaos. In several provincial towns there was organized burning down of Protestant shops, presumably on the assumption that the greater the sectarian animosity the easier it would be to consolidate the Catholic community behind the extremists.

I spent most of the forty-eight hours after the arrests locked away in my room at Stormont going through the papers of each individual the security forces thought dangerous enough to intern. I used quite stringent conditions for the evidence required, and my security adviser and the head of the RUC Special Branch spent much of this time explaining particular allegations or getting people to see me and produce further evidence. I had to be satisfied that the persons detained were members of the IRA or actively involved in the IRA campaign, or had played a part in promoting violence. Neither I as Minister nor any of my colleagues or staff had any say in the selection of the names of persons to be arrested, nor did we ever see the list which was compiled and used by the security forces. The first knowledge I had of a name was when a person in custody was recommended for a detention or internment order. I then had to examine the case personally and only if I was satisfied with the quality of the evidence was the order made. Later allegations that we had sought to lock up our political opponents were propagandist fabrications.

Of the 337 men arrested initially I released 97 and agreed to detention orders on the remainder. I have no reason to doubt today that I made the right decision in nearly all of these cases.

I had expected a bitter reaction from some quarters to internment, but not on the scale which occurred, both on the streets and among Nationalist politicians. However, it was a point of no return; we had taken the decision, we were still convinced that, given time, it would pay off, and we could not afford to allow ourselves to be deflected from carrying through the policy by what was obviously a planned and organized upsurge of violence. We did not believe that the IRA could for long sustain its efforts.

Terrorist morale was boosted, however, by two propaganda coups. The first and less important was a clever piece of IRA manipulation of the media; they had for long been acutely aware of the importance of using the media and were skilled in doing so. A few days after internment some men claiming to be the top IRA officers held a secret press conference in Belfast and claimed that their organization was untouched by internment. The resulting press reports did not subject these claims to the critical analysis which one normally expects from the experienced newsmen covering the Ulster situation.

The second and more important IRA propaganda success may in fact have done more than anything else to discredit the policy of internment. A few days after 9 August stories of the 'torture' of those detained began to appear in some newspapers, and this trickle soon became a flood of atrocity stories. After a particularly detailed series of allegations in the *Sunday Times* Harold Wilson contacted the Prime Minister and it was agreed that, in view of the seriousness of the allegations in a reputable newspaper, an inquiry should be held.

The Northern Ireland Government's involvement in this whole area was quite limited. We had initially assumed that the normal process of police questioning would be used and the whole matter of accommodation for those arrested was under the control of the Ministry of Defence. But shortly after the operation had started two senior security officers, one from the RUC and the other from Military Intelligence, came to see me in my office at Stormont. It became obvious from what they said that they had already been liaising on plans for the interrogation of IRA suspects and had come simply for my formal approval. They told me that the Army process of 'in depth' interrogation—rather than normal police questioning—of a small number of highly placed IRA members could yield valuable information vital to the success of the internment operation and to the stopping of the IRA campaign. This had, they said, already been cleared with the appropriate authorities in London and I saw no reason to object to the proposal if it had received political clearance. The possibility that Her Majesty's Government would authorize anything of dubious propriety did not, given the background of exaggerated caution on security, occur to me.

Thus, after the preliminary questioning, twelve of the most hard-core suspects were isolated from their comrades for 'in depth' questioning on the membership, organization and equipment of the IRA. The preliminary screening had taken place at three regional holding centres— Ballykelly Military Airport. Ballykinler Army Camp, County Down, and Girdwood Army Barracks in Belfast—and from there they went to the *Maidstone* in Belfast Lough or to Crumlin Road Jail in Belfast. But these twelve were taken off to a secret interrogation centre (the whereabouts of which has been frequently speculated on with little accuracy). RUC Special Branch men were involved in the questioning because of their specialized local knowledge, but they operated under the instructions of the Military Intelligence personnel who supervised the whole process.

The report of the Government Committee of Inquiry later described some of the techniques used—sleep deprivation, standing against a wall for long periods with head covered by a hood, total isolation—as 'ill-treatment', and a Committee of Privy Councillors which further investigated failed to agree on their legality or morality. The minority report by Lord Gardiner, a former Labour Lord Chancellor, said they were both immoral and illegal under domestic United Kingdom law, and was accepted by the Conservative Government, which ordered that the procedures be discontinued.

All sorts of arguments can be, and have been, put forward about interrogation methods: that we were dealing with a ruthless organization involved in a campaign of murder and destruction, that much valuable information was gained in the questioning of suspects which certainly saved lives, and that many of the techniques used were similar to those used by the Army in training their own intelligence men. All of this is true. The military were, on the whole, extremely pleased with the amount and quality of intelligence the whole internment operation was bringing in. I remember a senior officer saying to me one day: 'We used to have to search every room in several houses when looking for arms; but now we usually know which room we want, not to mention which house!' The figures for arms' finds at this time certainly support what he was saying. In the first seven months of 1971 we had found 41,000 rounds of ammunition, and 1,500 lbs of explosives in terrorist caches; in the five months after internment 115,795 rounds of ammunition and 2,157 lbs of explosives were recovered. Prior to internment we had taken 1 machine-gun from the IRA; in the next five months 25 were recovered.

But in spite of all this, the most important factor was the impact of these revelations on the Ulster situation in 1971. The papers, especially the Dublin papers, were full of lurid stories of 'torture' smuggled out from 'the lads' in detention; a great deal of what was being alleged was grossly exaggerated or total fabrication. But the substantiation of some of the claims in the case of 14 out of the 337 men arrested rapidly developed in Republican mythology to become proof that the most wild and exaggerated claims were also accurate. It was soon an established part of this mythology that over 300 Catholics had been dragged from their beds at dawn, taken to Army camps where they were beaten up and tortured, and then locked away simply because the Unionist Government did not like Catholics.

Sometimes the IRA propaganda was counter-productive, as when those arrested talked freely and expressed surprise at the humane treatment they received and the total absence of the 'torture' they had been led to expect. But the emotive impact of this whole interrogation controversy greatly helped the IRA in whipping up hysteria among

Catholics, and perhaps decisively tipped the balance against internment among political moderates in Britain.

Politics made little headway in the last four months of 1971. Those of us in London and Belfast still trying to hold the line against violence made various attempts to keep political dialogue going and to bring back elected representatives to the centre of the stage. But from inside and outside the State was coming under increasing challenge. The interplay between London, Belfast and Dublin was an important feature of developments in this period as politicians increasingly took sides for and against the existence of Northern Ireland and its Parliament.

The SDLP, having already abandoned constructive politics, found themselves almost overwhelmed by the upsurge of Republican jingoism. They needed to find a role which would keep them at least nominally at the head of the Nationalist population and which would show that they could play as effective a role as the IRA in undermining the Government. They reacted with something like panic to the upheaval in Catholic areas after internment and rushed off to Dublin to see Lynch, returning soon with plans for a campaign of civil disobedience, publicly supported by Lynch. All Nationalists were urged to withhold rents and rates, and to withdraw from all local councils and public authorities. Over a hundred councillors responded to this call, a particularly sad reversal of the demands for 'one man one vote' in local government, and several thousand public housing tenants and householders began to withhold rents and rates.

Lynch himself showed no apparent embarrassment about the long history of internment swoops against the IRA by Fianna Fail Governments in the Republic, and intensified his international campaign against us, calling on Westminster to suspend Stormont for its 'repression' of Catholics. The logic of Nationalists calling for a democratically elected parliament of Northern Irishmen to be suspended by Englishmen, and replaced by rule from London, always escaped me; it hardly coincided with the age-old Republican demand that the British should cut all links with Ireland. The Dublin Premier was, I believed, simply pouring fuel on the northern flame yet again in the hope that out of the chaos he would reap some benefits in terms of progress towards a united Ireland. A real statesman would have realized that all the democrats of Ireland needed to stand together against violent organizations. My utter disgust was expressed in a sharp statement denouncing his 'cant and hypocrisy' and pointing out that in recent years it had been his habit to speak in moderate terms of friendship and peaceful co-operation between North and South when Ulster was at peace, but immediately a crisis or conflagration broke out to exploit our difficulties in an opportunistic and irresponsible way. 'Mr Lynch now clearly commits himself and his Government to support by political means what the IRA seeks to achieve by violent means—the overthrow of the Northern Ireland Government.'

I pointed out that if his Government really wished to contribute towards peace they could begin by curbing the use of their territory as a base and training ground for terrorists who were killing our citizens. One cross-border town, Dundalk, was rapidly becoming known as 'Dodge City', and such was the atmosphere of general approval of the IRA that judges in the Republic were producing the most outrageous acquittals of IRA men caught red-handed with weapons. Even Lynch was becoming concerned that the judiciary were losing all credibility, as he admitted some months later.

On Wednesday 18 August, nine days after internment, I travelled to Chequers for two days' informal talks with Heath and his Ministers. I arrived late in the afternoon and found Heath deep in financial matters as a result of the dollar crisis, exchanging phone calls with the Chancellor, Anthony Barber, to sort out the British reaction. However, we soon settled down to dinner; Heath was on this occasion more relaxed and expansive than I ever found him before or since. He was full of chat about his newly acquired boat *Morning Cloud* and about how he had taught himself to sail. As someone with a little knowledge of sailing I found this an interesting subject and a welcome break from the weighty political discussions which would come soon enough. He explained to me at some length the problems he had discovered in mastering this sport, in improving the design of his boats, and in bullying manufacturers in the United Kingdom and the USA into producing the equipment he wanted. I was able to tell him some stories about sailing on the coast of County Down and the west coast of Scotland and the evening passed pleasantly. Later Heath played his hi-fi set in the vast inner room, formerly the Chequers coach-yard. He seemed to me a man at the height of his powers, confident, relaxed and happy.

Next day we got down to the more serious business of Ulster politics. The usual triumvirate of Maudling, Carrington and Home arrived to join us. A telegram from Lynch arrived uninvited; it repeated his denunciation of internment and his call for the suspension of Stormont. A few unprintable comments were volunteered all round, and Heath said he would send a reply after the meeting.

The weather was so hot that we sat out on the terrace in deckchairs for our discussion, Sir Alec with a knotted handkerchief on his head to keep off the sun. From the outset Heath made it clear that they were fully behind the Stormont Government in its policies. No constitutional changes were contemplated, and any political initiatives must come within the framework of existing democratic structures. Nothing could be contemplated which could even be interpreted as the first step towards direct rule. Later in the meeting I raised the subject of direct rule again; might it not come to that if things got worse? Sir Alec threw his hands in the air: 'Not direct rule,' he exclaimed, 'anything but direct rule.' It was a point of view clearly assented to by all present.

The rest of the meeting revolved around discussion of internment, the need to catch those IRA men still at large, and to counter the Republican propaganda now being poured out against the security forces. Heath and Home were in fighting mood, and appeared in no way intimidated by the Republican effort. I returned to Ulster much encouraged by this support.

In Belfast I discovered that Heath had issued a sharply worded reply to Lynch's telegram, telling him that he was 'interfering in the affairs of the UK' in a manner which was 'unwarranted, unhelpful, and in no way a contribution towards peace'. I was pleased that Heath should speak out so clearly. He was honouring the pledge made by his predecessor in the Downing Street Communiqué of 1969 that the United Kingdom Government would accept responsibility for asserting Northern Ireland's position as part of the United Kingdom in all international relationships, and the rebuff was well deserved. The problem was that Heath appeared to back down a few weeks later when he suddenly invited Lynch over to Chequers, probably as a result of pressures from the Foreign Office and the Labour Opposition.

Heath and Lynch held their talks at Chequers on 7 and 8 September, and, although nothing of importance was said afterwards, the breaches in Anglo-Irish relations seemed to have been partly repaired. The main proposal to emerge was for tripartite talks involving Heath, Lynch and myself, and I received an invitation from Heath to participate in such talks at Chequers three weeks later. Feelings in the Unionist Party were mixed; many had watched Lynch's journey to Chequers with concern, wondering what damaging stories this wily Irishman was going to plant in Heath's mind. This latest development seemed to them downright alarming, since it could represent acceptance of Dublin's right to interfere in the internal affairs of Northern Ireland. Paisley and Craig were, of course, warning of an impending 'sell-out'. From a Northern Ireland point of view it would have been easiest politically to decline the invitation, but from the United Kingdom viewpoint I knew this would be a mistake, placing us in the role of boycotters. Lynch had probably pointed out to Heath that no such tripartite meeting had taken place since the 1920s, and Heath was not a man to miss the opportunity of an historical first. It also made sense to meet Lynch face to face for some straight talking, rather than continuing to exchange statements across the border. Lynch clearly had it in his power to make the situation in Ulster much worse or much better; so far he had been concentrating on doing the former, but if he could be drawn into discussions he might be prevailed upon to make some moves against the IRA gangs roaming his territory. I had long lists of cross-border training camps from Army and police intelligence and such a meeting would give me the opportunity to put these in front of Lynch and demand that he do something about them.

I announced that I would agree to go, but issued a statement making it clear that I would not be prepared to discuss the constitutional position of Northern Ireland with Mr Lynch, but rather intended to seek inter-governmental co-operation against terrorism.

At Chequers the talks proceeded along these lines. I pressed Lynch on border security and IRA training camps, asked him to end the massive thefts of gelignite from Southern quarries (which were providing the main source of IRA explosives at this time), urged the extradition from the Republic of the forty or so known terrorists wanted in Northern Ireland, and pointed out that if internment were introduced in the South even now the defeat of the IRA would be a matter of months. Lynch eventually agreed to do something about the first two points, but insisted that extradition and internment were not on. The possibility of simultaneous introduction of internment in North and South had been cautiously explored by the Foreign Office before 9 August, but it had been clear that Lynch was hooked politically by his attacks on Stormont. He had actually prepared for internment in the Republic by activating the relevant legislation in December 1970 when there was talk of a plot to assassinate members of his Government—presumably because of the decision to stop the supply of money to the Provisionals. By 1971, however, he was once again the prisoner of the wild men in his party.

Throughout these talks Ted Heath was very helpful, backing me up on many points and urging Lynch to be more co-operative in the fight against terrorism. I felt sorry for Reggie Maudling, who was kept waiting at Chequers during the talks and had to ask various civil servants if they knew what was going on.

Meanwhile, Harold Wilson was rushing around proposing all manner of brilliant 'solutions' to the Irish problem, and the Nationalist campaign was gaining anti-Stormont converts in the Labour Party. Wilson took over responsibility for Irish affairs from Callaghan; I always thought that the size of the Irish vote in Huyton loomed rather larger in his mind than it should have done. In a statement timed to coincide with the Heath/Lynch talks he proposed a '12-point plan' including a Minister in the United Kingdom Cabinet for Northern Ireland, an all-Ireland Council and PR in Stormont elections. He also demanded the recall of the Westminster Parliament to hold an emergency debate on Ulster, a request to which the Government eventually acceded. But when Wilson accused the Government of departing from a position of 'neutrality' (a strange phrase to use of the role of the United Kingdom Government in a part of the United Kingdom where terrorism was rife), Maudling rightly retorted that he was being irresponsible.

In spite of these hiccups in Conservative/Labour relations the Opposition did agree not to vote against the Government at the end of the emergency debate, though some seventy Labour back benchers revolted and forced a division.

During this debate some important things were said by leaders on both sides. Mr Wilson deplored talk of direct rule and said it should only be thought of as a last resort. Mr Maudling called for all-party talks in Ulster to agree on means whereby 'an active, permanent, and guaranteed place in the life and public affairs of Northern Ireland shall be available both to the majority and the minority community'. This was a new formula, agreed between us in an exchange of telex messages shortly before, which he justified by an analysis of the political differences between Northern Ireland and Great Britain. He argued that the British system worked in practice 'by giving almost unlimited powers for a few years to the party that happens to possess a temporary majority in the House of Commons'. But, he said, this was only acceptable because the party in government changed. 'One must recognise that there are different circumstances in a country when the majority does not change.'

The analysis was fine as far as it went; but there was a fundamental problem of how one could have in government persons whose stated objective was to bring the existence of the State to an end, particularly when the position of Northern Ireland as part of the United Kingdom was, under the Ireland Act of 1949, dependent upon the will of the Stormont Parliament and Government, and Maudling had accepted this in our private discussions. I did not see that it was reasonably possible for me to go any further to meet the Opposition than my committee proposals of the previous June, especially in the absence of talks. These proposals had recognized the special needs of the Ulster situation and provided for a flexible and evolving response to them without in any way moving towards a sectarian constitutional arrangement. I was pleased, therefore, to note that on the second day of the debate Heath said they constituted an 'offer of major importance'.

Discussion and dialogue were the keys to political progress and the restoration of influence to elected representatives. I issued my own plea to members of other parties to come out of their trenches and talk. 'If Ulster people cannot find Ulster solutions, it will shame us all,' I said. 'This is a time for political leaders and community leaders to behave like men. We must turn from the tough words of re-stating our separate positions to the tougher deeds of seeking a common aim.' But my appeal, like that of the Home Secretary, went unheeded; the SDLP were adamant that there would be no talks involving them until internment was ended (though it is worth remembering that the SDLP withdrew from Stormont before the introduction of internment).

At the end of September the six months' term of office of the Labour member of my Cabinet, David Bleakley, Minister of Community Relations, was due to end. But a few days before the end of the month he gave me his resignation, expressing his disagreement with the policy of internment. I thought it was an unworthy end to an effective and useful ministerial term; internment had been introduced seven weeks earlier and that had been the time to resign.

However, having established the principle that Unionist Prime Ministers could bring members of other parties into the Cabinet I now had the opportunity to bring in a new face, if possible creating another new precedent and moving further towards the idea of community government. After some thought I asked Dr G. B. Newe, a prominent Catholic moderate who was founder and secretary of the Northern Ireland Council of Social Services. He agreed to accept a post as Minister of State in the Office of the Prime Minister, and thereby became the first Catholic member of a Unionist Government at Stormont. I regarded the appointment as symbolic, since it would indicate that in my office right at the heart of government there was an independent Catholic voice which commanded respect. Dr Newe deserves great credit for the courage he showed in accepting the appointment at a time when many of his fellow-Catholics were mounting total opposition to the State, and for the statesmanlike way in which he behaved in office. His daily concern for the welfare and interests of all the Ulster people, Protestant and Catholic, was an inspiration to those who came into contact with him. He performed very effectively the role which I had asked him to play, namely that of seeking out the various elements of thought in the Catholic community about the crisis and conveying them to me and the Cabinet as a whole.

When Stormont reconvened on 5 October after the summer recess the SDLP members continued their boycott and the Opposition benches were occupied by the lonely figure of Vivian Simpson, the only Northern Ireland Labour Party MP. But Paisley led his three henchmen, Boal, Beattie, and McQuade across the floor and they proceeded to adopt the role of a noisy and quarrelsome parliamentary Opposition. It was sad to return to the despatch box in such circumstances after all the hopes of the early summer, but we had the responsibility to govern, we had made every possible gesture of conciliation, and I for one was in no mood to give up. We were a democratic government facing direct challenges from a terrorist organization, from a neighbouring government, and from a minority political group within. To challenges of that nature there was only one possible response, a response which formed the keynote of my speech—defiance.

> We will respond to argument but never bow to ultimata. Let this message be heard by all who are working to destroy Ulster. We shall resist you. We shall resist you as a Parliament; we shall resist you as a government; we shall resist you as a people ... You have destroyed our property, bullied our people, and made many live in fear. All these things only increase our resolve to resist you. You shall not win for we shall not permit it.

That was the position as far as my Government was concerned. But as autumn moved on towards winter, and one atrocity by the IRA succeeded another, I began to watch with some concern the political developments at Westminster. Edward Heath I was confident I could rely on; our relationship had continued to be cordial and I believed him to be a man of principle and strong character who would stand by us when the going was rough. But I was less happy with the atmosphere developing among other parliamentarians, chiefly in the Labour Party, but also in the Conservative Party. There was a confused groping around for some political 'solution', which when applied to Ireland would quickly bring peace, rather in the manner of taking an aspirin to get rid of a headache. If one could only grant more concessions, ran this theory, the Nationalist politicians and the IRA would see the error of their ways and settle for some half-way position. War-weariness was creeping in early and resolve to defend the rights of Ulster's citizens was becoming weak.

The behaviour of Harold Wilson in the last few months of 1971 was foolish and unhelpful in the extreme. I have no desire to be unfair to him, but the benefit of hindsight has only confirmed this contemporary evaluation. I tried hard to keep the Labour Party informed about developments, and on 4 November I flew to London for a meeting with Wilson and Callaghan to bring them up to date. We met at Wilson's house in Lord North Street and were served with afternoon tea by Mrs Wilson while we discussed the security situation. Wilson and Callaghan listened attentively, posing the odd question, but making little comment. At one stage Callaghan said that he still got many letters from Ireland urging him not to be discouraged or give up, 'they say to me that I am one of the few British politicians who understands Ireland'. Wilson was puffing at one of the cigars he sometimes prefers at informal occasions. 'Yes,' he said thoughtfully, 'I get letters from crackpots too!' I returned to Belfast hoping I had made some impression, but without any evidence that I had done so.

A week later Wilson was over in Ulster on a fact-finding tour for several days. I met him and laid on a special dinner with all the Cabinet and senior civil servants present. Over coffee I opened up the discussion by saying, 'Perhaps, Mr Wilson, some of my colleagues would like to put some points to you.' No one responded, so I turned to Harry West, who had been particularly fierce in his demands at recent Cabinet meetings that I should tell Wilson off, and said, 'Harry, what about you?' He appeared a bit nonplussed at first, but then proceeded to tell two jokes which I am afraid entirely failed to relax our gathering.

Shortly afterwards I realized the limited success of our efforts to communicate the realities of Ulster to the Opposition Leader. A few days after his return to London he announced his latest, most comprehensive, most radical, and most dangerously destructive 'solution' of all. It was a '15-point plan' which, in a very Irish way, aimed at both honouring the pledges to Northern Ireland, but at the same time 'finding a means of achieving the aspirations envisaged half a century ago of progress towards a united Ireland'. To facilitate this the Republic of Ireland would have to rejoin the Commonwealth. The practical possibilities of the plan were nil, but the effects of putting it forward were dangerously explosive—perhaps literally so. By raising the fantasy of a united Ireland he was raising the hopes of the IRA and strengthening their resolve to continue the terrorist campaign; he was at the same time increasing

the fears of the Unionist population and the readiness of the more militant among them to create organizations which could be used to frus-
trate any future government actions interpreted as giving effect to this
plan. Over two years later under a Labour Government the chickens
of the 15-point plan came home to roost in fifteen dramatic and tragic
days. From the moment he made this speech Harold Wilson has been
regarded with the utmost suspicion and lack of confidence by almost
the whole spectrum of Ulster Unionism.

There was an important lesson on the nature of British politics to be
drawn from these developments. When I made my committee proposals
in June they were supported on all sides; but in October and November
there were many at Westminster critical of our Green Paper (which reiterated the committee proposals, raised the possibility of proportional
representation in Stormont elections, and supported a more active
Senate and an enlarged Commons at Stormont) on the grounds that it
did not go far enough to meet the 'new' situation.

But what was new about the situation? The political realities had not
changed: there were over one million people totally and passionately
opposed to a united Ireland and prepared to resist its imposition by
force if necessary, people passionately attached to the existence of their
own Parliament as the only safeguard of their rights; and there were
under half a million people who supported the idea of a united Ireland
with varying degrees of enthusiasm, the most militant of them having
taken up arms in the IRA terrorist organization. The voting figures had
not changed, the arguments for the two mutually exclusive points of
view had not altered.

What had changed was the scale of violence which the IRA was carrying out; it had escalated considerably. Thus applying the equation 'little
trouble equals little concession, big trouble equals big concession',
some British commentators were concluding that the IRA required a
big concession. That kind of approach may or may not be suitable for
solving the economic and other problems of the British mainland, but
it certainly is not suitable for dealing with the fundamental constitutional differences of Ulster. Either one accepted that the democratically expressed wish of the majority to remain in the United
Kingdom must be respected, and upheld it against all challenges, or one
did not. A choice had to be made and a stand taken on the basis of principle and justice. There was room for change within the existing constitutional framework, for ensuring a fair deal for everyone, but there
was no room for compromise on the basic constitutional issue. Yet the
idea of a choice was proving strangely repugnant, and a belief in the

virtue of ambiguity persisted. To the IRA and the Protestant militants the message was the same: future policy would be decided not on the basis of political principle but on the basis of conciliating whoever caused the most trouble. A premium was being placed on violence, and the price was to be dramatically raised a few months later.

It only remains for me here to make a few general points on the internment decision. Was it a disastrous mistake which did nothing to help combat violence? Was it a deviation from justice completely unjustifiable in a democratic state? My answer to both these questions is 'No'.

To deal with the second question first, I firmly believe that the primary duty of a democratic government is to protect the lives and property of its citizens. In times of emergency extraordinary measures may have to be adopted to achieve this. The European Court of Human Rights has recognized that preventive detention is a legitimate weapon in the hands of a democratic government when there is an organized threat to the life of the State.* Those who declare themselves 'morally' opposed to the measure are often persons fortunate enough to have been brought up in more peaceful societies than Ulster, and who have never learned by experience that governments are seldom blessed with a clear choice between good and evil. I respect the sincerity of many of these critics, but they are indulging in a moral gesture which costs them nothing, and which, if placed in a position of responsibility for the saving of lives, they would not be able to sustain. There was another type of 'moral' opponent of internment for whom I had less respect: the IRA propagandist in Ireland, Britain and America. The 'moral outrage' here was largely bogus; a great deal of time, effort, and money was spent denouncing internment as 'repression' etc., but very little, if any, in denouncing the murder and pillage which led to its introduction, and which was making its continued imposition necessary. The volume of such propaganda was so great at times the unknowing outsider might have been forgiven for believing that internment was the cause of the violence in Ireland, and were it to be abolished all would be well.

* Since Lord Faulkner completed this chapter the European Commission on Human Rights has produced a detailed report on the internment operation as a result of the case brought against the United Kingdom by the Irish Republic. The Commission found that intimidation had limited the use of normal court procedures, that detention without trial was 'strictly required by the exigencies of the situation', and that detention was applied without political or religious discrimination. But they also found that the interrogation-in-depth procedures constituted inhuman treatment and contravened the European Convention of Human Rights. The European Court of Human Rights, following up the case at the request of the Government, ruled in January 1978 that the procedures did not constitute torture.

But what of the practical value of internment? It is undeniable that the volume and seriousness of terrorist violence, already unacceptably high before internment, escalated immediately after its introduction. In the seventy-two hours after the arrests thirty people died in gun-battles and bomb attacks, and over the succeeding two months there was a daily toll of carnage and death. A small number of effective snipers, mainly Official (Marxist) IRA, were shooting soldiers, while the Provisional IRA bombers were hard at work, extending their attacks from so-called 'military and commercial' targets to direct attacks on the lives of scores of civilians. There was an attack on the offices of the Electricity Board in Belfast, a huge building where hundreds worked; a bomb was placed at one of the exits and a warning given which was just adequate for employees evacuating the building to reach the exit. By some miracle only one young man was in the immediate vicinity of the bomb when it exploded, and was killed, and sixteen were injured. There were three large explosions in the heart of Belfast on 2 September and thousands across the Province heard on the radio a man screaming with pain lying in a Belfast street. A bar was bombed in Sandy Row, injuring twenty-five. Another bar in the Shankill Road was reduced to rubble, leaving four dead, two of them children. A baby girl of seventeen months died from shots recklessly fired at soldiers in a busy street. ('One of the hazards of urban guerrilla warfare,' an IRA spokesman callously remarked a few days later.) And so one could continue; there have been so many fine people, Protestant and Catholic, young and old, needlessly cut down in this cruel violence, and whose deaths one feels ought at least to be recorded. We lost some brave men from the Ulster Defence Regiment and the RUC during these months too. And there was one particularly horrifying explosion which must be included: fifteen people died when a bomb exploded in the Catholic McGurk's bar in early December. The origin of the bomb is still uncertain, and numerous allegations that it was planted by Protestant extremists, or was an IRA bomb in transit, have been bandied about. I do not pretend to know which is accurate; all that matters is that more people died as a result of terrorism, either directly or through retaliation.

On the surface therefore it appeared that internment had made the security situation worse. Some commentators were busy with graphs of violence which purported to prove this point; there was more violence in the month after internment than in the month before, therefore, the argument ran, the measure had failed. But, as Dr Johnson said, there are 'lies, damned lies, and statistics'. The rate of increase of violence was in fact greater before internment than after, thus raising the question

'How much violence would there have been without internment?' The IRA were escalating a campaign against the State in July; if they were able to carry out such widespread terrorism after scores of their members were arrested in August, what might they have done were the arrests not made? From August onwards there was a gradual but steady decline in terrorist violence; August was the peak month. Can one therefore claim convincingly that internment caused greater violence?*

I have already outlined some of the reasons why internment was not as effective as it might have been: gaps in our intelligence due to 'No Go' areas, the emotive impact of the interrogation controversy, the manipulated outburst of hysteria, the abdication of leadership by Nationalist politicians, and the tacit support by Dublin for the objective of overthrowing the State. A deepening of the antagonism from Dublin and the Nationalists was the most obvious price of internment; we had anticipated this to some extent, but knew that deep down they were also concerned about the IRA, and if internment succeeded their criticisms would become muted.

Perhaps there was also a fault in our presentation; many people expected quick results and were very discouraged when they did not appear. Personally, I had expected a more speedy improvement and thus I did not point public attention sufficiently to the long-term nature of the anti-terrorist campaign. People were thinking of last week's bombing, or last night's shooting, rather than the improvement in intelligence which would lead to next week's or next month's arrests and arms' finds, and a reduction in violence the month after that. Those of us in the Government and the security forces were very conscious of the need to counter the Republican propaganda offensive immediately after internment, and in doing so we probably overstressed the advantages of the operation, rather than setting it in its context as one of many security measures.

All of this having been said, however, I still believe that our security measures, of which internment was a very important part, were, by the end of 1971, beginning to pay off and would, if consistently and firmly applied over succeeding months, have resulted in the virtual defeat of the IRA by the end of 1972. Intelligence was vastly improved as a result of questioning and tip-offs, and the inevitable exposure resulting from the all-out war following internment. More and more members of the

* A pamphlet published in 1975 by the moderate Conservative pressure group, the Bow Group, produced evidence that internment had cut off the increase in violence in 1971 and that peak periods of violence in 1972–4 were directly related to periods of large-scale releases of detainees.

Provisionals command were being picked up, especially in Belfast, and ammunition finds soared, as we have already seen. All but three small areas in Belfast were virtually free of IRA activity by January 1972 and it was hoped that it would soon be possible to move troops to the border area to deal with the continuing high level of activity there. IRA morale in Belfast was low and most of those still active seemed to be inexperienced youths in their teens whose random activities were alienating the population of the republican ghettos in which they were based. Most of the experienced leaders who had escaped arrest had fled across the border from where they operated hit-and-run attacks against isolated police stations and members of the security forces. The Government was moving civil servants to former terrorist strongholds in Belfast to speed up the restoration of normal community services.

This assessment of an improving security situation was backed up by two independent and influential observers who visited the Province in January—Lord Chalfont, the former Labour Minister, who wrote an assessment in *The Times*, and Peter Jenkins of the *Guardian*; the latter wrote that even the Dublin Government was convinced that 'virtual defeat' faced the Provisionals in Belfast.

The most decisive evidence of all was the appearance on reliable 'grapevines' of stories that the terrorists were interested in talking and reaching a compromise. When a terrorist organization with no negotiable demands whatever—which was and still is the position of the IRA—starts to suggest talks it is obvious that a breathing space is needed to reorganize and to extract evidence of a willingness to buy it off (i.e. weakness) on the opposing side. Unfortunately, democratic governments have a tendency to comply very easily with both requirements.

As far as internment (or detention) is concerned, it is worth adding that two Westminster Governments, one Conservative and the other Labour, found it an essential weapon for the security forces in dealing with the IRA while the intimidation of witnesses made normal prosecutions difficult to sustain, and that its eventual abandonment at the end of 1975 was followed by the worst year of violence in Northern Ireland since 1972.

12
Direct Rule

The year 1972 was to be a good one for Brian Faulkner, according to a well-known clairvoyant, Michael Woodruff. Writing in one of the Sunday papers he said that the 'portents were favourable', and that by March I would be able to relax. He was almost entirely wrong; it was for me a very bad year, perhaps one of the most difficult of my life. It was also the most violent year in Ulster's history. But by the end of March I did have an unexpected opportunity to relax.

Sunday 30 January was a decisive turning point. On that day—known in history as 'Bloody Sunday'—thirteen civilians were shot dead by the Army in Londonderry at the end of a Nationalist march. All parades, Protestant or Catholic, Nationalist or Unionist, had been banned by us since August the previous year to reduce the chances of sectarian conflict on the streets. This march was in defiance of that ban and therefore clearly illegal. The security forces had decided that the march could not be allowed to enter the city centre because of the danger of rioting and deployed their forces to stop it at a certain point. The bulk of the marchers stopped before they reached the Army lines and held a meeting, but a breakaway group began to stone the troops. What happened next is one of the most hotly disputed issues in Irish history; thousands of words have been written claiming to give the 'true' version of events, and I have no intention of raking over the ashes yet again. From relatives and friends of those killed there have been accusations of 'deliberate murder', while the paratroopers involved have insisted they were returning fire at snipers and nail bombers. A government inquiry under Lord Widgery, Lord Chief Justice of England and Wales, said that four of the dead appeared to have been firing weapons or using bombs, but in the case of the remaining nine evidence was either inconclusive or indicated they had no possession of arms. Subsequently the Government has paid compensation of varying amounts to the relatives of all thirteen.

It is with the effects of this tragic day that we are here primarily concerned. Nationalist Ireland, North and South, was in uproar. The age-old 'British oppressor' had done it again, and the accumulated fund of centuries of bitterness surfaced. John Hume, the Londonderry SDLP representative, was caught up in the emotional aftermath and declared 'now it's a united Ireland or nothing'. Lynch moved swiftly in the vanguard of the hysteria, recalling the Irish Ambassador from London and announcing that his government would provide funds for political action by 'the minority' in Northern Ireland. Bernadette Devlin attacked Maudling on the floor of the House of Commons and scratched his face. The propaganda vultures of the IRA were quick to exploit public feeling, and seemed to regard the tragedy as a coup. In the wake of Mr Lynch's reaction their task was easy; all over the Republic there were protests and factory walk-outs, and British papers and aircraft were blacked at the airports. Emotions reached their peak with the burning down of the British Embassy in Dublin by a huge mob on 2 February. Dominic Coyle accurately summed it up in the *Financial Times* when he reported from Dublin that 'a Pandora's Box of nationalism' had been opened up. The Irish Question was going to be solved once and for all, and in only one way—a united Ireland. In the minds of Irish Nationalists the Ulster Unionists, for a few heady weeks, simply ceased to exist.

The reaction of Dublin was particularly embarrassing for Heath. The Irish Republic and the United Kingdom were poised to enter the European Community as partners, and only a week before had met at Brussels on cordial terms to sign the Treaties. The Community would not take kindly to the entry of two members who were scarcely on diplomatic terms. A few days after the deaths the authoritative French paper *Le Nation* said in a front-page article that the Irish and British governments had a common duty to settle their differences before entering the Common Market: 'It is unthinkable that the Ten should not walk at the same pace along the paths of democracy and the right to self-determination of the people for whom they have responsibility,' it said, adding ominously, 'London and Dublin must both take note of this.' I have no doubt they did so, and particularly London. In America too, Britain was feeling international pressure. Patrick Hillery, the Dublin Minister for External Affairs, was mobilizing criticism of Britain at the UN, while, in Washington, Ted Kennedy was bitterly criticizing British policy and initiating Congressional hearings on Ireland to provide a platform for these criticisms.

In London 'political opinion was shaken', as *The Times* so aptly put it. I spoke to Heath on the telephone shortly after the shootings and he clearly did not, at that stage, regard this particular crisis as different in kind from the many others we had faced. He had received the Army report and believed the paratroops must have had good reason to shoot. He assured me that, despite all the clamour for the abolition of Stormont, direct rule was in no way made more likely by these events. During the next few days I think he began to appreciate the political repercussions. Wilson denounced the Government for 'foot-dragging', reiterated the need for a united Ireland, and divided the Commons on a critical motion. He also declared the bi-partisan agreement between Labour and Conservatives on Northern Ireland at an end, and demanded the transfer of all security powers from Stormont to Westminster. Maudling turned down this demand on the grounds that, quite apart from the practical difficulties involved, it would be regarded by Unionists as tantamount to direct rule—a very significant argument in view of later events. A few days later the *Guardian* political correspondent, Ian Aitken, was reporting that 'a significant number of Ministers' believed that the events of the previous Sunday had 'changed the situation entirely' and were urging 'an immediate and major gesture of conciliation'.

On Monday we held a Cabinet meeting to consider the crisis and issued a statement pointing out that 'violent deaths of any citizen or member of the security forces bringing as they do grief and pain to relatives and friends, are events of real sadness for the whole community' but that tragedies such as these 'can all too easily occur when the law is not respected and obeyed'. The same afternoon at Stormont I spoke to the Commons in very emphatic terms:

This is a very grave moment indeed in the history of Northern Ireland. Mounting unreason and hysteria surround us on every side. Impossible and outrageous demands are being made, which can do nothing but deepen the tragic conflict. It is right that I should sound a note of solemn warning. It is clear, as a result of the weekend shootings, that campaigns are being mounted in Northern Ireland and in the Republic to achieve a united Ireland without the consent of the Unionist majority. We in the Unionist community will not tolerate such a proposal. We are more than ready to discuss how the institutions of Northern Ireland may be framed on a renewed basis of general consent. We are more than ready to develop the most friendly and co-operative relationship with our neighbours in the South, if and when they manifest a matching goodwill. But there it ends.

We could see that it was a battle for survival, and the vultures were already beginning to circle over our Province. Mainstream Unionism rallied to the defence of Stormont, and even the voices of Paisley and Craig were, for a short time, silenced. I was speaking for the whole spectrum of Unionist opinion, for some one million people, in a responsible, democratic and forceful expression of fundamental belief. Beyond these limits lay an abyss of conflict the depth of which we could only guess at. For a moment the Unionist community paused and let its case rest on words and votes. But as events developed in succeeding weeks the fringes of those unwilling to rely on words alone grew and became organized and an impressive and dignified restraint began at last to crumble.

The fundamental nature of this crisis was underlined by two interventions. In the Stormont Commons Craig suggested that, since the Bogside and Creggan seemed more trouble than they were worth, we should consider ceding them to the Republic. And Dr Newe, in a rare political statement, addressed to his fellow-Catholics a warning: '. . . we as Catholics have a choice. We can pull down every frail bridge which links us with our Protestant fellow-citizens. If we do that, then indeed it will be a mockery to talk in any real sense of aspirations for unity.'

On Friday 4 February I went to London for talks with Heath and his Ministers at Downing Street. In the middle of the week there had been interparty talks at Westminster between Whitelaw, the Conservative Leader of the Commons and Lord President of the Council, and Harold Wilson. And the evening before our meeting at Downing Street, there had been a meeting of the Conservative Backbench Committee—the 1922 Committee—at which Northern Ireland had been the central topic. Maudling was reported to have told the meeting that an 'initiative' as meant by most people who were pressing for one would be a surrender. I was hopeful that our meeting would show that the Government was holding firm.

It was a testing and probing meeting for me. Discussions ranged widely over the spectrum of fundamental political issues, and the questions came at me thick and fast. There was no hint of hostility or criticism, but clearly they were casting around for a new line, for a means of diverting the storm of criticism which had followed the events of 30 January.

Heath was quite candid about the situation. He referred to the march planned (illegally) by the CRA for Newry the next day. 'I am afraid there will be great pressure, especially if things go wrong at Newry tomorrow, for a change of course,' he said. Home expressed his agreement, and Maudling added that the 1922 Committee felt the party could not continue indefinitely on its present course. Carrington elaborated: 'It is a question of being able to show that we are doing something positive about the situation,' he said. It sounded a bit like a rehearsed chorus and I could see I would have to convince them that our present course was the right one. I laid stress on the calm and restraint of the majority of the population. 'They are relatively calm and restrained because they still have confidence that our two Governments will not let them down or submit to the IRA. If they ever come to believe, or even suspect, that this is not so, that restraint could quickly crumble.'

'What about Craig's suggestion of ceding Republican areas on the border to the Republic,' asked Heath. 'Is there any support for that?'

'No, it has not been taken very seriously in Ulster,' I replied. 'And it would do nothing about the core of the problem, the 200,000 Catholics in Belfast.' I added that I could not see the Catholic section of the community being prepared to move, or to accept the lower living standards of the Republic.

'Would a referendum to test opinion on the constitutional position of Northern Ireland within the United Kingdom not be a good idea?' asked Heath. 'Could Lynch not accept that?' I said this was extremely unlikely since it would be seen as a device to tie the Catholic population to the existing constitutional position (an accurate assessment as events later showed). But Heath pressed it further, asking if Unionists would not welcome such a referendum. I replied again that Unionists saw the present constitutional position as settled, and to raise the matter in a referendum might be seen as re-opening it and going back on the 1949 Act, which placed the responsibility for expressing views about the Union on the Stormont Parliament.

And so the meeting progressed, with the four men raising targets for me to shoot at. Home wanted to know the effect of removing troops from Catholic areas, and I said it would mean surrendering the people of those areas into the control of the IRA. Heath wondered if some initiative in the security field might not be necessary to end violence. Maudling said that time was running against us. I referred to Tuzo's view, repeatedly expressed over the past two months, that the IRA in Belfast would be under control by the end of March, and said the facts bore out this prediction. We could then, but only then, consider a de-escalation of internment and other security measures. Carrington did not seem to accept Tuzo's view, and said that the Army always had a tendency to be over-optimistic.

A general discussion on the means of involving Catholics in the government of Northern Ireland ensued. I argued that to attempt some constitutional innovation of a major nature while IRA violence continued would be seen as setting democracy aside to appease the IRA. 'What would be the reaction to Catholic participation in the Cabinet if there was a constitutional referendum say every twenty years?' asked Maudling. I said that if we could get violence ended I would be in a strong position to urge magnanimity upon the majority, for example, in looking beyond party confines for members of the Government. When Wilson's proposition for the transfer of all law and order powers to London was raised I made my opposition very clear: it was a central power of Stormont under the Government of Ireland Act, and its removal now would reduce our government to a mere sham.

As the meeting neared its end some indications of Westminster thinking were given to me. The idea of a referendum arose yet again, and the view was expressed that, held at twenty-year intervals, it could help take the border out of politics. Heath said that whatever initiative was taken should be agreed between us. Direct rule was not being contemplated, he said, and only would be if there was a complete breakdown. 'In any case, why should Unionists worry about closer integration into the United Kingdom?' I explained that Unionists saw the existence of Stormont as the only effective political obstacle to a unification of Ireland against their wishes. As I walked to the door with Heath I said to him, 'I have been completely frank with you about our ideas. Are you absolutely sure there is nothing else on your mind?' He said very firmly that there was not.

I flew back to Belfast pondering our talks. It seemed to me that they had been setting up Aunt Sallys for me to knock down, and that the crucial remarks were those concerning an agreed initiative which we would meet again to discuss before anything was made public. We would have to put on our thinking caps yet again at Stormont and produce something which could act as a basis for new political talks in Ulster. This would, I thought, involve amendment of existing institutions and finding ways of broadening involvement in them. But there it would end.

Next Sunday, much to my annoyance, the first of a series of inspired press leaks appeared in the *Observer*. After some fairly accurate speculation about our discussions Nova Beloff reported that 'Mr Heath himself is particularly aware of the international repercussions ... He was astonished and disconcerted by the virulence of the Irish reactions to

Derry and in his gloomier moments envisages Ireland as our local Cuba.' I knew the reference to international pressures was accurate, though I was less convinced that Heath was 'disconcerted'. We knew there was a huge gap in the picture of Ulster which was filtering through to the outside world, and so we decided to step up our publicity effort. The Government Information Service at Stormont published a large glossy booklet entitled *The Terror and the Tears* which spelt out in simple words and pictures the horrors of the terrorist campaign Ulster was facing. The demand for it was overwhelming as Ulster folk circulated thousands of copies to friends and relatives across the globe. The Unionist Party set up a Publicity and Research Department and launched an appeal for funds. Public response was enormous; thousands of pounds poured in from all across the Province, accompanied by letters from pensioners and businessmen urging us to 'tell the world the truth about Ulster'. In retrospect our effort came too late.

Speculation and leaks in London multiplied over the next few weeks, and their direction was profoundly disturbing to Unionists. A belief in the efficacy of words and votes is essential to the working of democracy and our publicity effort therefore served a valuable function in Ulster, if not outside, in sustaining the belief that such weapons might prevail. But some of the divisions were beginning to surface again as new fears gained hold. On 12 February an organization called Vanguard was launched by Craig and he announced plans for rallies across the Province to express determination to resist any capitulation to the terrorists.

The rallies went ahead immediately, culminating in a massive display of strength in Belfast's Ormeau Park on 18 March by some fifty thousand supporters. The style of the rallies soon began to trouble me. Craig was arriving with motor-cycle escorts, or swooping down in a light private plane; and inspecting hundreds of men drawn up in military formation. On one occasion those present were asked to raise their hands in the air and indicate their assent to the objects of Vanguard by shouting 'I do' three times. Comparisons with Nazi rallies could scarcely be avoided. The Protestant backlash, so often derided by nationalists as a myth invented by Unionist politicians to frighten the British was beginning. I attacked these 'demonstrations with an alien and unconvincing flavour' adding that there was among Unionists a 'determination not to be coerced on basic matters which is a far more formidable thing than these comic opera parades can convey'. But I was concerned about the obvious attractions of such activities for those who had been saying for months, 'Can we not do something to show that we mean what we say?'

On the other wing of the party Phelim O'Neill left us on 18 February, and with two other Stormont MPs—one Nationalist and one independent Unionist—joined the Alliance Party, thereby becoming its first elected representatives. The Alliance Party had been formed in 1970 as an attempt to provide a non-sectarian party for both Protestants and Catholics. It was an admirable ideal but a rather naïve basis for a political party, and some of the liberal Unionists drawn away by Alliance could have played a much more useful role by staying in the Unionist Party and giving me their support, especially a couple of years later when a few votes at party meetings could have made all the difference. But these three men were reacting to a violent situation that February by making a gesture towards the middle ground which they hoped would express the general desire of the community for peace.

Immediately after the London meeting we began a major reassessment of the political situation at Stormont. We had to decide what would be necessary in order to get the SDLP back to the conference table in spite of all the hooks they had got themselves caught on, how far the London Government would press us to go as a result of the new pressures it was coming under, and how far we could afford to go ourselves without sacrificing some fundamental principle and without losing our political base in the community.

On 16 February, after a Cabinet meeting at Stormont the previous day, I sent a letter to Heath outlining the basis of our approach. I assured him that we fully appreciated the need to produce, as a matter of urgency and in agreement with his Government, the means of achieving the 'active, permanent and guaranteed role' to which both governments were publicly committed for the minority in Northern Ireland. I reminded him of what he had said to me at a previous meeting; that the two governments must stick together and on no account allow a wedge to be driven between them:

> Ever since, I have been concerned to conduct our relationship on a basis of complete frankness and I know that this has also been your objective . . . it is our understanding that any new, albeit provisional, conclusions reached by the UK Government will be put to our Cabinet for our consideration and comment before any concrete action is taken or any public disclosure made. In this context, we regard some recent press comment, which I realise is of a speculative nature, as distinctly unhelpful.

I also stressed that the security forces were at a crucial stage in the campaign against the terrorists, who must not, under any circumstances, be given a breathing space or have their standing and morale boosted.

I reminded the Prime Minister of our discussions at Chequers on 19 August and of the subsequent exchange of telex messages on 1 and 2 September between myself and the Home Secretary when we were agreeing on the phrase 'an active, permanent and guaranteed role'. Mr Maudling had then said, 'I quite agree that at Chequers we all recognized the suggestion of a coalition government was not a practical proposition.' We at Stormont had since then reviewed the whole basis of executive government and had concluded that we should not create by statutory means an entrenched position in the Cabinet for members of the Catholic community as such, since this would strengthen sectarian divisions and eliminate attempts to create non-sectarian political alignments. Nor was it possible to provide statutorily entrenched positions for the anti-partitionist (as distinct from the religious) minority, as this would lead inevitably to PR government, which we regarded as intrinsically unworkable and which would sterilize any real debate in Parliament. I told Heath that we were looking at other means of involving the minority, and were examining the idea of a referendum on the border issue. But it was our firm view that a transfer of 'law and order' powers would leave no credible basis of viable government, and that any transfer to the Republic of parts of Northern Ireland would create more problems than it would solve.

Two weeks later I wrote to Heath again, outlining the broad conclusions which the Cabinet had reached after much discussion. The objective, I said, must be to find a means of achieving for the institutions of Northern Ireland a general consensus, binding all sections of its population other than unreasonable and irreconcilable elements committed to the use of force. Such a consensus would be much easier to achieve with the co-operation and assistance of the Government of the Irish Republic. If the constitutional framework and governmental institutions were accepted as fair and reasonable throughout Ireland it would make possible on an all-Ireland basis determined action against terrorist organizations. We urged that, as a major contribution to peace, an attempt should be made to reach with the Republic a solemn and binding agreement on the constitutional status of Northern Ireland. This agreement would have to recognize the validity of efforts either to maintain or change that position by lawful, constitutional means and provide for an acceptable mechanism through which the people of Northern Ireland could decide in the future whether they wished to retain the existing position or change it.

We proposed that a referendum should provide this mechanism, treating Northern Ireland as a single constituency, the first to be held as soon as practically possible, and thereafter only when at least 40 per cent of MPs at Stormont presented an address to the Governor asking that one should be held. No question of a change in the constitutional position should arise unless more than 50 per cent of those entitled to vote registered a vote for a change. If the Republic's government accepted this as a proper mechanism—and we could see no reason why it should not if it really accepted that unity must be by consent—we would be able to adopt a common policy for the suppression of terrorism, dealing with fugitive offenders who were hiding behind the pretence of 'political' murder and thereby evading extradition, and a joint Inter-Governmental Council could be set up with equal members from the Dublin and Belfast governments to discuss economic and social matters.

I repeated our view that PR government in Northern Ireland would be unworkable. The active role for the minority which we were seeking to define could be achieved in various ways, involving mainly an elaboration of the proposals in our Green Paper of the previous October. The Stormont Commons should be enlarged, the Senate reconstituted to provide more representation for bodies such as trade unions, industrial interests, and local authorities, and the functional committee system should be expanded to include policy proposals. We also proposed that Offices of the House, such as Speaker and Chairman of Ways and Means, should be shared between Government and Opposition, and that all Ministers should, before making appointments such as for Chairman of Public bodies, consult the Minister of Community Relations to ensure that more members of the Nationalist community were given responsibility.

It was hard to think of further ways in which the minority could have their interests and rights safeguarded for, as I pointed out in the letter, the Government of Ireland Act which set up our State already expressly prohibited any public authority from imposing a disability or conferring an advantage on grounds of religion, and we had in the previous three years enacted the most far-reaching anti-discrimination measures. But, as a further gesture and to make our good faith clear beyond rational doubt, we proposed that the rights of citizens should be enacted with greater precision in a Bill of Rights providing quick and effective access to the courts for redress of grievances.

I placed these proposals before Heath and Maudling as a useful basis for discussion between Northern Ireland parties, and asked Heath to let me know his reaction to them before the further meeting with him and his colleagues which would obviously be necessary soon.

But at the very time we were sending this letter to London press speculation was again intensifying about a London 'initiative'. There was much activity and discussion going on at the top levels of Whitehall about Northern Ireland, and Ministerial meetings were taking place. The press reported the Cabinet split on a 'package', and some speculated that this 'package' would include a PR government, an end to internment and the transfer of all security powers to London. I warned London by telephone of the unsettling effect of these rumours on public opinion in Northern Ireland and urged that they be refuted. On 3 March, after another day of intense speculation in the media, I had to address an anxious gathering of Unionists in Belfast at the Ulster Unionist Council. Before the meeting I received a telegram from Heath in the following terms: 'You will have seen various articles in the Press claiming to describe the views of the UK Government on constitutional change in Northern Ireland. The articles are pure speculation and we have made this clear to the Press.'

It was carefully worded, but it was clearly designed to pour cold water on the speculation, and the frank and honest relationship which I believed existed between us seemed to justify placing an optimistic construction on Heath's words. So I read the telegram to the meeting with confidence, reassuring them that 'at the appropriate time the two governments would express for themselves their views on the best course for Northern Ireland beyond the ending of violence'. I was asking them to have confidence in me, and to have confidence in Ted Heath, and I believed that the Prime Minister would not send me a meaningless and misleading reassurance. My opponents on the right of the party muttered about an impending sell-out, but many of the six hundred Ulster citizens present were reassured and I was given a standing ovation. Thus, when at Downing Street three weeks later the rug was pulled out from under my feet, it came to me personally as a bitter blow.

IRA violence was continuing on a generally lower level due to the progress of the security forces, but the attacks were becoming more cold-blooded and callous to achieve maximum publicity and tension in the community. The dwindling calibre of the terrorists at large was shown by the deaths of fourteen of them in two months, blown up by their own bombs—what the Army called 'own goals'. On 22 February the terrorist war was carried to the mainland for the first time when the Official IRA tried to blow up the headquarters of the Parachute Regiment at Aldershot, and killed seven, most of them civilian cleaning staff.

Three days later John Taylor, our Minister of State at Home Affairs, miraculously escaped death when he was shot several times at point-blank range in Armagh. On 4 March the most horrible city centre bombing yet occurred in the crowded Abercorn restaurant when a bomb was left under a table. Two died and 135 were injured, many of them maimed for life without legs and arms. Such was the outrage among both Catholics and Protestants that the IRA hastily denied responsibility, but the RUC traced a telephone call giving a one-minute warning and an inaccurate location to a public kiosk on the Falls Road, an IRA stronghold.

All sorts of fingers were being dipped in the murky political waters to seek to gain credit for the forthcoming initiative. At Westminster Paisley was lobbying for the suspension of Stormont, presumably to discredit the Unionist Party. The IRA Provisionals announced a three-day cease-fire beginning on 11 March and reiterated three 'minimum' demands for a permanent end to their murder and destruction: withdrawal of troops from the streets and a declaration of intent for a total withdrawal from Northern Ireland, abolition of Stormont, and an amnesty for all IRA men. The *Guardian* rightly described this as 'a piece of hypocrisy which should fool no one'.

There was no government response to the IRA offer, and it was said privately by Ministers that they 'could not do business with murderers'. But Wilson went over to Dublin on the 13th and secretly met members of the IRA leadership. He went on television in Dublin and said that there must be an end to internment, a transfer of all security powers to London, and the Provisional IRA terms should be put on the agenda for talks. Even Dublin politicians were appalled by the last of these proposals, and by Wilson's comment that the truce had shown the IRA to be 'a well-disciplined' organization. I was outraged and attacked him fiercely:

> I think it most regrettable that at a time when a part of the UK is suffering daily from the outrages of a terrorist organization controlled from another country, the Leader of Her Majesty's Opposition should choose to visit the capital of that country in order to discuss circumstances in which Her Majesty's subjects who live in Northern Ireland may be separated from their fellow-citizens who live in Great Britain.

I also suggested that Mr Wilson should visit Northern Ireland hospitals to see some of the victims of this 'well-disciplined' organization. The Opposition Leader, asked by journalists for his response before boarding his plane to London, said it would be 'unprintable'. It was the bitterest exchange which ever took place between Wilson and I, but in retrospect I believe my anger was justified.

Unionist backbenchers, largely as a result of the 'united Ireland' hints of Wilson and the continuing speculation in the media, were beginning to dig in their heels against any concessions before the terrorists were beaten. And Heath had his own political problems with his backbench smarting after Wilberforce, Upper Clyde and the coal strike and hardened by the Aldershot atrocities into regarding the word 'initiative' as equivalent to 'concession'. But his Cabinet eventually reached agreement and on 15 March I received an invitation to go to Downing Street one week later for talks. Pompidou was visiting Chequers on the 18th and 19th, and the Budget was on the 21st, so it was a busy period for the Heath Government.

Our party assembled at Stormont Castle on the morning of Wednesday 22 March 1972. Jack Andrews, Deputy Prime Minister, was accompanying me, and we were supported by Sir Harold Black, Ken Bloomfield and Robert Ramsay. As usual for important London meetings we were keyed up to acquit ourselves well and put our case, and we were anxious to know what proposals the Heath Government would put to us. But it was one of many important meetings, we felt no sense of foreboding, and the usual cheerful good humour prevailed.

A helicopter arrived to take us to Aldergrove, coming in over the trees and landing on the smooth lawns in front of the Castle where such noisy manoeuvres were becoming increasingly common. We piled in, and in fifteen minutes were on the ground at Aldergrove walking towards the RAF Andover which was to take us to London. Soon we were soaring over Belfast Lough, looking down on the crowded industrial city where only a few hours later another bomb was to injure sixty people going about their work. Stormont Castle was never going to seem quite the same again after that morning.

Heath greeted us in the hallway at Downing Street at 11 a.m. with his usual brisk good humour. Upstairs in his study were the usual triumvirate, accompanied for the first time by Whitelaw. We wasted no time before getting down to business. We discussed the security situation briefly, reviewing the latest measures and the successes of the security forces in capturing many of the top IRA men in Belfast. Then Heath moved straight to the point outlining what he thought should be done: there should be a transfer to Westminster of all security powers and responsibility for criminal matters, followed by a constitutional referendum, a move towards ending internment, appointment of a Secretary of State for Northern Ireland at Westminster, and open-ended talks with the SDLP on the form of government with a view to reaching a 'community government'. This, said Heath, was the united view of the Cabinet.

We were puzzled more than angry. It was not a very impressive or cohesive package, its content in terms of how Northern Ireland should be governed was remarkably vague, and it did not seem like a thorough or finalized response to the comprehensive proposals we had forwarded. We had understood that this meeting would involve an exchange of ideas and provide room for compromise. So we decided that Heath was bluffing, and started to shoot down his target. The transfer of security powers would destroy the credibility of any Northern Ireland Government, I said, as this was the primary matter in most people's minds, and a government which had no power to enforce the laws it made would appear weak and ineffectual. Under the 1920 Government of Ireland Act we were charged with responsibility for the 'Peace, Order and Good Government' of Northern Ireland. Without control of law enforcement we could not discharge this responsibility. Nor could we agree to open-ended talks on constitutional formulæ; we had, I said, existing parliamentary structures which could be amended to safeguard legitimate minority interests, but only within agreed limits. I said we could agree to the referendum and the release of a hundred or so detainees.

After some time it was becoming clear that Heath had not been making an opening bid to soften us up, but had made up his mind before he met us and was presenting what amounted to an ultimatum.

When we adjourned for lunch at noon the Northern Ireland party was beginning to feel the effects of the blow Heath had dealt us. I was shaken and horrified, and felt completely betrayed. But in spite of the natural urge to give vent to these feelings, we were determined to exhaust every conceivable avenue of agreement, and to carry the talks through to whatever conclusion in the usual unemotional manner, and this we did.

We had a politely friendly lunch, during which we all tried to behave normally. One of my civil servants told me later that during the lunch Reggie Maudling, who was sitting near to him, pushed his glasses up to the top of his head, leaned back in his chair, stared at the ceiling, and said in a pensive voice, 'I wonder if Brian is bluffing'. We never quite decided if this was a ploy intended for the ears of my aides, or a genuine problem which Reggie was trying to solve.

The talks lasted for over nine hours. Sometimes we talked in full session with all the officials present, and at other times the politicians present withdrew into private session in Heath's sitting-room to allow some of the more sensitive things to be said frankly. Whitelaw had to go off to the Commons at one stage in the afternoon to carry out his duties as Lord President of the Council, and Heath, Maudling, Home, Andrews and I were in the sitting-room talking and drinking lime juice and soda till it was almost coming out of our ears. Maudling was arguing that we could accept their proposals and carry on, but—as he himself made clear to me later—they realized we could never survive politically if we did so, and that resignation was inevitable. Heath admitted, when pressed by us, that he saw government at Stormont as eventually something along the lines of a county council or the Greater London Council. To us that was insulting and completely unacceptable.

There was clearly no negotiable exit from the cul-de-sac into which we had been led, and no attempt was made to disguise this. Jack Andrews issued a particularly forceful warning that if they persisted in this course the Conservative Party and British Governments would never again be trusted by the people of Northern Ireland. When Heath escorted us down to the door of No. 10 at 9 p.m. after the discussions had eventually ended he said to me quietly: 'You may assume that the Cabinet will reaffirm this decision tomorrow. They have made up their minds and there is no going back.' I knew then without any doubt that we must resign, and that direct rule had arrived.

Before returning to Belfast the 'condemned men' ate a hearty meal of Aberdeen Angus rib of beef and baked alaska at the Carlton Tower Hotel. There was much gallows humour, though I was preoccupied, thinking about the effects of that day's discussions. Our conversation was not bitter, but I do recall several references to the Downing Street caucus as 'clots'. We felt they simply did not understand what they had done. Shortly after midnight we arrived back in Belfast quite shattered by the long meeting and the bad news we brought. Nothing was said to the press, who were naturally speculating wildly in the absence of any hard news.

Next morning the Stormont and Westminster Cabinets met almost simultaneously to consider the discussion of the previous day and make their final decisions. All the members of my Cabinet, including John Taylor, who had been recovering in hospital with immense courage and determination from the attempt on his life, turned up in the Cabinet room that morning. I admitted to them frankly that I had been wrong about the intentions of the London government; those who had said 'There is no smoke without fire' had been proved right. I explained the proposals which had been put to us and our reaction to them. Quietly and impressively each of the twelve men sitting with me around the long polished table expressed his unreserved support. The terms were impossible, said Bradford; we would be reduced to a bunch of marionettes. The Attorney-General, Basil Kelly, said it was an almost universal practice in democracies for devolved governments to have law and order powers. 'We must resign,' said Herbie Kirk, and the other Ministers expressed assent. One Minister suggested we should make Westminster throw us out of office, conducting a sort of protest sit-in in the Cabinet room, but I said that would be an unworthy end to a Northern Ireland Government, and the idea was dropped. It was unanimously agreed that we would refuse to accept the terms which Ted Heath had put to us.

I rang Heath and told him of our meeting. The conversation was curt and to the point. 'My colleagues have reaffirmed their previous decision,' said Heath. 'My Government then has no alternative but to resign,' I replied. It was agreed that I should fly to London that evening to complete whatever formalities would be involved. I lunched with a few of my colleagues at the Castle and then went over to the Commons to read out the business of the day, and to answer questions on security. At 4.15 p.m. we held another hastily summoned Cabinet meeting to agree on and sign a letter of resignation. It was a moving occasion and G. B. Newe summed up his feelings by saying, 'I am very sad to see a government of Irishmen being ended, but some day it will return again.' Our letter of resignation was brief:

Dear Prime Minister,

You have just conveyed to us by telephone the decision of the UK Cabinet that all responsibilities of the Northern Ireland Government and Parliament in relation to law and order should be transferred to Westminster. You have also made it clear that even this change is intended only to create a situation in which further radical changes, of a nature we believe to be unrealistic and unacceptable, will be discussed.

We now convey to you formally the unanimous view of the Cabinet of Northern Ireland that such a transfer is not justifiable and cannot be supported or accepted by us. It would wholly undermine the powers, authority and standing of this Government without justification and for no clear advantage to those who are suffering in Northern Ireland today.

We wish to point out with a sense of the heavy responsibility involved that the imposition of this proposal, involving as it will the resignation of the Government of Northern Ireland as a whole, may have the gravest consequences, the full extent of which cannot now be foreseen.

At around the time our meeting was ending at Stormont Heath and his senior Ministers were meeting at Downing Street again to prepare for their take-over of Northern Ireland's affairs. Jack Andrews and I, and our officials, left Stormont Castle again by helicopter for Aldergrove, and then flew to London, arriving at Downing Street at 7.45 p.m. Our discussions did not take long. We agreed to stay in office until the necessary legislation instituting direct rule could be passed at Westminster, so that Northern Ireland should not, even for a few days, be without a lawful government. I handed over our letter of resignation to take effect at that time.

A 'farewell dinner' had been laid on for us at Downing Street. It was for me a bit of a strain, but the normal chat about world and British affairs carried on around the table. I remember Ted Heath saying to Armstrong at one stage: 'Get the Prime Minister another cup of coffee.' I knew it was probably the last time he would ever refer to me by such a title. It was late when we took our leave and made our way back to Belfast, where the news of our impending resignation had already broken.

Next morning we held a 75-minute meeting with our Parliamentary Party, where once again I was given unanimous backing. That morning the first official statements were made simultaneously in London and Belfast announcing the result of our discussions. I made a statement giving a full account of the disagreement between the two Governments, as seen from our point of view:

On Wednesday Senator Andrews and I travelled to London for what we well knew would be a crucially important meeting with Mr Heath and his colleagues. We were determined to do anything we could reasonably do to restore peace and stability to Ulster and confident that we would hear from Mr Heath realistic proposals to help end the violence and find a new way forward for this community . . .

Our objective—and I had hoped the objective of the whole UK—was to end this violence, to end it completely, and to end it once and for all. We went to Downing Street fully prepared to acknowledge that, in defeating the violence, military means would have to be buttressed by *realistic* political proposals, designed to unite the communities and detach them from any sympathy or support for violent men. We had indeed, in a comprehensive letter, made such proposals to the UK Government.

But I was faced at the Cabinet Table not with a wide-ranging review of all these aspects, or with a comprehensive, coherent and 'final' package of proposals—which we ourselves had suggested—but with the idea of a constitutional Referendum and some movement on internment, both of which we found perfectly acceptable, and firm proposals to appoint a Secretary of State and to transfer to Westminster vital and fundamental powers which we have exercised for over half a century. The proposition put to us was that all statutory and executive responsibility for law and order should be vested in the UK Parliament and Government. These included criminal law and procedure (including the organisation of and appointments to the courts); public order; prisons and penal establishments; the creation of new penal offences; special powers; the public prosecuting power, and the police. Even these radical changes were simply to pave the way for further, entirely open-ended discussions, with continuing speculation and uncertainty as we have seen it in recent weeks.

I asked, naturally, whether the drastic proposal to transfer security powers was rooted in any conviction on their part that we had abused these powers. It was made clear to me that no such suggestion was made; that this diminution in the powers, prestige and authority of Stormont was in reality simply a response to the criticism of our opponents, which Mr Heath and his colleagues neither substantiated nor supported.

Of course, chief amongst those who have sought the emasculation and ultimately the downfall of Stormont have been the IRA terrorists themselves. And when it was made clear to me that the UK Government could not give an assurance of any further positive measures against terrorism, I felt bound to ask whether the end of violence was being sought, not—as we have always asserted—by defeating the terrorists, but by surrendering to them . . . I fear too that many people will draw a sinister and depressing message from these events: that violence can pay, that violence does pay; and that those who shout, lie, denigrate and even destroy earn for themselves an attention that responsible conduct and honourable behaviour do not. They may ask—if Belfast is to bow to violence today—where will it be next year? Birmingham? Glasgow? London? . . .

That afternoon Heath made a detailed statement in the House of Commons at Westminster, and there were rare scenes of emotion and unity as MPs sought to grapple with the mysteries of the Irish problem. Stormont was to be suspended for one year, plebiscites would be held on the border question at 'intervals of a substantial period of years', and a start would be made to the phasing out of internment. These proposals, said Heath, were 'put forward in an endeavour so to change the climate of political opinion in Northern Ireland that discussion could be resumed in an effort to reach agreement on a new way forward'. He was not ungenerous to me: 'I would like to pay tribute to the determination with which the Prime Minister of Northern Ireland and his government have sought to overcome the difficulties which have beset the Province and the House will wish to acknowledge the spirit in which he has agreed to remain in office until our legislation has been enacted.' Whitelaw was to be the new Secretary of State for Northern Ireland, and when Jeremy Thorpe wished him well in his new task Whitelaw, an emotional man, was seen to shed tears.

It was all over bar the shouting. Craig and the Vanguard organization called for a two-day Province-wide strike in protest against the suspension of Stormont and an estimated 200,000 workers responded on Monday and Tuesday 27 and 28 March, bringing the industrial life of the Province to a halt. Thankfully, the protest was reasonably disciplined and, with a few exceptions, peaceful.

Jack Lynch welcomed the initiative and sent the Irish Ambassador back to London. The SDLP also welcomed the latest developments, and issued a statement urging a cessation of the terrorist campaign. But both wings of the IRA denounced direct rule, and said the terrorist campaign would continue until 'total victory'—a 32-county Irish Republic.

On Monday 27th I addressed a meeting of the Ulster Unionist Council in Belfast, telling them that we had lost confidence in the Heath administration and denouncing the proposal for an 'Advisory Commission' of Ulstermen which would assist Whitelaw in governing Ulster. 'Northern Ireland is not a coconut colony; and no coconut commission will be able to muster any vestige of credibility or standing,' I said. It would be an 'undemocratic sham'. I urged people to rely on the strength of their numbers, the Unionist 'veto', and not to be led into any violent activity. It was an angry meeting, angry at what was seen as a betrayal and a surrender to the Province's enemies, and it was clear there were explosive frustrations in the Unionist community which we would have to express forcefully if extreme counsels were not to prevail.

On Tuesday morning the commercial life of the Province remained at a standstill and a massive crowd, estimated at 100,000, gathered outside Stormont, many of them carrying Ulster flags alongside the traditional Union Jacks and protest banners bearing unflattering references to Heath and Whitelaw. Just before lunch we were holding our last meeting as a Northern Ireland Cabinet, and as news came in about the huge crowd which was gathering we decided that we must all go out on to the balcony of the building and speak to them and give them a lead. The doors on to the balcony led off the Members' dining-room on the first floor where most MPs were eating lunch. Bill Craig, who was scheduled to address the crowd immediately after lunch, was there with some friends. I had a quiet word with him and we agreed that we should both address the crowd separately. At 1.15 p.m. I led my Cabinet out on to the balcony from where we could see the huge crowd stretching away down the long sweep of Stormont's one-mile long lawns and driveway almost to the gates at Newtownards Road. A cheer went up, and I began to speak through the loudspeaker:

> People of Ulster, I am speaking to you still as Prime Minister of Northern Ireland. I want to say, not just on my own behalf, but on behalf of every one of my colleagues in the Government and the Parliamentary Party here at Stormont, that we understand absolutely the feelings which have persuaded you to come out to Parliament Buildings today ... we share the resentment that you feel ... We have tremendous power. Our power is the power of our numbers; our power is the justice of our cause; our power is the responsibility of our conduct ... Let us never play the game of the murderers of the IRA. Let us show the world that, so far as we are concerned, violence and intimidation are out ... British we are, and British we remain!

I had scarcely started to address the crowd before I became aware that Bill Craig had come out on to the balcony and was standing beside me. It was an awkward moment, because Craig's record of right-wing politics was not one with which I or most of my colleagues wished to be identified, and I knew that liberal Unionists such as Bailie and Bradford would be angry at finding themselves on a joint platform with him. It transpired later that some of Craig's associates, together with Herbie Kirk, the Minister of Finance, had pushed Craig out on to the balcony, believing that a show of solidarity against the suspension of Stormont would be useful. Craig, never a personally vindictive man, did his best to ease my situation. He spoke to the crowd, supporting what I had said, and adding that, whatever differences we had in the past, I had done my best and had been shamefully treated. 'We will all stand together to win back Stormont for Ulster,' he said. Then he called for 'three cheers for the Prime Minister', and the crowd cheered loudly as Craig and I shook hands.

Most Unionists in Ulster were happy to see this apparent burying of the hatchet but, predictably, it was hailed in some of the national dailies as a 'pact of defiance', and the impression was created that Craig and I had formally joined forces. This was not, of course, the case, though I did my best to bring Craig along with my policies in the succeeding months.

The Stormont Parliament met for the last time that afternoon, while at Westminster a Second Reading was given to the Northern Ireland Temporary Provisions Bill by 483 votes to 18. We all went down from the Stormont balcony to the Commons as the crowd began to disperse peacefully, confident that their point had been made forcefully and effectively and that Westminster would have to pay attention. Procedure went ahead as usual, and there were no dramatic scenes as over fifty years of history came to an end. John Brooke, the acting Leader of the House, quoted in winding up the famous loyalist poem of Rudyard Kipling, 'Ulster 1912'. There was a general air of sadness, and an absence of the boisterous squabbling which had characterized some debates over the past few months. The adjournment of the House was moved for the Easter Recess as usual. I spoke briefly on the motion, paying tribute to the security forces, to the civil servants at Stormont who had served successive governments loyally and skilfully, and to my colleagues in the Cabinet:

> I conclude with this final word, as the Government of Ulster is about to pass, temporarily at least, into other hands. I have always been proud to lead the present team in Government but never so proud as last week. We stood firm and we stood together. When we faced a hard and unpalatable decision no hint of any other interest than the interest of the whole country was heard at the Cabinet Table. We did what we believed to be right, for that is the spirit in which Ulster should always be served.
>
> Could I express the hope and, since I believed in its power, the prayer, that we will see peace and that it will be peace with justice in our native land.

At 4.15 p.m. the House divided on the motion for the adjournment, four MPs registering a token protest against the situation in which we found ourselves, and twenty voting for the motion. At 5.15 p.m. the House stood adjourned, theoretically until after Easter, but in effect for at least one year. It was never to meet again.

13
'Willie Whitewash'

Willie Whitelaw came to Northern Ireland in 1972 in the worst possible circumstances. He arrived as the agent of a policy which had antagonized almost the whole Unionist population, but had failed to reconcile large elements in the Nationalist community. IRA violence was continuing and Protestant extremists were beginning to retaliate. All the Province's political structures had been swept aside at a stroke, and nothing was available to replace them. Dialogue between the political parties did not exist, nor was this changed by the Heath initiative. The SDLP continued to insist that they would not talk until internment was ended. I and my colleagues were, to say the least, not enthusiastic about Whitelaw's arrival.

So he was not a popular man in Northern Ireland. He became known in the Protestant Shankill Road as 'Willie Whitewash'. He came armed with all the wrong ideas about our problems and his policies for the first four months were an almost unmitigated disaster. But he had a priceless asset in his personality. He was a large, genial and humane man, deeply affected by the suffering of others, but possessing the necessary sense of humour to allow him to survive in Northern Ireland. He laughed deafeningly at things which amused him. He had many of the human characteristics which Ulster people like, and it was not long before many began to feel a certain affinity for him—even when arguing with or attacking him. The Shankhill Road jokes and caricatures took on a note of affection after a time.

I was convinced that, whatever our feelings about the switch in policy, we must try to work with Whitelaw, though not with his 'Advisory Commission'. To adopt the advice of those arguing for a policy of total boycott and abstention similar to that being practised by the SDLP would have been biting off our nose to spite our face. I issued a statement on 30 March saying that Unionists were 'Queen's Men' who respected the law and that the Sovereign Parliament did have the right to suspend

Stormont, however much one might disagree with its decision. We would co-operate with Mr Whitelaw, I said, on all proposals to meet the needs of the people and there must be no further disruption of the Province's economic life. A few days later I fulfilled a long-standing engagement to address the well-known Conservative organization, the Bow Group in London. I outlined in detail my objections to the course on which the Government had embarked—this 'unnecessary inter-regnum' as I described it. I pointed out that Northern Ireland was now in a constitutional limbo, under-represented at Westminster (Northern Ireland constituencies were, and still are at time of writing, on average some 40 per cent larger than those in Great Britain) and with the normal democratic processes of legislation effectively suppressed under government by Order in Council. I stressed that I could not conceive of these arrangements being acceptable for more than a year. 'The British Government, however good their intentions might be . . . have not got our will to win. For Mr Heath and Mr Wilson and Mr Thorpe, the affairs of Northern Ireland are a matter of political science . . . for us in Ulster, it is a matter of life and death.' Ultimately the solutions would have to be achieved by agreement between Ulster people themselves, but if there was not to be a worthwhile devolved parliament restored then Unionists would demand full integration on the Scottish model as their second choice.

This last point was a new departure in policy, and in a sense I was kite-flying to test reaction among Unionists and in Britain. I was concerned that if Mr Heath persisted in his GLC type view of devolved institutions for Northern Ireland we should be left without any fall-back position, and integration seemed the lesser of all the evils. I was quite clear that we could not acquiesce in a 'sham Stormont' giving a pretence of devolution but no substance, and depriving elected representatives of all public respect. In fact support for the public advocacy of integration was not widespread among members of my party, and both Mr White-law and Merlyn Rees, the Labour Spokesman on Northern Ireland, made it clear to me that there was no prospect of Westminster adopting such a policy. After more discussions with colleagues and supporters I decided to concentrate all my efforts on the primary objective of restoring a worthwhile Northern Ireland Parliament.

I had my first formal meeting with Whitelaw at the Governor's residence at Hillsborough. It was his first day in the Province as Secretary of State for Northern Ireland, and he made a point of meeting me first, a sign of his sensitivity for other people's feelings which I was to respect increasingly over succeeding months. On later occasions, when he was occupying my old room at Stormont Castle, he always made a point of meeting me in another office, recognizing the embarrassment I might feel as the ex-Prime Minister of a non-existent Parliament now making representations to him. Although his early policies often brought us into political conflict I rapidly gained a personal respect for Whitelaw. He was a well-meaning man doing what he thought was best in very difficult circumstances.

On this occasion I had a civilized conversation with Whitelaw and Lord Carrington, who was with him, and we posed afterwards for the pressmen, shaking hands. It was not a happy occasion for me, naturally, and looking at some of the press pictures afterwards I realized that I had not totally succeeded in disguising that fact. But I wanted to make a constructive contribution to Whitelaw's policies and co-operate in every reasonable way, and I knew that by this meeting and its publicity I was to some extent easing the transition to the new administration. Whitelaw had given me a general indication of the steps he contemplated, especially on the security front, but I was not very enthusiastic about them.

A crisis in my own career arose at this point. I was Leader of the largest party in the Province, but a member of no democratic forum. It seemed that for a time at least most of the important decisions about our future would be made at Westminster, and so I began thinking seriously again about the possibility of getting a Westminster seat.

Before coming to any decision my wife and I had a long-overdue holiday. It was the first time for twelve years that I had got away without strings of office of some sort, able to go where we liked, without a set itinerary of where we could be reached, and unhampered by telephone calls from colleagues or civil servants. Indeed, it was the first time for many years that we did not have to rush home for some crisis or other. We took our car to the Continent and spent a few nights in Paris, drove down to Geneva and then on to the French Riviera, which was at its best out of season and unspoilt by thousands of holiday-makers. It was a strange experience to be away from twenty-four-hour security surveillance, and a luxurious one, although the television coverage which had been given to Northern Ireland affairs made it difficult to pass unnoticed anywhere. We came back much refreshed and ready once again for the unending fray of Northern Ireland. I have often thought how much it would broaden the perspective of many people in Ulster if only they could get out of the Province more often and look at it from the outside.

I decided not to seek a Westminster seat. It could well have looked like running away from the domestic scene in search of a job and undermined the prospects of securing a restoration of devolved government in the future. I found some of the officers of the Unionist Council very opposed to my seeking a seat, though I never quite appreciated the logic of their approach to this. A factor no doubt was the traditional view of Westminster as a far-flung 'Imperial' parliament which had little to do with everyday life in Ulster and where the function of Unionist MPs was largely to protect the international interests of the Province. But I decided to keep my base in Ulster, and concentrate my energies on leading the party in what was now a pressure group situation. We would have to seek to dissuade Mr Whitelaw from the policies he was pursuing, urging on him better security policies, and adopt a new strategy to restart political dialogue leading to the restoration of effective devolved government.

The Heath and Whitelaw policy for the first four months of direct rule was one of killing the IRA by kindness. One of Whitelaw's first actions was to announce the freeing of 100 suspected terrorists from detention, and releases continued rapidly in succeeding weeks, reaching 500 by early June. 'No Go' areas of total lawlessness were allowed to exist in the Bogside and Creggan in Londonderry and in parts of West Belfast, and the idea of sending in the security forces to end this situation was rejected as likely to lead to a bloodbath. The security forces were given a low profile and expected to do nothing 'provocative'.

The results were predictable. There were hopeful rumours of 'doves' in the IRA camp who believed in a temporary tactical cessation of murder and bombing and of splits among their leaders. The SDLP campaigned hard in Catholic areas against the IRA activities, and clearly enjoyed much support among the population. 'Give the initiative a chance' Gerry Fitt appealed, and Cardinal Conway denounced the IRA. Women from Andersonstown in Belfast and from the Bogside and Creggan marched for peace and organized peace petitions.

But the IRA replied in their own inimitable fashion. At the Easter Republican celebrations their leaders announced that they would fight on 'for a united Ireland'. A pregnant Catholic woman was beaten up, her head shaved, and tar and feathers poured over her after she had been tied to a lamp-post in an exhibition of IRA 'justice' for some unspecified crime. The same treatment was meted out to a deaf and dumb man in Belfast a few days later. There were successive waves of bombing across the Province, causing massive destruction and injuries and deaths. The largest store in Belfast, the modern Co-op building, was destroyed by bombs and fire at a cost of some 750 jobs and £10 million. A young soldier from the Bogside, Ranger Best, who had returned on leave from

Germany to visit his parents, was brutally murdered. And so it went on. The message from the IRA was quite clear and unmistakable: 'We are not interested in reform of Northern Ireland, we want to overthrow the State whatever the wishes of its population, and we have the capacity to continue irrespective of the effect of political moves on opinions in the Catholic community.' It was a message which the Government did belatedly grasp, but only after immense damage had been done to the morale and discipline of the whole population, and after much tragic loss of life. The Official IRA, more sensitive to political movements in the Catholic community than the Provisionals, called a cease-fire on 29 May which they maintained sporadically for some time, concentrating on political agitation and subversion. But this had little effect on the level of violence. In the four months following direct rule 600 bombs exploded, 2,057 people were injured, and 192 died from terrorism.

On the other hand the Protestant backlash was becoming the ugly reality we had long feared and warned about. The Ulster Defence Association, which had grown into a large organization from the street vigilante groups formed in response to earlier violence, was becoming prominently active. Thousands of men marched through the streets in formation, many of them wearing masks and para-military uniform. At first their activities were accompanied by a surprising degree of discipline, which caused me some relief, accompanied by great apprehension about the future. To many of these men the democratic politics represented by my colleagues and I had failed in spite of majority support among the population, and they were now adopting the only form of pressure which the Government seemed to understand and to respond to, a show of naked force. The continued existence of Republican 'No Go' areas was at first the main target of their protests, and they started setting up their own 'No Go' areas in Protestant streets to dramatize their views and put pressure on the Government to act. More horrifying than this was the increasingly frequent violence from Protestant gunmen. One day there was a 24-hour gun-battle between the Protestant Springmartin estate and gunmen in the Catholic Ballymurphy estate beside it; and Protestant assassination gangs were beginning to search out victims for their 'retaliation' against the IRA.

The arrival of the Protestant assassination gangs on the streets of Northern Ireland coincided with the collapse of confidence among the Unionist population in the will of the Westminster Government to defeat the IRA and protect the rights of the majority. It introduced a new and sinister element into the security problem, deepening the fears of ordinary citizens for their safety and that of their friends. The IRA, being opposed to the State's existence, could bomb and destroy homes and businesses, and murder members of the security forces. But Protestant gunmen could not attack such targets; they wished to preserve the State, to defend what they saw as the rights of the majority against the violence of a truculent and unruly minority. It was inevitable therefore that they should turn on the IRA and those whom they regarded as their protectors and passive supporters, namely the Catholics of Northern Ireland. In April there were three assassinations; in May there were ten. Three of these were IRA killings of Catholics as they sought to consolidate their hold over the Catholic population by terror and intimidation; the rest appear to have been the work of Protestant extremists. The IRA leaders, the real culprits, seldom suffered. The Protestant killers could not penetrate deeply enough into Republican areas to find them, and their information on IRA activists was obviously poor. Thus it was the ordinary Catholic, going about his work in mixed Protestant/Catholic areas, or in Protestant areas, who was singled out for an act of symbolic vengeance. The divisions between Catholic and Protestant areas, already becoming increasingly marked, were reinforced when a 'religious' label became the only qualification for murder and a new all-pervading fear spread through the community.

What was the role for politics in this situation? There was a real danger of political disintegration as violent organizations held the stage and forced the pace. For the first time in fifty years the Unionist Party was not in Government, and for the first time in my career as a public representative I was not a member of a government party. We still represented the political views of a majority of the population, but our role had become essentially that of the major Opposition Party. It was not a role which I relished, nor one which I had any experience in handling. I have always preferred a positive rather than a negative and critical approach. But we had a government which was pursuing a policy we regarded as totally mistaken and counter-productive, and we had to express our criticisms of this policy forcefully and effectively if politicians were to retain any credibility. We had some hope that Mr Whitelaw would eventually realize we were right and adopt a new approach. I summed up our position in a speech to the Unionist Standing Committee in May:

As time goes on the Secretary of State and his colleagues in London will have to pay more attention to majority wishes and aspirations, for it will become increasingly clear that only with the general consent of the majority will any lasting settlement be possible, and that the appeasement of those who pursue violent or negative policies is a totally unrewarding exercise . . . the IRA has been enabled to regroup in Belfast. The strenuous efforts of the Army and of the Police over months have been sacrificed to a political policy which is not bringing results . . . We must not be deflected from the main task by 'knocking' the Whitelaw administration at every turn . . . We have no interest in seeing them fail . . . in the anarchy, chaos and bloodshed which would follow it would be little satisfaction to us to say 'we told you so'. No, what we must look to is not their failure, but rather a coming to their political senses. They will sooner or later have to face the fact that their task is not just to bring reconciliation, so that Protestant and Catholic can live together in peace, but that it is also to deal with an armed and vicious rebellion.

I embarked on a heavy programme of speeches in Ulster and in Britain, speaking almost every day for several months. Many of the speeches expressed strong criticisms of Whitelaw's security policies and some of the national media gave me a rough time, casting me in the role of a bitter loser now out to destroy the transparently well-meaning efforts of Mr Whitelaw. As in the O'Neill crisis of 1969 I had the full weight of government publicity machinery turned on me in an attempt to destroy my credibility. But I was convinced what I was saying was right and I went on saying it.

Positive leadership was also needed: the community required a political goal if any kind of political cohesion was to be sustained. I had to look to my party base and adopt a strategy round which we could unite and use political energies in spite of the absence of any democratic forum. It was becoming clear from contacts with Whitelaw that he saw himself in the role of catalyst in renewing dialogue between Unionist and Nationalist politicians, but he was making no progress with the SDLP who were refusing not only to talk to us, but also to him until internment was ended. I repeatedly stated—both in private and in public speeches—that we were ready and willing to talk to any party at any time about the future government of the Province, but the SDLP would not budge. I regarded their attitude as irresponsible and not entirely honest, as they had not left the negotiating table on the issue of internment, and had justified their position with a demand for the end of Stormont. On the other hand I was aware of some of their difficulties as politicians, largely deriving from the apparent weaknesses of the British Government. The limits to which Westminster could be pushed had yet to be fully probed, and no Nationalist Party was going to stick out its neck to produce an agreed system of devolved government for Northern Ireland within the United Kingdom when it seemed an open question whether or not the State was going to continue to survive. If a united Ireland really was on the cards—and there was a belief in some Nationalist quarters that it was—then the SDLP did not want to go down in history as the party which prevented it and made a British Northern Ireland workable. Austin Currie's crude and angry response to Maudling's call for talks in the autumn of 1971 may have been made in an emotional atmosphere, but it was not entirely unrepresentative of opinions among his followers: 'Why the hell should we talk to you?' he had said. 'We are winning and you are not.' To some extent the proposition still applied in the spring of 1972, even if the tone had moderated. It is sad, but true, that the real determination of Unionists not to join a united Ireland seems only to have been fully believed when Protestant assassins started killing Catholics.

We were, however, convinced that the SDLP would eventually have to find their way back to the negotiating table, if only as a means of asserting their independence from the terrorists in their own community. I knew that a united Ireland was not on, and I was reasonably satisfied that Whitelaw realized this. When Heath had announced direct rule he had also promised to hold a referendum to give the people an opportunity of expressing democratically their views on remaining within the United Kingdom or joining a United Ireland, and I had no doubts about the results of that vote, which would effectively tie the hands of any British Government however treacherous its intentions. So I set out our objectives as 'the mobilisation of support right across the community for our basic aim of the restoration of a meaningful NI Parliament and Government'. It was round this general objective that I sought to consolidate support. It was an objective which people understood and which appealed to the broadest spectrum of pro-Union opinion, and raising the possibility of its attainment by a political process was, I believe, very important in preventing the political disintegration from which only the men of violence could have benefited. But I warned against over-commitment on details. In a speech to the Standing Committee in May I said that people would try to commit us to the small print of our negotiating position, but should be ignored: '... there must be a certain amount of give and take about the detailed arrangements for the future'.

The immediate effect of direct rule on the Unionist Party had been to create solidarity and a common front of opposition. If my colleagues and I had been prepared to accept the ultimatum delivered to us at

Downing Street Craig was well positioned to carry away most of our support in the community. Our refusal to do so kept us at the head of public opinion and provided Craig with no clearly identifiable position unless he was prepared to advocate widespread disruption and abstention as a means of opposing the new administration. Fortunately the belligerent comments which had characterized many of his speeches before direct rule seemed for some time afterwards largely absent. I had attempted to hold my old Cabinet together for regular weekly meetings as a sort of 'Shadow Cabinet', and succeeded for some months in doing so. But the arrangement was not entirely successful as a means of giving leadership to our supporters. It simply did not pack enough punch politically, and some of its members, such as Robin Bailie, progressively got less interested and opted out of the meetings. I decided that I needed a body closer to the grass-roots if we were not to lose the solidarity created by direct rule, and in May set up a Policy Committee which was geographically and politically widely representative of Unionist Party membership to 'bring about the restoration of Parliamentary democracy to Northern Ireland and to decide on the negotiating position of the Unionist Party'. I asked Bill Craig to sit as one of the members of this committee and he accepted. I continued to rely heavily on several of my ex-Cabinet colleagues for advice, in particular Jack Andrews, Billy Fitzsimmons and Herbie Kirk, who were my closest associates. But looking ahead I could see that we were entering a period of negotiations when the support generated by our stand on 22 March could begin to evaporate and all the old accusations of a 'weak government' could be raked up again. It was important to create a broad-based framework for policy-making which could not be stigmatized as a failed government and which could show positive action towards achieving our political objectives.

Before we could make any further progress the Government's policy of appeasement reached its nadir, with further bloody consequences, and the affairs of Northern Ireland entered a new phase. Whitelaw was continuing his policy of releasing detainees, refusing to send the security forces into 'No Go' areas, and trying to persuade the SDLP to meet him for talks. I had been continuing to include in my speeches denunciations of this approach, calling the releases 'political sabotage' of the security forces, and demanding that a date be set for the ending of all 'No Go' areas. On 15 June Whitelaw eventually persuaded the SDLP to meet him for the first time. It was in fact their first gesture towards dialogue since they had walked out of Stormont the previous July, and it was therefore an encouraging sign; perhaps they might soon be persuaded to sit round a table with us and discuss the future of our province. What emerged from the meeting was not, however, very encouraging. The pressures of the IRA on the SDLP constituencies showed in the appeal from John Hume to the Provisionals for a cease-fire to 'help create an atmosphere for peaceful negotiations'. The next day Mr Whitelaw made a major statement, attempting to give something to everybody. No one was going to change the border against the will of the majority, he said, but there would be a fair deal for everyone who lived in the Province. He added that 'a cease-fire now would provide new opportunities for us all. Sanity and commonsense must prevail before it is too late.' This transparent olive branch to the IRA did not please me in the slightest, since I did not see sanity and common-sense playing any more of a part in their counsels than cricket, and I wondered what 'new opportunities for us all' had transpired from the talks with the SDLP.

Three days later, on Monday 19 June, the SDLP and Whitelaw met again, and a statement issued by the SDLP said they believed that they had made real progress in securing their objectives. It transpired that Mr Whitelaw had agreed to grant 'political status' to convicted terrorists. Several IRA prisoners had been on hunger strike for some days demanding to be exempted from normal prison discipline and given special privileges like the non-convicted internees, and this agreement ended that strike. It is important to remember the chain of events leading up to the granting of 'Special Category Status', and the events which followed shortly after, if we are to understand the decision, which had disastrous consequences recognized by the Gardiner Committee and Mr Whitelaw himself over two years later. It was all part of the process of wheedling the SDLP into co-operation, and the SDLP's mistaken tactic of acting as honest brokers between the Government and the IRA. If the SDLP were later to regret that thugs and murderers were glorified by the title 'political prisoners' they were to some extent the authors of their own misfortune.

However, the mere fact that the SDLP were talking showed some progress. It was probably inevitable that they should want to show definite gains from their first talks in order to ward off attacks from their own hard-liners for talking at all while internment lasted. I was in London on the day of the second meeting, and in a speech to the Society for Individual Freedom I tried to strike a tentatively hopeful note, saying that the SDLP now seemed to be off some of the hooks they had got themselves on, and that the political situation was offering some prospect of movement.

On Thursday 22 June the Provisional IRA announced that they

would start a cease-fire from midnight on the following Monday. Since Mr Whitelaw's talks with the SDLP the idea of a cease-fire was in the air, but my only comment had been that if there was a cease-fire it must be unconditional. It was hardly a great gesture towards humanity for an organization of murderers to agree for a time to cease murdering, and I felt it would be intolerable if the Government felt in some way bound to respond. It was typical of the Provisionals that they should announce a cease-fire to take place four days later and continue their nefarious activities right up to the deadline; in these four days there were scores of explosions and armed robberies, thousands of rounds of ammunition were fired in gun-battles, and ten people died, one of them a soldier killed in East Belfast a few minutes before midnight on Monday. My comment on the cease-fire summed up, I think, the reaction of most of the citizens of Northern Ireland: 'It must be remembered that the truce has come 379 lives, 1,682 explosions, and 7,258 injuries too late.' For this comment I was attacked by the SDLP as attempting to sabotage the prospects of peace, but that worried me less than the fear that the Heath administration was about to commit the ultimate blunder. Seamus Twomey, leader of the IRA in Belfast, appeared on BBC television stating that the Provisionals had agreed to a 'bilateral truce' so that their proposals could be discussed with British representatives. I had already arranged to go to America for a week on a coast-to-coast speaking tour, but on the eve of the Provisionals' truce I issued a warning that it would create disastrous precedents for the future if, in the pursuit of peace in the short term, the IRA were allowed to shoot their way into a negotiating position with the British Government.

When I returned from America the truce was still in existence, but the UDA were mounting a major protest against the continued existence of Republican 'No Go' areas. Over a hundred barricades were set up in Protestant areas, many of which involved drilling the roadway with pneumatic drills, and on 3 July a confrontation between the Army and some 7,000 UDA men took place in Ainsworth Avenue as the Army tried to dismantle some barricades. A compromise was agreed which averted what could have been the most serious clash yet between the Army and the Protestant para-military.

These activities allowed the para-military to let off steam about the general security situation and the idea of a deal with the IRA—which was rightly interpreted as the purpose of the truce. They were illegal and potentially lethal activities, but not as ruthless and lethal as those of the minority in the assassination gangs who decided to step up sectarian killing. In the fifteen days that the truce between the IRA and the security forces lasted eighteen people died in tit-for-tat killings between Protestant extremists and the Provisional IRA. Usually it was innocent civilians who suffered. The objective of the Protestants involved was clear; they were telling the Government that if it was thought peace could be bought cheaply by a deal with the IRA, they would be buying more trouble from another source. That such a message should be conveyed in such a grisly way was a symbol of how politics had become devalued in Northern Ireland.

The truce ended on Sunday 9 July when the IRA, clearly no longer anxious to maintain it, staged a confrontation with the Army in the Lenadoon area of Belfast which led to a gun-battle. The Dublin leaders used this incident to call the truce off. The next day Mr Whitelaw admitted that talks had been held with IRA leaders during the truce. The admission brought roars of outrage, which became more intense as details of these talks leaked out. Six IRA leaders, probably the most wanted men in the United Kingdom, men who had for several years been master-minding the murders of British citizens, were flown across to London in an RAF jet at public expense for talks with senior British Cabinet Ministers in the Chelsea flat of Paul Channon, Minister of State at the Northern Ireland Office. They had, it appeared, put forward a list of demands: the Government must publicly state its support for the principle of an all-Ireland vote on the future of Northern Ireland, and there must be an amnesty for all terrorists in prison. There had been some discussion on these demands, and Mr Whitelaw had agreed to explain them to the Cabinet.

These talks were the logical conclusion of the policy of appeasement which direct rule had initiated. But they represented pragmatism gone mad. The IRA were not a liberation army, they enjoyed no substantial support among the population, they had consistently refused to put forward candidates in elections, and their only claim to be listened to by anyone derived from their ability to kill and destroy. They had no negotiable objectives; they sought the total overthrow of the democratically expressed wishes of the Northern Ireland population, and the desertion by the British Government of all the pledges made to the people of the Province. That any government should even consider that something could be gained from talking to the IRA shows either an appalling ignorance about the nature of the organization with which it was dealing, or else a willingness to consider conceding some of the demands (which were already well known). I favour the former interpretation.

Mr Whitelaw, to give him his due, quickly realized and was later to admit that the talks had been a serious mistake. His realization of this and of the dangerously inflamed passions and fears of the community was sharply underlined by the IRA's response to the end of the truce. On Friday 21 July Belfast experienced a bombing blitz which is still remembered with horror by most of its citizens. A total of 22 bombs exploded within a short period of time all over the city, and as people found their escape routes from the first bombs blocked by new explosions panic and fear rapidly spread. First estimates were that 11 had died and 130 were injured, but it was later realized that 9 had died; it was difficult for the police to be precise about dismembered human bodies. Few Ulster people will forget seeing on television young policemen shovelling human remains into plastic bags in Belfast's Oxford Street, where the worst carnage took place. The IRA issued a brief and chilling statement: 'We accept responsibility,' they said.

It was the end of the road for the Government's policy. Concessions had failed, and they had either to govern or get out, to take on the IRA or surrender. I saw Willie Whitelaw at Stormont Castle, and he made it clear that a new phase of policy had arrived, and that the Government now realized that the IRA would have to be beaten. A two-pronged campaign was, he said, going to be pursued; he would try to build up political momentum towards an all-party political conference in the autumn, and the law was going to be enforced throughout the Province. The next day I was speaking to the Conservative Party Back Bench Committee and I made a more hopeful speech:

> After Direct Rule had been imposed I said here in London in April that the critical period would come when Mr Whitelaw came to the end of the policies he was then pursuing and that I could not see how that stage could be further away than a matter of months. Clearly that point has now been reached.

The same day the SDLP, who had been holding a conference at Dungloe in County Donegal, issued a statement indicating a willingness to talk and to put forward definite political proposals. They were obviously shocked by the events of 'Bloody Friday', as it has now become known, and condemned the IRA in very forthright terms. We seemed at last to be set on the road back to political dialogue, with the IRA effectively isolated.

Mr Whitelaw acted swiftly to put his words into effect. All the Republican barricades in Belfast were removed by the Army at dawn on 24 July. Several thousand troop reinforcements were flown in, bringing the total of troops in the Province at the end of July to 21,000. On the

morning of 31 July a massive operation, known as Operation Motorman, was mounted in Londonderry to remove the barricades behind
which the IRA had been ruling for many months. Centurion tanks,
fitted with bulldozer equipment but stripped of their guns, rolled up to
the barricades. The IRA left the area and fled across the border into the
Republic, and the operation which we had long demanded but which,
it was said, would cause a bloodbath, was completed almost without
a shot being fired. The UDA immediately began removing their own
barricades, in some places working alongside the Army, thus under-
lining that their activities, frightening though they might be, existed
mainly as a reaction to the IRA campaign and were unlikely to continue if that campaign was brought to an end.

The public were delighted at this set-back for the IRA. It is one of the
characteristics of a terrorist war that the community can seldom see the
victories or defeats that occur in conventional wars; it is a long, slow
battle of nerves and determination, and it is easy for people to feel that
not enough is being done to protect them. It was a sign of Whitelaw's
political agility that he was able to recover so swiftly from his dramatic
and almost disastrous reverses of a few weeks earlier. He was never quite
forgiven for the ultimate treachery of negotiating with the IRA, and it
was a long time before public confidence began to recover. He was also
in a sense fortunate to have immediately available such a dramatic
action as the ending of 'No Go' areas. None the less, his willingness to
admit to mistakes, and his ability to take decisive remedial action, were
admirable, and I began to have more confidence in the administration,
though I was not entirely happy that the possibilities offered by Motorman were adequately followed up in succeeding months.

But the day was not to end on this satisfactory note. Some twisted
and hate-crazed mind dreamed up an act of defiance for which the sleepy
little village of Claudy, some twelve miles from Londonderry and with
a mixed Protestant and Catholic population, provided the victims.
Three large car bombs exploded without warning in the village street,
killing six people and wrecking half of the village. The IRA hastily
denied responsibility, but the SDLP representative for the area, Ivan
Cooper, called them liars and accused them of responsibility, and he
seems to have been right on both counts.

14
Constitution Building

The political scene developed rapidly but became no less confused. The diffuse nature of Unionist Party organization was causing many problems, not all of which I was able to overcome.

By the autumn the old Cabinet had virtually collapsed as an effective political force, and we stopped meeting regularly. Roy Bradford, one of the party's TV performers, had gone off at a tangent and was doing his own thing with the media. It was being said that if a 'genuine liberal', such as he, was running the Unionist show a political solution would not be long in coming. For most of the direct rule period he remained in this unhelpful and ambitious frame of mind. On the other wing of the party Harry West seemed more interested in farming and stayed at his farm in Fermanagh. Those members who remained loyal I continued to consult with, and brought some of them on to the Policy Committee.

At the same time the officers of the Ulster Unionist Council were beginning to assert a new political importance and agreement with them was an increasing problem. Led by Sir George (Tony) Clark, a county gentleman of the old school, and Orange Leader, they represented generally the older and traditional element of the party, and were less receptive to new ideas. I brought one of the more forward-thinking of them, George Hyde, on to the Policy Committee.

Then there was the problem of liaison with Unionist MPs at Westminster, who were also asserting a new independence now that the Stormont Parliament no longer met, and this caused serious difficulties over the following months. I was fighting to keep the old Stormont Parliamentary Party together in spite of having no democratic forum, to consolidate and sustain the support we enjoyed in the community, and to push ahead the work on policy, and so I probably failed to pay enough attention to problems of party liaison and organization.

The party was fortunate in its servants at this time. J. O. Bailie, the

General Secretary, was an able man who had given the best years of his life to the organization of the party electoral machine. Though he was disheartened by the new turn of affairs and unwell he remained a key figure in the party organization. For the first time the party was building up a professional research and publicity machine, and the driving force behind this was Fred Tughan, businessman and former Mayor of Bangor, who was chairman of the Publicity Finance Committee which had been set up to give impetus to our publicity drive.

Such professional assistance was all the more vital now that we had no government machine at our disposal. Peter McLachlan, a young and enthusiastic Englishman with strong Ulster connections, and with a first-class degree from Cambridge, was recruited into the Westminster organization to liaise with the Conservative Research organization and help our rather quarrelsome brethren in the Westminster Parliamentary Party. David Smyth, an able young Ulsterman with similar academic credentials from Queen's University Belfast, became our first Research Officer in Belfast. Sam Butler, another Queen's graduate, became our Press Officer, and towards the end of 1972 John Houston, who had just finished a year as President of the Student's Union at Queen's joined and completed our new intake of young men. Unfortunately they were almost all inexperienced and found themselves thrown in at the deep end of a party which was undergoing an enormous political upheaval and which left them with a great deal of work in public relations and research. But without the Publicity and Research Department of the party and the loyalty of its staff our work during this direct rule period would have been even more difficult.

Willie Whitelaw and his team had been pursuing what was generally held by the media to be a worthy objective, the splitting of the Unionist Party and the promotion of 'moderate' and 'centre' groups such as the Alliance Party. This party contained men who were patently civilized and well meaning and who put forward admirable non-sectarian sentiments which were music to the ears of British politicians. Some of them even spoke with English accents. It was obvious, so the theory ran, that any hopeful future would have to be built on such people. To help this the strength of the Unionist Party would have to be broken, so that the sensible elements would move towards the 'centre' and the rest would go where they belonged, out into the cold. The techniques employed to pursue this end were a subtle combination of media and political pressures which imposed demands that the old Unionist structures could not accommodate. But the policy was, in my view, mistaken. It misunderstood Ulster politics and applied Westminster attitudes to a different political situation. It underestimated the strength of Unionist sentiment and miscalculated the position of the real political 'centre', which was represented by my colleagues and I. New parties with a 'clean hands' approach could not hope to achieve the political leadership which was necessary in order to deliver support for any settlement. It was some months before the Government came to realize this.

By the beginning of September the Policy Committee had prepared its proposals, and they were published as a 'Unionist Blueprint' for the future government of Northern Ireland. My Government's Committee proposals of June 1971 and the Green Paper of the following autumn had never yet been the subject of inter-party discussions in Northern Ireland, so we were reluctant to go a lot further in new concessions to mere intransigence on the part of the SDLP. Our proposals were based on the assumption that a powerful committee system constituted the limit of institutionalized participation possible in a democratic system. We developed our committee system as much as possible, proposing that the chairmen should be privy councillors, should have a salary similar to that of Cabinet Ministers and should have the opportunity to attend the Cabinet to discuss the affairs of their committees. We also proposed that the committees should have power to amend Bills, subject to subsequent approval of the Commons. But we did not anticipate that any anti-partitionist party would be acceptable as a partner in a Northern Ireland Cabinet, giving the attitudes of the SDLP on the right of the Ulster people to self-determination. We shall return to this important point later.

Willie Whitelaw was still trying to persuade some of the other parties to join in the 'all-party conference', and he announced that it would be held in England in September. Other parties hastily produced proposals which varied greatly. Among the more silly were the SDLP proposals for a 'Condominium'. They suggested that joint sovereignty over Northern Ireland should be exercised by the Republic and the United Kingdom, but were unable to produce any precedent other than German Sudetenland for the idea. It was another symptom of their determination at this time not to recognize Northern Ireland as an entity. The Alliance and Northern Ireland Labour Parties argued for committee government along the lines of a British regional authority, with controversial matters such as security and the police permanently run from Westminster. Paisley's party also published proposals for a form of total integration with Westminster and a county council set-up at Stormont.

We preferred, and we were convinced that the majority of voters preferred, a devolved legislature with real power. It was the best way of keeping government near the people, it was more efficient than remote bureaucracy, and it coincided with the attitudes of mind and the expectations built up over half a century of devolved government. I was also convinced that the possibility of Ulstermen sinking their differences and getting together to work for the prosperity of the whole community depended on the existence of a devolved legislature in which they could co-operate. The removal of political argument to Westminster seemed likely to lead to continued talking at each other through the major British parties.

The 'Darlington Conference' as it has become known, began on 24 September at the Europa Lodge Hotel which had just opened a few miles outside Darlington in County Durham. Only three Northern Ireland parties sent delegations. The SDLP declined to participate on the grounds that internment had not yet been ended (Willie Whitelaw had stopped the releases after Bloody Friday). There may have been a political calculation here also; the SDLP proposals were patently unrealistic and a party deputation at Darlington arguing them would be seen as totally isolated sharing virtually no common ground with the other parties. It was easier and safer to stay at home. Paisley announced that he could not attend unless there was an inquiry into incidents in the Shankill when the Army shot some civilians. It was a sad parroting of the SDLP excuse for opting out in July 1971. Paisley wanted to be in a position to benefit from any mistakes we made at the conference. He had not found the role of 'statesman', adopted at the time of direct rule to win support at Westminster, as successful as expected and began to revert to the old belligerent attitude we all knew well. Darlington provided him with the perfect occasion to switch tacks.

There was one other important absentee from the conference. Each party had been invited to send one spokesman and six advisers, and I decided to ask Bill Craig, who had worked well on the Policy Committee and signed the final proposals, to be one of my advisers. It was the acid test as to whether I was going to be able to bring him along with me or whether the pressures on him from his Vanguard organization would lead to a renewed split between us. I was hopeful that he would agree to come and help us argue our case, and it was a disappointment when he replied to my invitation by saying

I have come to the conclusion that I can in no way participate in a conference which is an attempt to set aside the constitutional and democratic processes and, in any event, cannot succeed. ... In

Vanguard we are proceeding with preparations to make a loyalist veto effective, and if need be, something more positive than a veto.

He attacked all the other parties and indicated that he regarded the very idea of talking to them as 'foolish'. It was obvious that he had defected from the ranks of those on whom I could rely, and was determined not to be associated with any of the concessions which would inevitably be involved in the process of discussion and negotiation on which we were embarking.

The refusal of these parties and political figures to attend meant that only my party, the Ulster Unionist Party, plus the Alliance Party and the Northern Labour Party—both small parties in terms of public support in Northern Ireland—would be joining Whitelaw and his Ministers at Darlington for discussions. This reduced the usefulness and credibility of the conference considerably, but we decided to go none the less. It was the only forum we could find to publicize our policies, and it was important to get political thinking going along positive lines to start a process which could eventually produce a restoration of democratic regional government. There was no future for us in the belligerent style now being reverted to by Paisley and Craig, even if we had wished to add to the competition for that kind of support. Equally importantly, we had to show up the barrenness of ideas coming from the other parties and try to win the respect of Mr Whitelaw and his associates so that we could influence their thinking about the future. It had already become clear that the views of the Alliance Party and the New Ulster Movement—an associated organization of liberals and do-gooders—were commanding attention and respect with the Government and media, and Darlington was for us an opportunity to redress the balance.

Our deputation consisted of Herbert Kirk, Billy Fitzimmons, Robert Babington, Commander Anderson, Jim Bailie and David Smyth as advisers, with myself as the spokesman. Robert Babington was MP for North Down and a QC, and I hoped his legal knowledge would be useful; Albert Anderson was MP for Londonderry, and had a sharp political brain. The team worked well together, though there was not a lot for all of them to do. David Smyth, the youngest of the team, performed brilliantly in his handling of the press, and also worked closely with me on policy briefing.

On the first day of the conference there was a minor hitch in the arrangements. When I arrived I was invited up to Whitelaw's room, and found Phelim O'Neill, Leader of the Alliance Party, and Vivian

Simpson, the widely respected spokesman for NILP, both there. They had proposed to Whitelaw that all seven representatives of each party should be entitled to participate in the formal discussions, and not just one spokesman for each party as had been agreed beforehand. Whitelaw said that if this was unanimously agreed he would go along with it, but if anyone objected he would stand by the previous arrangements. Obviously Phelim O'Neill and Vivian Simpson had been got at by their parties who were fearful of relying on their leaders' powers of exposition—they were neither of them very fluent speakers. In particular Oliver Napier and Bob Cooper, both energetic and able leading members of Alliance, were anxious to have their say. I refused to agree to the change, pointing out that the proposal should have come earlier, since we might have wished to select different delegations if all were to speak. Besides, I did not relish the prospect of dozens of people all airing their views, and it was not in our interests as a party to agree; I was confident that I could deal with the other two leaders.

The talks proceeded amicably, and developed largely into an opportunity for me to expound our proposals and to answer questions from the other parties, from Lord Windlesham, Minister of State, and from Willie Whitelaw, who chaired the sessions. We all agreed that Northern Ireland should remain part of the United Kingdom for as long as a majority of its citizens so wished, and that some form of provincial administration and assembly should be restored as soon as possible. We differed on the powers of this assembly and the form of its executive. The other two parties opposed any devolved responsibility for security or policing, while we insisted that some such powers were essential to the credibility of the institutions. Alliance and NILP opposed Cabinet-style government and proposed differing forms of committee government, arguing that this was the best way of securing minority participation. We argued our case for an executive exercising collective responsibility and providing extensive safeguards, including powerful committees, for minorities. On this second issue we were most closely questioned by Windlesham, and it soon became clear that they were concerned to find a means of SDLP participation in government. I argued our case on the second day as follows,

I can visualise active opposition politicians who would not want to belong to an Executive, a Cabinet, because their aims would be so fundamentally different from the aims of the Cabinet itself. They might be very strong Irish republicans and would not wish to be members of an administration which was basically a UK administration. But we would hope that such people would be very ready to serve as chairmen of committees, giving them a very prominent place in the working of Parliament. We have suggested they should be Privy Councillors, because we think that this would not only give them a recognised standing in the community, but the freedom to discuss proposals on a Privy Council basis.

Windlesham summed up what he saw as the nub of the argument:

> Both the Unionist Party and the Labour Party proposals do depend on the premise that NI, in any revised local institutions that might emerge, could be governed by an executive based on one party alone, whereas the Alliance Party do not subscribe to that view, as I understand it.

He went on to ask me if our proposals could operate equally well in conditions of coalition government, and I replied that if such a coalition were agreed between parties, our proposals should work equally well in that situation. But I could see the way British thinking was developing, and this was underlined by the Government's Green Paper produced soon after.

We came away from Darlington feeling that we had achieved several useful things. First, I thought we had impressed the Whitelaw team with our sincerity in seeking constructive proposals, and the logic and determination of our case. Secondly, the massive media coverage for the talks had provided us with a unique opportunity to be seen by our supporters putting their case, thus helping to isolate the negative bandwagon hunters who had stayed at home. And finally the weakness of the Alliance and NILP arguments had reached the press, making the conference in general a propaganda success for us. Both Government and media treated us more seriously thereafter. We were no longer dismissed as bitter losers in the direct rule revolution, backwoodsmen with no real case. We had shown that we were prepared to take our policy anywhere and argue it cogently and rationally, and that was something worth doing.

The conference ended in an amusing way. The management of the Europa Lodge gave each of us, as a souvenir of our stay, a bottle of mead. When our plane arrived in Ulster a crowd of photographers and reporters was waiting for us and, suddenly realizing that I was carrying my souvenir, I thrust it into the hands of David Smyth, who was nearest to me. It would not have done to allow the spread of rumours, backed up by photographs, that Brian Faulkner had eventually taken to drink!

The Government published its Green Paper on the future of Northern Ireland in October 1972. It was a comprehensive and extremely fair summary of the range of options open to us, and gave general indications of the Government's view as to the proper way forward. In his foreword Whitelaw declared his objectives as trying to find 'a system of government which will enjoy the support and respect of the overwhelming majority' adding that, 'if it is to do so such a system must in large measure emerge from the ideas and the convictions of the NI people themselves. This is why there has to be a long process of consultation.'

The summary of options was so comprehensive, and pre-empted so much of the later discussions on the subject that it is worth mentioning some of them here. On sovereignty and citizenship it pointed out that the Government was bound by pledges given in the 1949 Act and the Downing Street Declaration of 1969, and Mr Heath had already promised that a referendum would be held to provide an opportunity for people to express their views on where Northern Ireland belonged. But the Discussion Paper also argued that there was an 'Irish Dimension' which must be taken into account, not only because a large minority in Northern Ireland sought unity with the Republic but also because Northern Ireland and the Republic shared a common land frontier and many common economic and other problems. The desired arrangements should seek to secure the acceptance, in Northern Ireland and the Republic, of the existing status of Northern Ireland, 'and of the possibility—which should be compatible with the principle of consent—of subsequent change in that status'. There should also be provision for consultation and co-operation between the two parts of Ireland, and for concerted governmental and community action against those terrorist organizations which 'represent a threat to free democratic institutions in Ireland as a whole'.

Within that context, it said, one needed to find the best way of governing Northern Ireland. The full range of schemes from integration to semi-dominion status for a regional parliament were outlined. It was made clear that the Government would not favour either of these two extremes; integration would represent the reversal of the traditions of half a century, impose a substantial new legislative burden on Westminster, and hinder the possibility of co-operation with the Republic. If there were to be devolved institutions they must allow the United Kingdom Government to 'have an effective and continuing voice in NI affairs, commensurate with the commitment of financial and military resources in the Province'. Possibilities of

'executive'devolution alone, limited legislative devolution (for example
with certain stages of all legislation taken at Westminster), or powerful
legislative and executive devolution were outlined. But it was clearly
stated that all security powers must remain with Westminster, because
of their 'divisive' nature within Northern Ireland. No commitment
was made on the type of devolution which would be envisaged, but
any division of powers between Westminster and a regional authority
'must be logical, open and clearly understood'—a hint that the powers
and the pretensions of the previous Stormont Parliament had not
always coincided. Their function must be to 'work efficiently' and to
help produce 'a much wider consensus than has hitherto existed'.

The means of producing this 'consensus' were of course central to
the whole discussion. The various institutional ideas for its achievement were listed: entrenched government (like the then Lebanese system), PR government, weighted majority government and committee
government. Most of these were subject to the objections which we
had already outlined before direct rule and again at Darlington, since
they assumed that executive power, rather than increased influence
and human rights guarantees, would have to be available to minority
representatives. We did not see how this could be done, not only
because we regarded the idea of institutionalized sectarianism as intolerable, but also because we saw the attitudes then being adopted
towards the existence of Northern Ireland by the SDLP as totally unacceptable for a party with any pretensions to govern the Province.

The Government did not however commit themselves in this paper,
observing only that 'as a minimum' minority groups would have to
be assured of an effective voice and real influence, though there were
'strong arguments that the objective of minority participation should
be achieved by giving minority interests a share in the exercise of executive power if this can be achieved by means which are not unduly
complex or artificial and which do not represent an obstacle to effective government'.

In November Ted Heath visited Northern Ireland and announced
that the referendum or 'Border Poll' as the British constitutional pur-
ists now wished to call it, would be held in early spring 1973, and
a White Paper outlining firm constitutional decisions would be
published. He also talked about the cost of Northern Ireland to the
United Kingdom Exchequer, which soured his visit and antagonized
local opinion. While the proposals were being hatched the various
political and para-military groupings continued to flex their muscles,
stand on their heads, or stay sullenly silent, in their own particular

way. Bill Craig rushed around organizing rallies and making outrageous and newsworthy speeches. He eventually made himself ill with
the strain and had to retire for a rest. The sectarian assassinations
continued, and the IRA campaign continued at a reduced level—the
benefits of Motorman were still being felt by the security forces. The
UDA clashed seriously with the Army and shots were exchanged: I
condemned the UDA and said there could be no excuse for adding
to the problems of the security forces. The Government made the
first detention orders against 'loyalist' terrorists. Serious explosions
occurred in Dublin for the first time, on the eve of an important law
and order debate in the Dail. The SDLP were busy finding excuses
for postponing talks with Whitelaw, and Paisley was busy finding
excuses for not attending Vanguard rallies.

Our main problem in the Unionist Party involved the continued
operation of the Vanguard organization and its members as a sub-
grouping inside the party. The increasingly strident comments of Vanguard, particularly a speech by Craig at the Monday Club in London
when he talked of 'shooting to kill', brought an increasingly strident
reaction from the liberal wing of the party. Stratton Mills, MP at
Westminster for North Belfast and well known as a conscientious if
somewhat dogmatic moderate, put a motion to the Standing Committee urging that membership of Vanguard should be declared incom-
patible with membership of the Unionist Party.

I had sympathy with the position of Stratton and his supporters, but
there was no chance that the motion could be carried; the whole ethos
of Unionism had been its inclusiveness across the spectrum of Unionist opinion, and the idea of ideological expulsions was repugnant.
Theoretically the policy of Vanguard was still to support our blueprint,
so we had no adequate grounds for expulsion, other than inflammatory
speeches, which are not usually held as adequate grounds in other
parties in Britain. So I played it straight down the middle on this
occasion, condemning the attitudes of Vanguard but not supporting the
motion, which was not taken. Unfortunately, the whole issue had been
blown up by the media into a test of the liberality of the party and our
inability to come out with a neat solution was taken by some as a 'moral'
failure which should justify the defection of all men of conscience to a
party with more unsullied principles. Stratton and some of those supporting him eventually joined the Alliance Party, much to my regret.

The spring of 1973 was a crucial time in the development of events.
The UDA, which had initially enjoyed considerable sympathy
for seeming to show the mailed fist to the Government, became

over-ambitious, attracted numerous racketeers and petty criminals, and antagonized public opinion by trying to hold general strikes which degenerated into violence and intimidation and rapidly collapsed. They had overplayed their hand, they were becoming associated with violence and criminality, and their political importance declined.

Craig began to develop more overtly the ideas of independence and 'dominion status' for Northern Ireland which had for some time been inherent in many of his attacks on the Westminster Government, and the SDLP were going through a crucial period of finding their political direction which led them to express interest in Craig's ideas and meet him for discussions. The SDLP were having to decide whether or not they were prepared to make a British Northern Ireland work by making a push for power within the United Kingdom framework. They were also having to decide which section of the Unionist political leadership they could cultivate most profitably—the more anti-British who were also the more anti-Catholic, such as Paisley and Craig, or the more pro-British but also more conciliatory Unionists, such as the Official Unionist Party which I led. There were obvious attractions for a nationalist party in making common cause against the British with those Protestant politicians who were becoming increasingly bitter about the way in which Northern Ireland was being treated by the Government, and who were inclined to blame all our ills on mishandling and blundering at Westminster. The problem for the SDLP was whether or not to risk the safety of the Catholic community by abandoning the British guarantee for the sake of Nationalist doctrine. Craig's new theory of finding common cause in a new 'Ulster' identity was superficially attractive, but provided no guarantee as to how the minority would be treated in an independent Ulster.

The SDLP emerged from these talks speaking of 'common ground' but clearly unconvinced that this offered a definite new strategy for them. They were becoming involved in talks with Whitelaw, and the problem of putting forward positive proposals was urgent. The 'condominium' idea was irrelevant as a practical proposition, and the imminent publication of a Government White Paper underlined the necessity for them to become involved in the constitution-making process now well under way. I made my own position quite clear; I was committed to the Union with no 'ifs' and 'buts', and I was anxious to find a constructive role for minority representatives within the United Kingdom framework if they would meet me half way. I attacked Craig's talk of independence and said that as far as I was concerned he was no longer a Unionist and I could foresee no future co-operation between us.

He had become more and more closely tied up with the para-military organizations and this set the seal on the split between us; I was interested only in a constitutional way forward.

A few weeks later the arrival of a new political phase was decisively underlined by the holding of the long-awaited 'Border Poll', which ended all the speculation and discussion on what the views of Ulstermen really were on the issue of citizenship. A simple choice was posed between two questions, 'Do you want Northern Ireland to remain part of the UK?' or 'Do you want Northern Ireland to be joined with the Republic of Ireland outside the UK?' The SDLP and the Nationalist Party—which still existed in name—called for a boycott of the poll; it was not very surprising that they did so. Their support in the Catholic community came from both doctrinaire Nationalists, and from those whose primary interest was to secure the maximum possible influence for their community within Northern Ireland and were in no hurry to join with the less prosperous Republic. None the less some 600,000 electors voted in a 59 per cent poll; 98 per cent of them voted to remain in the UK and 1 per cent voted to join a united Ireland. Even allowing for an exceptionally high poll of 80 per cent among Unionists, it was clear that some 20 to 25 per cent of the Catholic community had voted for the British link in spite of the boycott campaign.

The whole strategy of the Lynch government in Dublin and the SDLP in Northern Ireland over the previous eighteen months had been based on the assumption that Britain wanted to get shot of Northern Ireland and therefore a united Ireland was on the cards. It seemed to be assumed that the combination of intense propaganda from Dublin and intransigence by the minority inside Northern Ireland would lead to a British declaration of intent to withdraw on a 'post-colonial' basis. Mr Lynch had often said that unification of Ireland could only come about by 'peaceful means', but it was clear that he was not averse to 'peaceful coercion' from London.

These assumptions about the direction of events and the intentions of British policy were dealt a blow by the Green Paper, which made it clear that a decision that Northern Ireland should cease to be part of the United Kingdom was up to the people of Northern Ireland themselves, and shattered by the Border Poll, which told the world clearly and decisively that the people of Ulster wanted to remain British citizens and were in no way part of any 'colonial' situation. Henceforth discussions were to centre on the possibilities of co-operation within a British Northern Ireland, and on possible schemes for co-operation between Northern Ireland and the Irish Republic. One heard no more talk of a 'united Ireland or nothing'; the long road back from undiluted nationalism to constructive policies for participation in Northern Ireland had begun.

15
The Assembly

The security situation improved in 1973. The previous year had seen Ulster almost collapse into civil war. It had been by far the worst year we had ever known, and the statistics tell only part of the horrors. There were over 1,300 explosions, 10,000 shooting incidents, and 1,200 armed robberies providing funds for terrorist organizations. A total of 467 people died violently, and over 5,000 were injured in terrorist activities—one person in every 300 of the population.

It is not surprising that it was difficult to make people believe that constitutional schemes had any relevance, or to reconcile them to making concessions to those they regarded as largely responsible for their suffering. But even by the end of 1972 it was obvious that the increased flow of intelligence brought about by the freeing of the former 'No Go' areas from IRA dictatorship was paying off gradually and that the security forces were making progress in the war of attrition. By the early summer of 1973 violence was down on almost every measurement. The IRA were still operating a terrorist campaign, and Protestant assassins were still retaliating in a way which suggested their initial political motivation had become submerged in sheer hate and criminality. But there was a demonstrable improvement, and when people who are close to despair see some hope of alleviation of their plight it gives them new heart to work for a way to improve things and to give constructive ideas the benefit of any doubt. Such was the climate as the Government produced its constitutional proposals at the end of March, almost exactly one year after the suspension of the Stormont Parliament.

Tensions were also being eased by the defeat of Jack Lynch's Fianna Fail Party in the Republic and the accession to office of a new Labour and Fine Gael coalition Government led by Mr Cosgrave and containing progressive thinkers such as Conor Cruse O'Brien and Garret Fitzgerald who commanded some respect in Northern Ireland. A new era of neighbourly co-existence appeared possible.

Just before the White Paper was published there was an attempt to dislodge me from the Leadership of the party. Willie Orr, Leader of the Ulster Unionist MPs at Westminster, announced the formation of a united front with Paisley and Craig to demand 'the immediate restoration of parliamentary government to Northern Ireland'. He did not consult me before the announcement, but sent me a belated invitation to join the group. I turned it down flat, as I could see little common ground between me and Paisley or Craig. Orr may have thought that Unionist opinion would rally to the call and he would be leader of a grand alliance, but after being ignored humiliatingly by reporters at the initial press conference he realized his mistake. I met him the next day privately at the Stormont Hotel and persuaded him that the most useful thing he could do was to cease to give credibility to this unholy alliance. He issued a statement along these lines and then went to ground for some days. It was a sad episode which probably destroyed the political reputation of Willie Orr in Northern Ireland. His undoubted parliamentary talents could have been more constructively used.

The White Paper was one of the most controversial documents ever produced by a British Government. Controversy raged for months, and indeed years, over whether its proposals, shortly afterwards embodied in the Northern Ireland Constitution Act 1973, provided an acceptable and practicable scheme for the government of Northern Ireland. This is not surprising, as they represented an attempt to reconcile widely varying proposals and political traditions. A new unicameral Assembly was to be elected by PR, was to determine its own rules of procedure, seek to agree on the setting up of an Executive, and then have legislative powers over a certain number of matters devolved to it. Argument centred on three main aspects of the proposals: the conditions placed on the formation of an Executive, the extent of powers it was proposed should be devolved, and the style and status of the new institutions.

The central issue was that of who would govern Northern Ireland. The White Paper said, 'It is the view of the Government that the Executive itself can no longer be based solely upon any single party if that party draws its support and its elected representatives virtually entirely from only one section of a divided community.' The Secretary of State for Northern Ireland, who was to continue to have certain responsibilities for Northern Ireland in the new scheme of devolution, would have the discretion to decide after the election of the Assembly whether or not any proposed Executive met these criteria, and would in fact play an active part in discussions leading up to the formation of the Executive. It was a cleverly flexible scheme, which avoided most of the objec-

tions which we had to put to PR government or an institutionalized sectarian government, as there would obviously have to be a freely agreed
coalition of parties subject to the interpretative phrase of 'widespread
consent'.

The question people immediately asked was 'Will the SDLP be in the
government?', and the press rather crudely interpreted the scheme as
meaning that Whitelaw was going to guarantee the SDLP a place in the
Executive. Given the history of the SDLP over the previous years, and
particularly their attitude that Northern Ireland had no right to exist,
it was natural that Unionists should feel strongly against SDLP participation in government. I simply did not know the answer; the paper
placed the onus of 'constructive participation' on any party which
aspired to power and it would depend on how the SDLP handled themselves whether or not that embraced them when the time came. To date
their performance had not been encouraging, but if I was right about
the changing direction of their policy it could be to our advantage and
the advantage of Northern Ireland to seek to bind them to the new institutions by participation in government. One thing was clear in my
mind; the new scheme did not provide any absolute right for the SDLP
to be in government, and it was conceivable that an unco-operative
SDLP would pave the way for a Unionist/Alliance coalition involving
elected representatives of the Catholic community.

Most important of all was the guarantee, later written into the Constitution Act as the second clause, that the people of Northern Ireland
would remain citizens of the United Kingdom unless they decided
otherwise in a Border Poll—and under the Border Poll Act another one
could not be held for at least ten years. The Border Poll was central to
our attitude to the SDLP, since it was a doctrine of traditional die-hard
republicanism that Ireland as a whole was a political unit and only a
vote of the whole of Ireland was valid in determining the future of any
part of the island. Now that the poll was in the Constitution Act any
party seeking participation in government would have to accept the
validity of a vote of the Northern Ireland people alone, and if the SDLP
did so they would be abandoning doctrinaire nationalism for the more
practical and worthwhile task of preserving the interests of their
supporters and making Northern Ireland a better place for us all to
live in.

The question of the powers of the new Assembly was also highly
charged emotionally. Stormont had been suspended because we in the
Cabinet had refused to accept a 'sham Parliament' with no real
power. The new scheme proposed by Whitelaw divided the powers of

government into three categories. First, reserved matters which would be permanently exercised from Westminster: foreign relations, defence, all electoral arrangements, the judiciary, emergency powers and prosecutions; second, transferred matters, those devolved to the Northern Ireland Assembly: social services, industry, education, planning and agriculture. Third, reserved matters, a new 'in between' category of powers for the time-being reserved to Westminster, but on which the Assembly could legislate with the agreement of the United Kingdom Government, and which might in time be transferred to the Assembly. This last category included organization of the police, criminal law, courts and prisons, which were the most controversial powers formerly exercised by Stormont. It was a policy designed to remove from the Assembly, at least initially, those powers about which there was likely to be most disagreement between Nationalists and Unionists.

One could see the logic of this argument, but it ignored the point that there were important issues which had to be faced and overcome, rather than simply removed from the political arena. I never regarded a devolved legislature as wholly credible without some control on policing matters, preferably from the very beginning, but at least in normal peace-time circumstances. I realized, however, that there was little possibility of Westminster agreeing to this while the campaign of terrorism continued or before the new Assembly gave evidence of evolving a stable political system within which Protestants and Catholics co-operated. But many Unionists judged the new scheme by the extent of devolution which had been exercised in the Stormont Parliament, and saw the Whitelaw proposals as a drastic down-grading of local institutions. Northern Ireland was outside the mainstream of the devolution debate in the United Kingdom and it was not realized that the scheme of devolution here proposed for Northern Ireland offered greater local scope, with the possibility of continuing enlargement of powers in the future, than was being considered for Scotland or Wales.

Unionists were offended also by the terminology of the White Paper. We were not to have a Parliament, but an Assembly; not a Cabinet but an Executive; the Governor and the Northern Ireland Privy Council were to be abolished and the position of Secretary of State for Northern Ireland in the Westminster Government was to continue; the Assembly would pass Measures and not Acts. To people used to fifty years of extensive devolution in a Parliament adopting all the titles and paraphernalia of the Sovereign Parliament this was a down-grading of their institutions which they resented. I did not regard most of these matters as significant, though I soon found out that I was moving too fast here for most of my colleagues. In a speech made several months earlier I had outlined my attitude to parliamentary ceremonial: 'I am no preservationist when it comes to Parliament, any rituals, titles, procedures and hallowed patterns. Indeed I agree with those who feel that the Mother of Parliaments herself could do with a facelift.'

By nature I was attracted to business-like and practical arrangements, and quite welcomed what I saw as a modernization of the legislative style. But popular indignation about the Governor in particular became evident, heightened by the regard in which the then Governor, Lord Grey, was generally held. My colleagues insisted that the party must express this opposition to the abolition of the Governor—with which most of them agreed—and mount a campaign to have the office retained. I always regarded this campaign as one based on sentiment rather than any clear understanding of the constitutional role fulfilled by the Governor. The title smacked of colonialism and damaged rather than strengthened our position as part of the United Kingdom.

How then was the Unionist Party to react to the overall constitutional scheme proposed in this White Paper? We could, as some were urging, reject it out of hand and declare that if it were implemented in legislation we would refuse to participate in the institutions set up. That was the easy road of negative politics which would win us a few cheap cheers in the short term and re-erect the old siege mentality. But we already had a resident expert in negative politics in the person of Ian Paisley, and I had no inclination to follow him down that road. Such a course would discredit Unionism abroad and in Britain and seriously endanger our position as citizens of the United Kingdom.

We had before us a detailed and flexible constitutional scheme worked out after months of consultation and negotiation and backed by all major parties in the Sovereign Parliament. It guaranteed our place as British citizens, and would for the first time in history secure the support of all three major British parties for the Union. It provided for a devolved legislature and executive government, without the inflexibility of entrenched sectarian or PR government. It was closer to the proposals for which we in the Unionist Party had argued than those of any other party. I had been aware, from trips to Britain and contacts with Westminster politicians, of the real possibility of being presented with a much less acceptable scheme, and was quite pleased with the extent to which many of the points we had made to Whitelaw and his team had been incorporated in the proposals.

Practical politics demanded that I qualify my welcome. The scheme could only work if I could get a sufficient number of Unionists to agree to try to make it work, and there were powerful forces of sentiment and tradition to be overcome. Ulster people have a very stubborn streak, and the easy way British commentators had talked about the need to 'impose' a solution on Northern Ireland in the wake of direct rule made many Unionists ready to reject anything which had the appearance of being imposed on them, irrespective of its merits. In any case I did have reservations about the scheme, particularly the decision not to devolve police powers to the new Executive. So I welcomed the White Paper in principle, describing it as a 'constructive document' and referring to the need to clarify some points which had been left deliberately flexible. Three days later at a special meeting of the Ulster Unionist Council I elaborated on this, asking people to look only at essentials:

A system of government is not to be imposed on us. It has to be worked out by the elected representatives of the new Assembly ... The composition of the Executive is to be worked out by the Assembly itself, in consultation with the Secretary of State ... our own proposals envisaged a role for 'all reasonable men' and that does not necessarily mean one-party government ... It is up to us today to decide whether the things we dispute about the White Paper are of fundamental importance. I believe we have in fact secured almost all of our fundamentals.

This position was vocally opposed by a large minority of the 700-strong audience, led by Craig. The latter denounced the new proposals and called for their total repudiation by the Unionist Party. When it became clear that he could not succeed in this he staged a walk-out from the meeting with some hundred supporters, and those left passed a motion giving a qualified welcome to the White Paper by a substantial majority. This occasion marked the formal ending of Bill Craig's links with the Unionist Party, links which had been increasingly tenuous and anomalous. Shortly afterwards it was announced that the Vanguard organization was setting up a new political party, the clumsily named 'Vanguard Unionist Progressive Party', thereafter referred to as VUPP.

Unease about the White Paper was widespread among Unionists and I mounted a campaign throughout the country to explain the advantages I saw in it and the dangers of failing to grasp the opportunity it offered. The 'Parliamentary Party' discussed it at length, and though I was given backing it was made clear that I was thought to have reacted too enthusiastically. The issues were confused and the party divided on what the White Paper actually meant and on what our reaction should be. There was much talk of 'negotiating' further with Mr Whitelaw, but as far as I could see the die was cast and the post-White Paper situation was a completely new one. There might still be room for flexibility on the question of police control, which I was determined to take every opportunity to press, and on the working out of the power-sharing concept. There was also a possibility that Whitelaw might agree to restore the Governor as a gesture to Unionist sentiment. But the constitutional framework was decided, it was essentially workable, and we needed now to prepare for the elections to the new Assembly and the important role we would almost certainly have to play in it.

In an attempt to sort out some of the confusion I led a deputation to the Secretary of State to discuss some of the points which concerned us. Then I and my colleagues made a firm decision that we would work the new scheme, and published a pamphlet entitled *The White Paper—a Constructive Approach*. This was circulated in thousands around the Province. It outlined our attitude to all the major aspects of the proposals, and it is worth quoting the section entitled 'Power-Sharing' because it encapsulated the position I was to maintain consistently over succeeding months:

> It has not been Unionist policy to insist on one-party government. The White Paper intends to make one-party government impossible. That is a limitation on the natural course of democracy which our Blueprint did not propose. But it is not something to which we have been fundamentally opposed.
>
> We have one important reservation. There can be no place in any new Executive for those who are not prepared to accept the right of the people of Northern Ireland to decide their future by a free vote, to accept that decision and to work for the benefit of the community inside the framework thereby decided ... What is clear is that the proposals are flexible, and the more Unionist representatives are elected to the new Assembly the more we can mould these proposals to the form of government we advocate.

The majority of Unionists rallied to this position of qualified acceptance, but quite a few of those who sympathized with Craig were not prepared to leave the Unionist Party and join him. A massive pro- and anti-White Paper campaign developed with some constituency organizations taking one side, and some the other. The assembly elections were announced for late June 1973 and the intervening months were an exhausting time. My colleagues and I not only had to prepare and publicize manifestos for local government and assembly elections (the local elections took place on 30 May) but we had to fight every inch of the way against the dissidents in our own party who were uniting with Craig and Paisley to whip up resentment and fear about the new constitutional scheme. The Orange Order, or rather a politically motivated group at its head, pronounced that the White Paper held the 'seeds of our destruction'.

When the Constitution Bill implementing the White Paper proposals was given its second reading at Westminster, some of our Unionist MPs decided without any consultation with me to oppose it in principle, and I had to issue a statement repudiating their action, and urging that amendments only should be sought at the Committee Stage. The so-called 'Loyalist Coalition' of Paisley and Craig met and decided on all-out opposition to the White Paper and to any Executive formed under its provisions. The battle lines were being drawn and the choice seemed clear—constructive politics versus the wreckers.

I got together a committee representative of the party to draw up the election manifesto. It contained some of those who were two years later elected to the Convention as my opponents, such as James Armstrong from County Armagh, and William Bell, from Belfast's Shankill Road. We worked rapidly to agree on a wide-ranging policy statement—not only confined to current security and constitutional issues, but covering also the 'bread and butter' issues such as industrial development, education, housing, health and social services, and the environment—which had been prepared by our research staff.

Our main problem was what to say about the White Paper and the issue of power-sharing. I said frankly to the committee that I did not want to adopt a form of words which would prevent us having an SDLP member of the Executive if this turned out to be necessary to get devolved government going again after the election. Reactions in the committee varied and it was proposed that we say we could not share power with Republicans, nor with anyone whose central aim was to see Northern Ireland absorbed into a united Ireland. I pointed out that this might not apply to the SDLP if they were prepared to work for the good of Northern Ireland. It was then proposed that we adopt the formula 'we are not prepared to participate in government with those whose primary objective is to break the Union with Great Britain', and this went into our manifesto. It was a phrase which was to become very controversial as the election campaign progressed.

Constituencies were busy selecting candidates and if the election was to mean anything the electorate would have to know where they stood on the new constitutional set-up. I sent out a letter from party HQ to all constituency chairmen enclosing a summary of the agreed manifesto and a form for all officially selected candidates to sign. The form said, 'I undertake to support the Statement of Party Policy issued on 9 May 1973, and, if elected to the Assembly, to serve loyally as a member of the Unionist Party.' This form became known as the 'Pledge' and the 39 Unionist candidates who signed it became known as the 'Pledged Unionists' while the 10 refusing to do so were known as the 'Unpledged'. (Outside observers unaware of this might have been forgiven for thinking that the election was concerned with drinking habits.) Some were later to say that the Pledge had been divisive and precipitated the break-up of the party. But there are times in politics when party unity has to take second place to the interests of the community, when issues cannot be fudged or cracks papered over, and this was one of them.

We published our manifesto at the end of May under the title 'Peace, Order and Good Government', and I was questioned intensely about it at our press conferences and in television appearances. Once again interest centred on our views about the Executive. Was the SDLP a party whose 'primary objective' was to break the Union? Would I participate in the government with the SDLP? Time and time again I had to reiterate our position; that we wanted to secure the election of the maximum possible number of sensible Unionists, that we hoped to play the major role in the formation of a regional government which would set about the reconstruction of the social and economic life of our province, and that I was willing to enter a coalition with any party prepared to dedicate itself to the same objective. The Constitution Act laid down an oath for members of the Executive to take:

I swear by Almighty God that I will uphold the laws of Northern Ireland and conscientiously fulfil, as a member of the Northern Ireland Executive, my duties under the Constitution Act 1973 in the interests of Northern Ireland and its people.

It was an oath which no Republican dedicated to the destruction of Northern Ireland could take. 'If any other party is prepared to take this oath in good faith it will provide a starting point for discussions about power-sharing,' I told the reporters. 'But no party can be in government and support rent and rate strikes.' I also pointed out that the Act which the oath referred to had in its second clause the guarantee that the people of Northern Ireland would have the right to determine their own future by democratic means through the Border Poll, and that any politician taking the oath would be supporting that provision.

It was up to the SDLP to make it clear whether they would operate within that framework and on those principles. Their position was equivocal at first, but as the election approached they began to take a conciliatory line and my responses became increasingly specific. *The Times* headlined a report of a radio interview I had done saying 'Northern Ireland party leaders prepared to share power in new assembly', and the *Observer* came out the Sunday before the election with the headline 'Faulkner: I'll share power with the Catholics'. I specifically stated that a long-term objective of a united Ireland was acceptable in a potential coalition partner, provided the Act and the constitutional position under it were accepted. My personal election address to the voters of South Down said simply: 'I shall co-operate in the Assembly with all those who are prepared to make the new institutions of government effective.'

The facts about the campaign are important because it was later to be said by the 'Loyalists' in order to justify their wrecking tactics in the Assembly that my actions after the election in sharing power with the SDLP were inconsistent with my pledges to the electors. This is simply untrue.

The election campaign was hectic and more hard-fought than any I could remember. Violence continued, but for once the spotlight was on the politicians and there was hope that democratic politics could achieve some result. The IRA campaigned in their own murderous way, firing a mortar bomb at a polling booth and attempting to step up the violence so that extreme positions would be taken up and the chances of compromise destroyed. But everywhere I went I found hope: 'Let's give the news system a chance', people were saying. 'We are not happy about all of it, but at least there is the chance of getting politics off the streets and into an Assembly of our own.' I campaigned all over the Province and on election day itself, a day of brilliant sunshine, I went to help candidates in the constituency of North Belfast, travelling around the Shankill Road area I had once known so well. There were hecklers and critics of course, but the warmth and enthusiasm of my reception were almost overwhelming, and there were many good-natured wisecracks when I called in to a well-known Shankill pub for a glass of orange juice.

This was the first Northern Ireland general election held under the PR system in multi-member constituencies since 1929—there had already been a trial run on local government elections, and contrary to the expectations of pundits, the Ulster people had taken to the system like ducks to water. There was a tiny percentage of spoilt votes, and the results in candidates returned were overwhelmingly Unionist as under the old system. I do not believe that many communities could handle the technicalities of politics as intelligently as the voter in Northern Ireland, on either side of the fence. No election in Northern Ireland had ever held so many imponderables: the new electoral system, divisions within the once solid Unionist block, a proliferation of parties and so many new issues. The results could not be forecast this time with any degree of certainty. None the less I ended my campaigning much reassured about the basic good sense of Ulster people and went off to the count in Downpatrick to discover how the voters of my own constituency had determined my fate.

The South Down election count in Downpatrick brought me a bonus in the form of more than 16,000 first preference votes. My two colleagues on the pro-Assembly Unionist ticket were my loyal friend Brigadier Ronnie Broadhurst, who was also elected, and a candidate from the Mourne area who was not. I had expected to run close to the top SDLP contender, as there was a large SDLP vote in the constituency. But I ended up with more than twice the number of votes needed to get elected on the first count, and I was pleased and encouraged that so many people were prepared to support me.

Elsewhere the results were mixed. In North Antrim Paisley topped the poll with 14,000 votes, beating Craig into third place below the quota. But in the same constituency John Baxter, a young lawyer supporting me and making his début in politics, ran a good second to Paisley and was elected on the first count. In three other constituencies our candidates had topped the poll, and we had won more seats and votes than any other party. The Unionist Party had 32 representatives in the new 78-seat Assembly, but 10 of these had refused to sign the pledge I had circulated and were equivocal about their attitude to the Constitution. The Loyalist Coalition of Paisley and Craig and their associates had 18 seats, the Alliance Party had 8, the SDLP had 19 and once again the Northern Ireland Labour Party had only one representative.

My pleasure at some of the results was mixed with regret that more of our candidates had not been elected. The anti-Constitution lobby, divided though they appeared to be, had returned a substantial minority. Fear and suspicion still existed among Unionists that the new set-up was designed to sell out their interests and we would have to tread cautiously and reassure them. But the men of violence had been decisively defeated. All candidates clearly associated with a para-military tag had failed to gain election. The SDLP had smashed the Republican Clubs, the political arm of the Official IRA, who received less than two per cent of the votes, and the Provisionals' call for spoiled votes had received derisory support. Clearly the IRA of either wing did not represent the democratic voice of Catholic Ulster, and the SDLP was established as the party with which anyone wishing to accommodate the Catholic community would have to do business.

No one was quite sure what should happen next. An assembly had been elected and it would have to meet and decide its procedures, but there was no obvious government in view. All six party leaders were invited to Stormont separately for a brief meeting with Whitelaw to test which way the wind was blowing. 'I take it you are in favour of negotiations to try to form an Executive?' Whitelaw asked me. 'We are,' I said. We agreed to talk again when he had met all the other parties. But no further talks took place for some weeks. Whitelaw was having difficulty with the SDLP who were still rather uncertain about the right line to take and were playing for position.

For some weeks the in-fighting in my own party provided the central political spectacle. Immediately after the election I made a tactical error by holding a meeting of the twenty-two Unionist Assemblymen who had signed the 'Pledge', thereafter referred to as the 'Pro-Assembly Unionists', and not sending an invitation to the ten who had refused to do so. It seemed quite natural, as we had fought a different election campaign, and they were out of sympathy with us on fundamental issues. But they had not fought the election as members of the Paisley and Craig coalition and gained many of their votes as official Unionist representatives, particularly in constituencies where we had not been able to get sympathetic candidates selected by Unionist Associations and had lost perhaps two or three seats as a result. Most of them had used our manifesto with some expressed reservations on the controversial areas such as power-sharing. When I had attacked them as wreckers they had insisted they were not out to wreck the new constitution. Our failure to invite them to our initial meeting saved them the embarrassment of having either to refuse—and be seen as a rebel breakaway group—or to attend and be seen as a minority within the party. Thereafter they were to cry 'persecution' and 'lock-out' and had more freedom to operate as a separate political grouping. They would have done this anyway, but psychologically they had an easier start to their rebellion due to our decision.

We quickly realized this and issued invitations to everyone for our second meeting, but these were turned down. Later they elected their own leader, Harry West, my former Cabinet colleague, who had organized them since the early days of the election campaign. Although we made several attempts to get them to attend meetings of the Assembly Party, their true sympathies soon became clear. The first meeting of the Assembly was fixed for 31 July, when there would be a formal opening and election of a Presiding Officer. On the day before the meeting Craig's VUPP, Paisley's DUP and the 'Unpledged Unionists' issued a joint statement for the first time, announcing that they would vote as a bloc in the Assembly and would oppose *in toto* the new institutions which were not 'parliamentary democracy'. I attacked them for 'conning the electorate'. If that was their position they should have had the courage to tell people before the election, openly joining a wrecking coalition.

The approach of the first formal meeting of the Northern Ireland Assembly brought several practical problems to the fore, in particular where we would meet and who would be elected to the normally uncontroversial position of Presiding Officer. All parties except the SDLP had told Mr Whitelaw that they considered the precincts of Parliament Buildings at Stormont the natural meeting place. But the SDLP were reluctant to agree to this and it was obviously essential from the Secretary of State's point of view to reach some compromise which would avoid an SDLP boycott before we even got started. Stormont, they said, symbolized the old régime which they had been glad to see brought down, and if their supporters were to believe that a new era had dawned a new meeting place would have to be found. But it soon became obvious that the only practical premises available were at Stormont, which had all the necessary parliamentary facilities. A compromise was arranged whereby the initial meeting would be held in the stately surroundings of the Great Hall at Stormont, pending the appointment of a Standing Orders Committee which would recommend permanent arrangements.

Agreement on a Presiding Officer also turned out to be no simple task. We had already lost one of our pro-Assembly Unionist members, David McCarthy from North Antrim, who had died tragically in a motoring accident on holiday, and we could ill afford to lose another member by seeking to place him in the chair. We also felt that, since there had often been accusations in the old Stormont that offices were not adequately shared around, it might be a good idea for the Assembly to have a non-Unionist as Presiding Officer. But David Bleakley, the only NILP member turned down the job, and both the SDLP and Alliance refused to produce a candidate. So we had to do so. Roy Bradford proposed Nat Minford; we were given to understand that he was unlikely to be opposed by the loyalists, and he was selected as our candidate.

The first meeting of the Northern Ireland Assembly was a very unnatural occasion. Sitting in the Great Hall under the massive chandeliers and ornate ceiling and with the statue of Lord Craigavon looking down on us from the top of the marble staircase, the disadvantages of meeting in an environment which was neither architecturally nor acoustically designed for debate soon became obvious. Those of us on the floor had great difficulty in hearing what was going on, while the guests and press in the gallery round the top of the Hall could hear even whispered conversations between members. At one stage, my wife, who was sitting in the balcony, sent a note down to me by an attendant saying, 'For heaven's sake be careful what you say. I can hear every word up here, and so can the people beside me.' I do not recall if the note was stimulated by some impolite remark I had made, but I should not be surprised if it was, considering the way the meeting developed.

Ronnie Blackburn, the Clerk to the Assembly, took the Chair to open and struggled bravely to move the proceedings towards the election of a Presiding Officer. I moved the nomination of Nat Minford and Roy Bradford seconded. We took two minutes between us. Immediately afterwards Craig proposed William Beattie, Paisley's deputy and a clergyman in his Free Presbyterian Church, for the post, attempting to widen out his speech into a long sermon about the new Constitution. He was repeatedly ruled out of order by the Chair, but the obstructionist tactics of the loyalists, orchestrated by Paisley, soon became clear as a continuous stream of points of order challenging the Chair were made, most of them spurious and deliberately irrelevant. Insults, barracking and noise rapidly reduced the meeting to an undignified shambles. It took some $2\frac{1}{2}$ hours before we reached the election of the Presiding Officer and the quality of the intervening contributions can best be illustrated by an extract from Hansard. Kennedy-Lindsay, a 'Professor' of uncertain academic pedigree at an African institution, and one of the intellectuals of the loyalist group, made a long and incoherent speech revolving around the following sentiments: 'We need a strong man. This is a weak Parliament; it is not a Parliament; it is a weak organisation. Mr. Beattie is a very strong man.'

The rest of his speech ranged over aspirins, gundogs and swivel chairs. It was not untypical of that day.

We attempted to maintain a dignified detachment from the rowdy goings-on, as did Alliance and the SDLP. The last party had worried us a little by its refusal to participate in any way in the election of a Presiding Officer even by voting in a division. The options were obviously still being kept open. But John Hume made a constructive and dignified contribution in which he said that the presence of the SDLP was an earnest of its seriousness to attempt to work out a fair system of government through the Assembly, and that was reassuring. The behaviour of the loyalists dramatized the issue of the 'wreckers versus the rest' as never before, and made the SDLP seem by contrast a responsible party—for them an important transition. It pushed a little nearer and made ultimately inevitable, the day when we would be able to work with them.

Nat Minford was eventually elected as Presiding Officer by 32 votes to 26, the Alliance Party voting with us. Further wrangling followed the appointment of a Standing Orders Committee and the Assembly was adjourned amid disorderly scenes. Hansard records it as follows:

MR McQUADE: You leave that chair. Have the courage to leave that chair.

REV. DR PAISLEY: Let the Assembly vote. We will be satisfied with the vote.

THE PRESIDING OFFICER: I am taking no vote now.

MR McQUADE: Then get out of the Chair.

MR BARR: Get out of the Chair.

REV. DR PAISLEY: Vote, vote.

THE PRESIDING OFFICER: I adjourn the Assembly.

But Hansard does not record what followed. The loyalists refused to leave the Chamber, installed their own chairman, and carried on a mock Assembly in what the press described as a 'back to school atmosphere'. It was a disgusting performance which made me feel thoroughly ashamed. It was difficult to believe that we were the elected representatives of people who were suffering grievously from terrorism, and that some eight hundred people had already died. We had a serious job to do in creating as soon as possible a regional government which could set about the social reconstruction of our Province. Public reaction was so strong that Paisley, realizing he had overplayed his hand, agreed a few days later to sit on the representative Standing Orders Committee, and there was much speculation that he had abandoned the wrecking tactics. Craig, a less flexible but more principled politician, remained consistent by refusing to accept the place offered to him.

For several weeks this committee busied itself with numerous matters which, if not irrelevant, seemed to me very minor in comparison to the central political issues. That did not prevent them generating a great deal of heat. It was an argument over symbols, and to many Irish politicians symbols are the central issue in politics. Where the new Assembly would meet, what shape the debating chamber should be, whether we should have a Speaker or a Presiding Officer, whether we should open with a prayer and whether the prayer should include a reference to the Queen, and whether we should have a mace in the Assembly—all these issues were fiercely argued in the Standing Orders Committee. The SDLP wanted meetings of the Assembly to be held in Armagh for historical reasons, but no other party supported this and it was agreed that the Stormont Commons chamber, redesigned to a horse-shoe shape so that seating was a continuum, should provide the forum for our debates. On all the other controversial issues, however, the SDLP, supported by the votes of the Alliance representative on the Committee and the Presiding Officer, got its way because of Bill Craig's refusal to attend. All the traditional ceremony was absent from the Draft Standing Orders brought back to the second meeting of the Assembly, this time in the House of Commons chamber, on 15 October. But this was not acceptable to any of the Unionist parties—Paisley's, Craig's, West's or mine. So the Assembly spent two days debating whether or not to change the Standing Orders, three more days debating whether the new Constitution was 'democratic' or not, and four more sittings changing the Standing Orders again to reverse all the controversial votes in the committee.

I had little taste for any of the meetings of the Assembly before Christmas 1973, regarding them as an empty talking-shop which offered little of practical value to the population of Northern Ireland, and I attended as few of them as was compatible with my position as Leader of the largest Assembly party. On the other hand, at least people were talking and though the loyalists were still somewhat unruly they had clearly changed their tactics away from outright wrecking towards using the platform offered by the Assembly to make numerous lengthy speeches. But I knew they still held the same objectives and were simply biding their time, watching and hoping we would make mistakes on which they could capitalize.

16
The Castle Talks

The chances of success or failure for the new institutions were already being decided elsewhere. Deputations from three parties—Alliance, pro-Assembly Unionists, and SDLP—representing a majority in the Assembly met in the old Cabinet Room at Stormont Castle at 11 a.m. on Friday 5 October 1973 for the first formal inter-party talks on the formation of a coalition Executive.

All the other parties were asked to participate, but they all refused, Paisley saying that he could not talk to the SDLP while they continued to support a rent and rates strike. There had been no real dialogue between representatives of the Unionist and Nationalist communities during the two bloody years since the SDLP had walked out of Stormont, so this was an important new opportunity to restore a basis for peaceful co-existence and political reconciliation in the Province. The hesitation of the SDLP even after the elections seemed to be due to two things: uncertainty and perhaps division in their own party about the political repercussions of committing themselves to the new system, especially while detention continued, and secondly, uncertainty about me personally. But when even the patient Willie Whitelaw began to tire of their delaying tactics and the Northern Ireland Office to leak stories to the press blaming the SDLP for obstruction they realized that the political repercussions of not participating would be even worse and decided to ignore the extremists in their own ranks.

It had also become clear that Roy Bradford, who was thought to be more sympathetic to the SDLP position than I, was not going to get any support from Unionists to take over as Leader, and so the SDLP agreed to do business with me. Because I had been the Prime Minister responsible for internment I had personally suffered uniquely from the bitter opposition to that measure, and some of that feeling remained. There were thus real problems for the SDLP which I recognized; we both had to deliver significant electoral support for whatever agreement was reached. But I think it is true to say that, just as I learned to respect the integrity and ability of the SDLP leaders over the next few months, they developed a respect for me.

We all entered the talks under the chairmanship of Whitelaw with some hope but also considerable hesitation. So much still seemed to divide us and our supporters, and the bitter memories were no longer deep in history but in the recent past. To many Unionists the SDLP were the party whose leaders had started off the violence with irresponsible demonstrations on the streets, who had criticized and undermined the security forces ever since, and who had encouraged their supporters to opt out of the system by a rent and rates strike which largely continued. There was still some doubt as to their attitude on the very right of the State to exist. These matters all had to be clarified if there was to be any prospect of reaching agreement on an Executive.

After some discussion before the talks, the Unionist Assemblymen had agreed on certain conditions for sharing power in a coalition Executive with the SDLP: the discussions could only begin after a clear commitment by all concerned to the Constitution Act and in particular to Section 2 of that Act which guaranteed the right of self-determination to the people of Northern Ireland voting in a Border Poll; the SDLP would have to call off the rent and rates strike, and give firm general backing to the security forces—including the RUC; there would have to be a Unionist majority on the Executive to reflect the overwhelming unionist sentiments of the electorate; and any Council of Ireland set up in conjunction with the Government of the Republic would have to contain safeguards and limitations which would make it clear that it was not designed to lead to the absorption of Northern Ireland in an all-Ireland Republic. These things seemed a minimum for any reasonable basis for a coalition Executive with any party.

We were very conscious of the serious step we were taking in entering the talks. As we walked up the steps of Stormont Castle on the first day Basil MacIvor said, 'Someone has to do what we are doing. But it could be the end of a political career for all of us.'

Willie Whitelaw was, as always, very careful about protocol. He invited each of the two main parties, the SDLP and the Unionists, to bring a deputation of six to the talks, and the smaller Alliance Party to bring three. Our positions around the long mahogany table were carefully arranged. Whitelaw sat at the top, flanked on the one side by his senior civil servant, Frank Cooper, who was obviously an important influence on government thinking, and on the other by his Ministers, David Howell and William Van Straubenzee, neither of whom intervened much in the discussions as a matter of policy, though Howell played a useful role as chairman of the social and economic affairs sub-committee. Our deputation sat along the table on Whitelaw's right, the SDLP sat opposite us, and the Alliance Party occupied the other end of the table. The SDLP deputation led by Gerry Fitt consisted of John Hume, a formidable political thinker with great personal integrity but a sometimes exasperating dogmatism; Austin Currie, an able and conciliatory young man; the refreshingly unpredictable Paddy Devlin; Eddie McGrady, an old friend and political opponent of mine from South Down; and Ivan Cooper, dubbed by the press 'the token Protestant'. I tried to bring some new talent into my deputation, which, in addition to the experienced Herbie Kirk, Roy Bradford and Basil McIvor, included new boys Leslie Morell, from County Londonderry and John Baxter from North Antrim, both of whom made an important contribution to our efforts. The Alliance Party deputation consisted of Oliver Napier, their outspoken and very fair-minded leader, Robert Cooper, his deputy, and Basil Glass, the Alliance Chief Whip.

At first the talks were tense, with everyone very sensitive about their position and prickly about the attitude of other parties. But we rapidly became convinced of the seriousness of each other's intentions to secure, within the political limitations upon us, an agreement which could provide hope for the Province. In the achievement of this understanding the sensitive and skilful handling of the talks by the Chairman, Willie Whitelaw, played an important part. On several occasions when it looked as if deadlock had been reached on some issue he would move the discussions on to another and then find a formula which allowed talks to restart on the controversial issue later. He opened our first meeting by reading from a statement outlining the basis on which the talks were being held. Forming an Executive by itself could not solve all Northern Ireland's problems, he said:

> But I am convinced that the great majority of people wish to see their elected representatives managing, in large measure, their own affairs. The forces of violence can only be defeated if those who believe in democratic processes stand together ... The Constitution Act is the only basis on which we can all move forward. We must all accept that the Constitution Act is the law and that an Executive must conscientiously fulfil its duties under it in the interests of Northern Ireland and its people.

The three party leaders then spoke and each of them committed themselves to the Constitution Act without any reservations. 'We accept the

Oath,' said Gerry Fitt, and Austin Currie added later, 'We are agreed on Section 2 of the Act.' As far as I was concerned that marked the formal end of the 'united Ireland or nothing' party and my willingness to continue talks with the SDLP rested on the belief that they made this commitment in good faith. Controversy arose, however, over the working of the Standing Orders Committee when Gerry Fitt brought them into the discussion and criticized the attitude which Jim Stronge and Herbie Kirk, our two representatives on the Committee, were adopting. It was controversial and unnecessary, he said, to include a prayer for the Queen, and we should accept the majority report which omitted it. 'If the Report is not accepted there will be no Executive,' Paddy Devlin added ominously. I pointed out that we had to make a clear assertion of our attachment to the Crown, as the loyalists were already trying to dub us 'republican-unionists'. Whitelaw smoothed over the argument, pointing out that disagreement on the Standing Orders need not prejudice the setting up of an Executive, and we agreed to differ. We then discussed how the talks should proceed and sought to define the issues of disagreement. Our party was much heartened when Gerry Fitt volunteered the view that the rent and rates strike would have to be ended. Paddy Devlin intervened again: 'It would be incongruous for me to hold the Office of Chief Executive and at the same time be on rent strike!' he said. One possible obstacle to agreement had been quickly removed.

When we ended our discussions around 4 p.m. that Friday our hopes had been a little strengthened. We had defined major areas of disagreement, but the willingness of everyone to spend time trying to resolve them was plain. We were to meet the Secretary of State separately the following Monday to discuss them further, with formal inter-party talks again the following day. We agreed to maintain strict confidentiality for the duration of the talks. We had also set up a sub-committee to prepare a social and economic programme for a potential Executive, as a brief summary of the views of our three parties seemed to indicate no major problems in the way of agreement. To people in other societies this may seem ironic, but in Northern Ireland it seemed quite natural that this should be so, and that it was issues of allegiance and inter-communal confidence which divided us. In fact our optimism on this point almost turned out to be misplaced.

Policing, detention and the Council of Ireland rapidly emerged as the three points of controversy and on these much of our discussion over the following weeks centred. The Assembly would not initially have any policing or security powers devolved to it but the problem of violence and security tactics was so central to the crisis in our province that we felt a coalition Executive which lacked a generally agreed approach on these subjects would not be able to command any credibility. We have already seen how the break-down of the RUC in early 1969 was followed by the Hunt Report and sweeping reforms intended to restore Catholic confidence in the police, and how the initially favourable impact of these changes in the Catholic community was lost in the upsurge of IRA terrorism and the recriminations over the security tactics with which the Government responded. Attempts to move the RUC back into the former 'No Go' areas gradually had resulted in the killing and attempted killing of several officers, and the Army had become established as the only effective representative of authority there. RUC patrols, although rearmed for their own protection, operated in some parts of the Province only with an Army escort.

The SDLP had been fiercely critical of the RUC and the Army over the previous three years and had refused to assist in restoring regular policing. If we were now to make a fresh start and if the SDLP were to make the transition from unconstitutional political opposition to partners in a coalition of reconstruction they would have to be seen to support those whose task it was to uphold the law under the new system. They had an important role to play in securing more support in their community for the police and improving Catholic recruitment, which was now at an all-time low due to IRA intimidation. This was in spite of the fact that the Chief Constable of the RUC was a Catholic (indeed, the head of the Special Branch until quite recently had also been a Catholic). If the Executive was to have any relevance to the ending of violence, the central concern of us all, it would have to be in terms of an open commitment from leaders of the Catholic community to co-operate with and assist the security forces in every way possible.

Detention was for the SDLP the major obstacle to making this commitment. They had become firmly impaled on a political hook by making opposition to detention and demands for its end their central political theme for over two years, and they were now anxious to avoid accusations from their own hard-liners of having 'sold out'. But we were convinced that detention was an essential weapon against the terrorists, the attempted abandonment of which in 1972 had already provided disastrous.

Arrangements for a Council of Ireland were, at least partially, within the powers of the proposed Executive, though the international responsibilities of the Westminster Government demanded that they play an important part. We had always recognized the importance of our relationship with the Irish Republic, and this aspect had been increasingly borne in upon us by the effect of the Dublin Government's actions on our violent situation over the last few years. The detailed proposals for an inter-governmental Council of Ireland put to Ted Heath before direct rule had been reiterated in our blueprint for the Darlington Conference. The idea of a Council of Ireland, in the recent history of Northern Ireland at least, was therefore Unionist originated. This is not really surprising, as it was Northern Ireland which was suffering and had suffered from political aggression and terrorist incursions, and it was in our interests to secure the co-operation of the Dublin Government against the IRA if we were to succeed in defeating them. The absence of this co-operation in the early years of the campaign had been a major factor in the terrorist's success. It was also important for our domestic political stability, as the process of achieving consensus and co-operation from the minority within Northern Ireland would inevitably be much easier to achieve if the institutions of government were accepted as fair throughout Ireland.

But in spite of the obvious advantages of such a deal for Northern Ireland some of the loyalists had been becoming increasingly unenthusiastic about the whole idea in recent months. Bill Craig, in appending his signature to our Darlington proposals, had in fact approved the Council of Ireland idea, and the Unionist Council had supported it too. But 'loyalist' candidates during the Assembly elections had attacked any Council of Ireland, arguing that it would only lead to a united Ireland, and an Orange Order statement had urged support only for those candidates opposed to it. These pronouncements were a reaction to the fact that the SDLP and the Dublin Government had been increasingly taking over the Council of Ireland idea and building it up into a grand design for the whole of Ireland on the European model in order to express Nationalist aspirations. We saw it as the only vehicle through which we could secure progress on the important matters of recognition and security, but we would obviously have to approach the idea cautiously if the loyalists were not to capitalize on the fears which statements emanating from Dublin were creating among Unionists.

On none of these subjects did any easy or immediate solution present itself. We talked our way through them during October and November in Stormont Castle, learning increasingly to understand each other's point of view and trying to find new solutions which would benefit us all. We were conscious all the time of an historic responsibility; no one had succeeded in establishing generally accepted institutions throughout Ireland and the result had been violence in each generation. We were determined to end that. The Constitution Act, supported as it was by all the parties at Westminster and approved by the Dublin Government, offered the prospect of a new relationship between all the people of these islands, British and Irish. It was this feeling of responsibility and this vision which kept us talking when all routes seemed already blocked.

On Tuesday we met again in full session as planned. The Social and Economic sub-committee had met the previous day under the chairmanship of David Howell and drafted an outline programme. Roy Bradford, who was one of our two representatives on the sub-committee, had been caught on the hop when the SDLP, with typical efficiency, produced an already prepared programme covering a wide range of policies, and he had been forced to agree to use it as the basis for discussion. We had in fact included a comprehensive statement on industry, agriculture, education, transport, etc. in our election manifesto which our research department had prepared after a great deal of work, and so there was no need for us to be caught out like this if Roy had done his homework. But on this as on some other occasions he relied too much on his verbal skill and general manœuvrability and too little on hard work. The draft was agreed as a basis, and the sub-committee was instructed to meet again to consider amendments.

Then came the discussion which Willie Whitelaw was clearly worried about—policing. All the parties had already explained their views to him, though not yet to each other, and he was all too aware of the gap which divided us. He emphasized that under the Act this was the responsibility of Westminster and not the Executive and proposed that he should draw up a paper stating government policy on the police, which we might all then be able to support. I said that as far as we were concerned the RUC provided the police force of Northern Ireland and we could not even proceed with discussions unless that basis was accepted. There had been rumours that the SDLP wanted a completely new police force with a new name, or two different police forces, and it had to be clear from the start that we were not prepared even to start moving down that road. The RUC had already been booted around too much as a political football and we did not see that they could be shuffled around again for some spurious political reason. If it was accepted that the RUC was and would remain our police force, I said, we were quite willing to discuss details which might help to restore normal policing.

But the SDLP, and John Hume in particular, were insistent that we must discuss this issue in full and without pre-conditions. 'We in the Catholic community need policing more than anyone,' said Hume, 'but identification with the police by the community is the key to effective policing, and we need to create this identification.' He went on to argue that the Council of Ireland should control both the Northern Ireland Police Authority and a Police Authority in the Republic, since the problems of security north and south of the border were essentially the same. He saw the Council of Ireland being associated with a court which would deal with terrorists from both jurisdictions.

'I think these proposals are totally impracticable,' I said.

'But getting Catholics to identify with the police is the only way to restore policing,' Austin Currie said. 'We want Paddy Devlin and John Hume to be able to say, "This is our police force".'

'You can say that now,' I pointed out.

Whitelaw then intervened to avoid what was beginning to look like a deadlock, emphasizing that policing was the responsibility of HMG at Westminster. He suggested that he should prepare a paper for the next meeting outlining the government position on the RUC, taking account of the points made, and this could then be discussed and provide a basis for agreement. We decided to meet again the following Tuesday after the second meeting of the Assembly with policing and the Council of Ireland on the agenda. I felt the need to emphasize yet again our position lest there should be leaks that we were discussing fundamental changes in the RUC.

'There can be no discussion on policing outside the framework that the RUC is the police force of Northern Ireland,' I said.

Whitelaw added with good humour, 'We will discuss next Tuesday whether we can discuss the police.'

A press statement was agreed saying that 'satisfactory progress' was being made in clarifying the party attitudes.

At the next meeting Whitelaw produced a draft paper expressing government policy on the problems of law and order. It restated that the Secretary of State would remain accountable to Parliament for all security, but the Assembly would have an advisory role. The Government's objectives were to end all politically motivated violence, to restore effective policing to all parts of the Province so that the Army could be progressively withdrawn from its existing role, and to bring about public support for and identification with the police. The RUC would continue to provide the police force of Northern Ireland, much had already been done to reorganize them, and further constructive suggestions would be welcomed. It was proposed to reconstitute the Police Authority to introduce a minority of elected representatives from the Assembly, and an independent complaints system would be drawn up. The Government of the Republic had a significant contribution to make to the ending of politically motivated violence, and this could be discussed at a tripartite conference, though normal policing would remain the responsibility of the respective governments.

I was quite happy with this as it expressed views similar to ours. The only problem concerned the role which a Council of Ireland might play, which was still vague. What contribution was the tripartite conference expected to make to the resolution of our policing problems, I asked. We accepted the importance of co-operation with the security forces of the Republic against violence, and the need for a common law enforcement area or extradition, but the problem was how to formalize this co-operation. We could not accept that the Republic had any role to play in the internal policing of Northern Ireland. I also argued that control of the police in Northern Ireland should be devolved to the Executive, as this might in fact help to provide widespread acceptance of the R U C if the Executive contained S D L P members. But, I added, we must remember that the R U C were acceptable throughout nearly all of Northern Ireland and we could not base our entire policy on a few problem areas.

John Hume took a tough line. He agreed with the proposal for Assembly members on the Authority, as we had tended in the past to appoint non-aligned individuals who gave confidence to nobody. It was better to have people who fought their corner. But, he said, the statement approving the R U C did not meet the problems of the situation. He understood our position, and we all needed the police, but he could not see how the name and uniform of the R U C could be accepted and defended in certain areas. We had to find a way of ending the violence if any settlement was not to be upset, and this involved finding the means of achieving acceptance of some form of policing. He agreed that there were many fine men in the R U C, but there were some who had disgraced the uniform and must be weeded out. The attitude of the Dublin Government was most important, and the problem of fugitive offenders must be dealt with, but he could not see how we could ask a government to accept responsibility for offences in another jurisdiction without some kind of authority.

Roy Bradford then came in with a constructive contribution. There was general agreement that Ireland had an integral security problem, he said, the issue was how to formalize co-operation. Clearly the Council of Ireland was appropriate, but could this not be achieved by a joint consultative committee on security rather than by setting up a mechanism of joint government control of policing?

Austin Currie matched this with a conciliatory contribution. He thought it might be a good idea for policing to be devolved, as there was a danger of the Executive having responsibility without authority (it was the first time a member of the SDLP had expressed this view in my hearing). He referred to Bradford's proposal for consultative machinery and said a development of this could lead to 'fruitful discussion'.

But it was clear that the SDLP were not ready to give firm backing to the paper, although Whitelaw pointed out that we were known to be discussing policing and some statement from him would soon be required about government intentions, and the sooner the better in view of the speculation. He needed general assent to his statement. We agreed to discuss further with our parties and meet again to consider a revised paper from the Secretary of State.

John Hume then raised the thorny problem of detention. We must make progress towards bringing it to an end, he said. I said this was not a question of politics; people should only be held if they were a security risk, and released when they ceased to be so. Whitelaw added that the safety of the community must come first, and ending violence was the first priority. 'Do we not accept that something must be done about the ending of detention to help establish the Executive?' asked Ivan Cooper. 'We would agree to a formula.' I said this was no problem if it was related to the ending of violence.

We moved on to discuss the Northern Ireland Civil Service. John Hume said there was a serious imbalance in the civil service, particularly in senior posts and in strategic areas such as the Northern Ireland Office, Home Affairs and Finance, where there were few Catholics. I rejected the idea that there had been any religious discrimination in promotions, but agreed that there was not a balance in senior posts largely due to the fact that fifteen to thirty years earlier few Catholics had been joining. Change would take time, but it would come. Hume said that he accepted this, and knew there were real pressures on Catholic civil servants in some areas such as Home Affairs, but we should speed up the process of change by a deliberate policy. Whitelaw intervened to say that merit could not be set aside, as efficiency was the criterion for a good civil service.

Three days later we met again and Whitelaw produced his revised draft on policing. We suggested some minor amendments. But John Hume said that the total commitment to the RUC was not acceptable to the SDLP without knowledge of the final package agreement, including the tripartite discussions. The paper should be published by the Secretary of State on his own responsibility with a statement that the parties had agreed to consider it. Mr Whitelaw was displeased with this, and urged the SDLP to think again. They did not have to agree entirely with the statement, but general approval would be helpful. But the SDLP were adamant that they would have to take the statement back to their party. The important thing was that they would not express any dissent from the Secretary of State's published proposals, they said. It was agreed that the statement should be issued and we would consider the subject again later.

Hume then proposed that we should sign the draft social and economic policy, but Bradford emphatically rejected this and said we needed time to consult our parties. The SDLP complained a little but this was eventually agreed. At our next meeting, however, on Monday 28 October, a blazing row broke out on the policy. Bradford's handling of the matter was bitterly criticized by the SDLP and I learned that at the sub-committee meeting held in the intervening week Bradford and Devlin had been standing on their feet shouting at each other, thumping the table and exchanging insults. I never quite gauged the real depths of feeling involved, for both men were political animals with a keen sense of the dramatic, but it seemed unnecessary to place further obstacles in the way of agreement. It appeared that Bradford had produced a list of proposed amendments to the document and the SDLP, who had thought it essentially agreed and requiring only the formality of signatures, felt some pique at having their ideas amended at the last minute. The Alliance Party backed up the SDLP saying they had already obtained party signatures to the agreed final document. Paddy Devlin intervened in typically dramatic fashion: 'You can't have a totally Unionist document. You are pushing our generosity to the limit,' he said. 'This is going to end here. We are not accepting your amendments.' We were getting nowhere fast and I tried to cool things. The seeds of the dispute became evident when Bradford said that it was very difficult to produce a 'revolutionary document welding two different philosophies'. Roy, with his trendy middle-class tendencies, had seen himself as the defender of the citadels of capitalism against the 'socialist' onslaught of the SDLP, an unrealistic pose in a non-existent conflict between two parties with differences of emphasis only. After more argument we agreed to consider the amendments at a later meeting. Gerry Fitt approached me after the meeting urging me to take over the handling of the document for our party if any progress was to be made, and I agreed to do so. It was quite a dramatic change from Bradford's 'special relationship' with the SDLP a few months earlier. A week later we agreed on a final draft, including our proposals on industrial development, growth centres, and the important concession from the SDLP that they recognized the principle of priority in employment for Northern Ireland people.

It took three more weeks of tough bargaining before we reached agreement on the basis for an Executive. The SDLP were still worried about detention, and argument ranged over whether or not this was tied up with politics or was entirely a security matter. The SDLP stressed the emotional effect on Catholics and the feeling that it was unfairly directed against them. They accepted that phased releases might be better than a sudden release of all detainees, but said the establishment of the Executive should coincide with a substantial release of detainees to give it a boost in Catholic eyes. I contended that this was not a political issue, but if it was safe to let out any of these men they should be released immediately. Peace was more important than the formation of an Executive, I said. Whitelaw agreed to consider our views but said that detention, like policing, was a matter for the Secretary of State and the Westminster Government.

On 31 October we first discussed the Council of Ireland. We were all well aware that this was another potential area of breakdown. When we started at 6 p.m. I decided to lay down our position clearly. The Council of Ireland would be an inter-governmental body dealing only with social and economic matters, I said. Recognition of the right of the people of Northern Ireland to order their own affairs was an essential prerequisite. If the Council could help to deal with terrorism by providing the formal machinery of co-operation that would be excellent, but the structure must be functional and not some great bureaucratic network. Gerry Fitt said that there was much scope for harmonization between North and South and the tripartite conference was the best place to discuss all these matters. 'Everything must be agreed before the Executive is formed,' said Hume. I pointed out that we were committed to the view that the Executive must be formed first, so that the Northern Ireland delegates at the tripartite conference would speak with a united voice. 'If the Executive is in embryo form we would have to invite all parties to the conference,' pointed out Whitelaw. Austin Currie was fiercely against this. Only people prepared to work the Constitution should go to the conference he said. We all agreed to prepare position papers on the Council of Ireland and circulate them before our next meeting.

These papers revealed very clearly the different conceptions of a Council of Ireland held by the three parties. The SDLP wanted a powerful two-tier Council with both inter-governmental and inter-parliamen-

tary tiers, a powerful permanent secretariat modelled on the European
Commission, and an all-Ireland Court interpreting 'Orders' and 'Laws'
made by the Council and with human rights functions. They wanted the
Council to have exclusive executive functions in certain fields, as well
as harmonizing and advisory roles, and with 'a major role in the control
of the Police in both parts of Ireland'. It was also envisaged as having
its own independent sources of finance. The Alliance Party's proposals did not go as far as this, though they went further than we were
prepared to go on some issues. They accepted the idea of a two-tier
body, with a powerful secretariat and executive functions, and independent sources of finance, but they included the important proviso that
all decisions of the Council should have to be unanimous. Our document gave three reasons for supporting the idea of a Council: all the
people of Ireland had a common interest in the achievement and main-
tenance of peace and therefore in arrangements whereby no part of the
British Isles could provide a haven for terrorists; there was a need for the
co-ordination of Government activities on many social and economic
matters, given our geographical situation; and there was a need to pro-
mote mutual understanding and tolerance of the different Irish traditions. We proposed a single-tier inter-governmental Council operating
on the basis of unanimous decisions to provide a forum for the discussion of these matters which the respective governments would then be
separately responsible for implementing.

On Monday 5 November we discussed these proposals. I knew we
would have to make some concessions if any progress was to be made,
and thought we could possibly do this on the second tier by proposing
an alternative inter-parliamentary forum. John Hume began by stressing that the Council proposed by the SDLP was modelled on the EEC
and, like the Community, would have built into it the capacity and the
intention of evolving into something increasingly powerful. It should
also have its own taxes, such as a percentage of VAT or the GNP of
both States. I said we were all agreed on the need for an inter-governmental tier, but the second tier was unnecessary and would only be a
mischievous talking shop. After pressure from both Alliance and
SDLP on this point I suggested that an inter-parliamentary Association of the Dail and the Assembly could serve equally well to provide
contact between politicians North and South. But everyone else, including the Secretary of State, clearly was wedded to the idea of a second
tier, and Oliver Napier argued that it could help to involve people like
Paisley and Craig, so I agreed to consider it. But I added that the essential thing was for the Council to be seen to have a practical role; if it

was seen as purely political it would not be politically saleable. It was not and could not be an all-Ireland Parliament, as the SDLP seemed to envisage it becoming, and any powers it had could only be delegated by the respective governments. It was agreed that the position of the Unionists, as a potential minority in the Council, would be safeguarded either by the unanimity principle or by the Northern Ireland Executive always adopting a collective approach. We agreed to have further discussions with our parties and to look again at this subject.

Next day we moved on to the nuts and bolts of Executive government—how departments should be organized, and which departments should be held by which members of the coalition. This problem was to absorb us for the remainder of our meetings. The political issue at stake was a simple one but, for us, crucial to the success of the whole exercise. We had always said that there must be a Unionist majority on any Executive if it was to have any credibility with the community at large, but the defection of ten members of our party to the loyalist coalition very seriously weakened our argument. It left us with only twenty-one Assembly Members, still the largest party, but with only two members more than the SDLP and with less members than the SDLP and Alliance Parties combined. I had to argue that, irrespective of the precise number of representatives each of the negotiating parties had, the overwhelming majority of the population of Northern Ireland was committed to the Union and would have no confidence in an Executive which did not have a Unionist majority. I also argued that in a sense I was representing those who had voted for Unionists who had now opted out.

We made fair progress at first on the question of how departments should be organized to provide for the maximum of twelve Executive members laid down in the Constitution Act. We worked from a paper prepared for us by Ken Bloomfield, who had been one of Whitelaw's senior advisers from the Northern Ireland Civil Service since direct rule. It outlined the existing departmental structure, the possible alternatives, and the administrative problems which would have to be borne in mind. Under the Stormont Cabinet we had nine departments: the Prime Minister's department, Finance, Home Affairs, Education, Health and Social Services, Agriculture, Commerce, Development, and Community Relations. At the time of direct rule I was running Home Affairs as well as the Prime Minister's Department, but we had four Ministers of State who, together with the Leader of the Senate, made up a total Cabinet membership of fourteen. But since all twelve members of the Executive, apart from the Chief Executive and his

Deputy, were envisaged as having equal Ministerial status, we were in effect short of posts under the existing administrative structure. All the major functions of Home Affairs—police, administration of justice, treatment of offenders—had been reserved to Westminster under the Constitution Act and the remaining functions of child care, fire services and road safety did not leave it a viable separate department. We needed three new departments, and had to decide on the most practical redistribution of functions.

Ken Bloomfield's paper was, quite rightly, concerned to point out the dangers of administrative disruption which could be caused by too much hacking around of functions for political convenience, but made it clear that there were three departments which lent themselves most naturally to re-organization—Finance, Development, and Health and Social Services. Health and Social Services had a natural break between Labour Affairs and Social Services; Finance could retain its Treasury-type function but the Civil Service and Works Division could be hived off and combined with legal services to form a Central Services Department; but in Development there was no obvious break although it now constituted one of the largest departments.

We found easy agreement that none of the 'single-subject' departments should be split up, and that Health and Social Services should be divided into departments of Manpower and Health and Social Services. We also agreed that the Ministry of Community Relations should be strengthened by taking over the functions of the Community Relations Commission, with which it had never developed an effective working relationship. The problem then was what to do with Development and Finance and whether it was desirable or practicable to create a new department. After much discussion we seemed to be moving towards an agreed structure. 'Right,' said Paddy Devlin. 'Now let's decide who gets what.' Whitelaw intervened to point out that we had already held a long meeting and should not move on to the 'numbers' argument without some preparation. The minutes of our discussion should be passed on to civil service heads of departments for comments as this subject vitally concerned them and we must ensure adequate consultation. Quite a few senior civil servants were in fact present at this particular session of the talks, and Willie no doubt felt that a smaller audience was more appropriate to the sometimes bloody business of political bargaining. He proposed we discuss a final draft on the Council of Ireland at our next meeting, and if we survived that 'cruncher' we could then discuss Executive numbers. 'Numbers are a crunch issue too.' muttered Paddy Devlin darkly.

One week later we met at the Castle again. It was a day of serious violence in the Province and before we met there had been nine explosions in Belfast including one at the SDLP headquarters. They were all directed against Catholic property and clearly the work of Protestant extremists who believed that by raising community tension they would destroy the talks and the prospects of a coalition government involving the SDLP. Willie Whitelaw told us he was announcing the proscription of the so-called 'Ulster Freedom Fighters' and the 'Red Hand Commandos' which had frequently accepted responsibility for acts of violence and we all agreed that we would not be deterred from the search for compromise by these activities. In a sense they made us more determined.

It was not, however, our most successful day of talks; more than once it seemed we had reached complete deadlock. On the Council of Ireland there was still no agreement on the question of a second tier and on the basis for holding a tripartite conference. We argued that it could only take place after the formation of an Executive so that the Ulster delegates would go with a common approach and the formation of the Executive would not be seen to be dependent on the approval of the Dublin Government. John Hume and Oliver Napier were insistent that the second tier Assembly would strengthen the Council from a loyalist point of view, as it would provide the loyalists with an opportunity to air their views and to scrutinize the activities of the Council of Ministers and would prevent allegations of operating behind closed doors. I was doubtful about this and warned that in proposing North–South cooperation we were dealing with a tender plant which should not be expected to grow too fast. There was constant reference to European parallels, especially by Whitelaw, who suggested we look at the Western European Union and circulated a paper outlining how it was organized. I always thought these parallels unrealistic both because we were dealing only with relationships between two states, the United Kingdom and the Irish Republic, and because of the long-standing hostility between Northern Ireland and the Republic which had only recently diminished. But I was aiming for the supreme prize of co-operation against terrorism based on an agreed *status quo* in Ireland and to achieve it I was prepared to go along with a limited amount of nonsense from the Nationalists. We left the subject of the Council of Ireland at this meeting without making any progress towards agreement, but with our side admitting there might be some merit in the arguments for a second tier and agreeing to reconsider.

Then began the numbers game. I restated our absolute commitment to a Unionist majority on the Executive. Gerry Fitt countered by saying I had only nineteen supporters—with some truth, as two of them, Whitten and Stronge from Armagh, wanted the talks only as a whitewashing exercise and were not prepared to accept the SDLP in government under any circumstances—and described me as 'the weakest man at this table'. Oliver Napier said Executive membership must be proportional to our party strengths.

'It is in the Act that this Executive must be "widely accepted"—in fact that is the purpose of the new Constitution,' I said. 'It cannot be widely accepted without a Unionist majority.'

'You want the Chief Executive to be a Unionist and to have a Unionist majority as well,' said Hume. 'You are not entitled to this.'

'Any seats at all in government is an advance for Alliance and the SDLP,' I pointed out.

'We will only accept 5 Unionists, 5 SDLP and 2 Alliance,' said Gerry Fitt.

'Agreed,' said Oliver Napier.

'Seven Unionists or nothing,' I said.

'Is that your last word?'

'No,' said Whitelaw. 'We need to review the position on this. I will hold talks with the leaders.' Once again complete breakdown had been averted.

During the following week Whitelaw met all the parties separately to try to get some movement. He clearly understood my insistence on this point and accepted the need for a Unionist majority, but he was not finding the SDLP or Alliance very easy to budge. He was increasingly anxious to see the talks brought to a successful conclusion, partly because of the scope for press speculation which their protracted nature was providing, and partly because his apparent success as a conciliator in Northern Ireland was leading to demands at Westminster that he be brought back to help deal with the industrial relations problems which the Heath Government was now facing. But with a maximum of twelve Executive places fixed by law, with the politically virginal Alliance Party proving less the unambitious honest broker than might have been expected, and with the SDLP insisting on at least five Executive places, all his ingenuity was being taxed in seeking to devise an acceptable compromise.

On Monday 19 November we met at 3.30 p.m. for what was widely heralded as our final and make-or-break session. The meeting was scheduled for noon but was postponed to allow last-minute private talks between Whitelaw and the SDLP and Alliance Party. Whitelaw opened by introducing a paper he had circulated outlining a draft agreement on all the major issues, including an 11-member Executive consisting of 6 Unionists, 4 SDLP and 1 Alliance member, with a non-Executive post each for Alliance and SDLP. He stressed the urgency of bringing our talks to a conclusion and warned that further delay could only help the men of violence. But Alliance and the SDLP were not at all happy. Oliver Napier regretted the production of the document and said it should be ignored. Gerry Fitt said that six weeks was not a very long time to take to try and overcome the problems of decades, and referred to speculation that Whitelaw was going to be moved back to Westminster soon, saying that the problems of industry in Britain had not caused 900 deaths and the services of the Secretary of State were still needed in Northern Ireland. A 6:4:1 Executive was an insult to the SDLP he said; it must be 5:5:2 as proportionate support would dictate.

Whitelaw said that if he fell down dead another Secretary of State would have to take on the job, and the important thing was to fill the political vacuum in Northern Ireland. An Executive would not command widespread support in Northern Ireland as required by the Constitution Act unless it had a Unionist majority, and this was simply a fact of life which we had to recognize. John Hume said that we (the Unionists) had got an Assembly like Stormont, a Unionist Presiding Officer, I was going to be Chief Executive, and now we were demanding an Executive majority as well. 'The basis of these talks is acceptance of the Constitution Act,' he said. 'So the criterion is how many Unionists accept the Act, not how many were elected to the Assembly.' Paddy Devlin asked if Willie Whitelaw was saying that an Executive of 5:5:2 would not be acceptable under Section 2 of the Act (which provided that the Secretary of State could only appoint an Executive which 'having regard to the support it commands in the Assembly and to the electorate on which that support is based, is likely to be widely accepted throughout the community'). Whitelaw said that was exactly what he was saying.

There seemed nothing more to be said if Alliance and the SDLP would not move, and our talks were on the verge of collapse. A fifteen-minute adjournment was agreed to give us time to consider, and it was some time before we reconvened. None of us wanted a breakdown on this point. We had learned to recognize each other's problems, and we were determined that if there was any acceptable solution it should be found. We decided to adjourn until Wednesday and try again. Whitelaw stressed the need to maintain the utmost secrecy about our talks in the meantime. The document was not agreed, he said, though he recognized that I would probably restate in public at a meeting of the Ulster Unionist Council which I had the next day the Unionist position that we must have a majority on the Executive. I said I would, but there was no question of claiming that this had been agreed.

The Unionist Council meeting that Tuesday brought home to me again the many anomalies of our party organization. My opponents, led now by John Taylor, had been busy in the constituencies sowing fear and despondency about the talks and the dangers of a 'sell-out' to the SDLP and were hopeful of defeating my policy. Once again at a crucial stage in the politics of Northern Ireland they were able to make progress difficult by calling a meeting of the governing body of the party to try to undermine the credibility of the party's elected representatives. While we were working very hard trying to thrash out a political solution they were busily trying to weaken an already difficult negotiating position. How much stronger and more effective our position could have been if they had given us support. It did not seem to me honest that they should undermine our position and at the same time attack the agreements reached on the grounds that they were not satisfactory from the Unionist point of view. My exasperation was given further point when we realized that Taylor and his colleagues had ensured a full turn-out of the Orange delegates to the Council and that many of these were not members of our party at all, some of them even being members of other parties. The Unionist Council was rapidly coming to seem an irrelevant and out-dated body for organizing Unionist opinion in the Province. However, we scraped through by a majority of 10 votes out of the 700-odd delegates attending and were able to return to the talks claiming a mandate for our position.

We met again at the Castle at 10 a.m. on Wednesday for what was to prove the final long session of talks. Whitelaw had redrafted his paper slightly to take account of various points and we now had in front of us a draft agreement on the Council of Ireland, detention, policing, the social and economic programme, and procedure for appointing the Executive. It proposed a Council of Ireland confined to representatives of North and Southern Ireland but with arrangements to protect Her Majesty's Government's interests on reserved matters, consisting of a Council of Ministers operating on the unanimity principle and having executive and harmonization functions and a permanent secretariat, and a second tier inter-parliamentary consultative Assembly. The Council, said the paper, could play a useful role in certain reserved matters, particularly the problem of fugitive offenders and the law and order field, though how this would be done would have to be discussed between the three governments concerned. It was proposed that this discussion would take place at a preliminary tripartite conference held once agreement had been reached on the appointment of the Executive. If agreement was reached there would then be the formal appointment of the Executive followed by a formal Tripartite Conference to ratify the Council of Ireland agreements.

There were several important matters here, particularly the second tier, the 'law and order' role of the Council, the 'executive and harmonizing' functions, and the procedure concerning the formation of the Executive. We were prepared to accept, though with some misgivings, that the second tier could, as everyone else seemed to think, provide for participation by dissident loyalist elements. I queried what law and order role the Council could have, stressing that we were anxious to see it assisting in improving co-operation between the Gardai and the RUC and producing agreement on extradition of terrorists, but that there could be no question of any kind of dual national control of the police through the Council. Whitelaw agreed. 'That is our view as well,' he said. We accepted that the Council could have some executive functions in minor social and economic matters where this was in our common interest, seeing no real danger in this in view of the unanimity rule—a decision we were later to regret. The announcement of an Executive Designate, but not its formal appointment before the Tripartite Conference, seemed the only possible compromise between the SDLP position that 'until everything is agreed nothing is agreed', and our position that the Executive should be appointed first to establish the principle that the Republic was not interfering in the internal affairs of Northern Ireland.

One problem remained; should those invited from Northern Ireland to attend include all political parties in the Assembly, as the White Paper of the previous March had suggested, or should only the parties in the Executive Designate attend? Whitelaw's paper for the previous Monday had proposed to invite all parties, but the one now in front of us had changed it to members of the Executive Designate only. The SDLP and Alliance Parties had fiercely opposed the attendance of Paisley and his wrecking hordes, arguing that the whole purpose of the Conference was to make the new Constitution work and that constructive discussion, or any kind of confidentiality, was unlikely if invitations went out to everyone. I said I thought everyone should be invited, though I doubted if the loyalists would attend in any case. Whitelaw expressed the view that Paisley wanted an invitation only in order to make an issue out of turning it down, a view with which we were all inclined to concur. It was agreed to leave the matter in the hands of the Secretary of State.

On detention Whitelaw had found a position broadly acceptable to all of us. He restated his desire to bring it to an end as soon as the security position permitted, and as an earnest of his intentions he proposed to release a number before Christmas—again if the security situation permitted. He would also consider compassionate cases on a wider basis than hitherto and introduce new measures for the rehabilitation of released detainees. If the political developments created a new atmosphere in the community which led to an improvement in the security situation there could be a progressive phasing out of detention. I confined myself to restating that the security of the community must always take precedence over any political considerations and that we must not be seen to be trying to buy the Executive with releases. Whitelaw agreed and said he envisaged a maximum of 100 releases at Christmas.

After lunch we returned to the numbers controversy. Oliver Napier said Alliance was entitled to two seats and would not accept Mr Whitelaw's line at any price. Hume and Devlin restated their rejection of the 'widespread acceptance' thesis and insistence that posts should be distributed on the basis of a head count of Assembly support. But Whitelaw had come prepared with a few tricks up his sleeve. We could amend the Act, he said, to change the Executive numbers from twelve to whatever number we felt necessary. There could also be flexibility on the numbers holding office outside the Executive, so that within the Executive, where all decisions which came to a vote would be taken, there would be a Unionist majority, but within the Administration as a whole there could be a more even spread of posts. This opened infinite possibilities, and there followed several hours of intense bargaining, numerous adjournments for party discussions, private talks with the Secretary of State, and short plenary sessions. Every conceivable numerical permutation was canvassed, and at 7.10 p.m. agreement was reached that the Act should be amended to provide for a maximum of 11 voting members, of whom 6 would be Unionists, 4 SDLP and 1 Alliance. There would be 4 non-Executive members of the Administration of whom 2 would be SDLP, 1 Unionist and 1 Alliance, the Chief Whip for the Executive being one of these four. It was all over bar the allocation of portfolios.

It is difficult to explain to people not involved in these talks how we felt at that point. We were united as people who had come through an ordeal together, pushed closer together by the attacks made on us from outside by politicians and terrorists who shared the common objective of wishing to see us fail, if not a common rationale for their hopes. The ending of the tension of long hours of negotiation when we all knew we had to fight our corners and when a false step could have either destroyed the talks or destroyed our own political standing with our supporters left us now with a certain optimism and some emotion. Gerry Fitt, always very direct at expressing his feelings, said he felt very emotional. 'Let's wrap it all up,' he said. 'I have decided not to take a Ministry myself so that I can work full-time with Brian as Deputy Chief Executive.'

A list of nine departments was then prepared by Ken Bloomfield, Frank Cooper and David Holden—the Head of the Northern Ireland Civil Service—while we went off to have some overdue nourishment. It took us just an hour to allocate the various departments to the three parties, as it was done in a friendly co-operative atmosphere rather than in terms of negotiation and bargaining. The civil servants had drawn up a list of Executive posts which were: Chief Executive; Deputy Chief Executive; Legal Member and Law Reform; Finance; Commerce; Health and Social Services; Information Services; Housing; Planning and Local Government (formerly part of Development); Environment (the other part of Development); Education; Agriculture. The four offices outside the Executive would be Chief Whip, Community Relations, Manpower and Executive Planning and Co-ordination.

There were obvious candidates in my party for particular posts and I tried to choose them with that in mind. SDLP took Housing, Planning and Local Government, Health and Social Services, Community Relations and Executive Planning and Co-ordination. We took Agriculture, Education, Environment, Information Services and Chief Whip. The only problem was which of the two important posts remaining, Finance and Commerce, should go to the SDLP and which to us. Finance had always been regarded as the senior Ministry, held by the Deputy Premier and controlling the purse-strings and the Civil Service Department. On the other hand I was well aware from my own experience that Commerce offered a publicly active role to an enterprising Minister. But in Herbie Kirk I had an experienced Minister of Finance, the SDLP expressed a preference for Commerce, and so that was the way we divided. It was agreed that the allocation of particular posts within the framework decided was a matter for the respective party leaders and we agreed to prepare lists and submit them to the Secretary of State. I was already satisfied that my negotiating team provided adequate scope for appointments to our six executive posts and later indicated this to Whitelaw.

The meeting ended in great harmony with mutual congratulations all round, especially to the Secretary of State, who was delighted to be able to announce at Westminster the next day the formation of an embryo Executive. There was one sombre reminder of the situation to come, however. Whitelaw said he was assigning armed guards to all members of the delegations immediately.

17
Sunningdale

The Tripartite Conference at Sunningdale was for its supporters the climax of many months of constitution building and patient negotiation. For its opponents it was the nadir of Unionist treachery. It was designed to draw together all the threads of Anglo-Irish relations in a new settlement which would provide a stable basis for the constitutional experiment in Northern Ireland. In the end it was to be the unanswered questions, the loose ends of the threads, that brought about its downfall.

The announcement of the Executive agreement, contrary to persistently hopeful predictions of failure from the loyalist camp, galvanized Paisley and his cohorts into new militancy. Denunciations of an impending 'sell-out' reached a new crescendo and the next meeting of the Assembly had to be adjourned in 'grave disorder' when the loyalists persisted in interrupting a debate on unemployment by chanting in unison 'traitors, traitors, out, out' at my colleagues.

The ordinary citizens of Northern Ireland remained a little confused but hopeful that the agreement marked some progress towards improving their unhappy lot. The British press was delighted and Whitelaw was hailed as a miracle-worker. He was whisked off to London as the new Secretary of State for Employment, where it was hoped he would perform similar feats with the trade unions. He was succeeded by Francis Pym, who started his Ministerial career at a grave disadvantage by being thrown in at the deep end of Ulster politics. He moved into the Northern Ireland Office a matter of days before the holding of the Tripartite Conference, and could not possibly have been expected to master the background to this event in the time available to him, although he made admirable efforts to do so. The removal of Whitelaw was, in my opinion, overhasty and ill-timed and showed an inadequate appreciation of the importance to the whole United Kingdom of the successful conclusion of his efforts in Northern Ireland.

On Wednesday 5 December, the day before the Sunningdale Conference was due to begin, the Assembly met again. All the wrecking tactics we had seen had not prepared us for the viciousness that was to be displayed that day. Paisley made a long verbose speech expounding various fantasies about the Council of Ireland and the Tripartite Conference, where, he alleged, we were going to commit the heinous crime of sitting under the chairmanship of Liam Cosgrave, the Prime Minister of the Republic (which was in any case untrue). He went on to complain that the loyalists had not been invited, but in the middle of his speech an invitation from the Secretary of State to attend the first session was handed to him. He then proceeded to explain why he could not accept the invitation. When business moved on to a renewed debate of the unemployment motion Paisley arose on a spurious point of order, which was clearly a pre-arranged signal for what followed. There was a concerted physical assault on the members of my party by the loyalists. Peter McLachlan was rugger-tackled by Professor Kennedy Lindsay, fell over the bar of the House, and was then kicked in the groin as he lay half-stunned on the floor. Herbie Kirk received a wound on the head which drew blood, and all around the benches members were trading punches and struggling. Basil McIvor was seized by the tie and half-strangled before he hit his attacker so hard he almost knocked him down. Once again, the Assembly was adjourned by the Speaker in 'grave disorder'.

I had taken some relaxation that day on the hunting field to prepare for the gruelling work at Sunningdale and so I heard about these events when I met up with my colleagues at the airport. All three delegations had travelled to the airport together in one bus with a police escort. Some of them had been concerned about the attractive target for terrorists on either side provided by a bus containing the complete Executive Designate. But soon we were winging our way across the Irish Sea. The efficiency that greeted us at Northolt and the elaborate security precautions closing all junctions on our route into the pleasant English countryside at Ascot perked up our spirits a bit, and the SDLP delegation began to entertain us all with rousing songs.

For four days the biggest gathering on record of senior politicians and civil servants from Westminster, the Irish Republic, and Northern Ireland deliberated at the Sunningdale Civil Service College. The whole area was under intense security, patrolled by police with guard dogs and with other police manning road blocks which diverted everyone other than local residents.

The British team was led by Ted Heath, who chaired the Conference, and included Sir Alec Douglas-Home, Francis Pym, David Howell and Peter Rawlinson, the Attorney-General. They were supported by a team of around forty civil servants from numerous government departments, led by the ubiquitous Permanent Secretary, Frank Cooper, who sat beside Heath throughout. From Dublin there were eight Cabinet Ministers led by the Prime Minister, Liam Cosgrave, and including the leader of the Labour Party in the Coalition, Brendan Corish, and the well-known figures of Garret Fitzgerald, Foreign Minister, and Conor Cruse O'Brien. They were supported by a similarly large civil service contingent. This array of back-up machinery highlighted for the twenty-three Northern Ireland representatives, who operated as three separate party groupings, the problems of meeting a government in negotiations on equal terms. This was especially true for the Unionists, as the SDLP could largely rely on the support of the Dublin side, while we found ourselves several times at loggerheads with Ted Heath. Each of the Northern Ireland parties had been invited to augment their usual negotiating team with a few advisers. We had three: Professor Harry Calvert, author of the most authoritative book on the constitutional law of Northern Ireland; Reggie Magee, Chairman of our Backbench Committee; and Sam Butler, our Press Officer.

The Conference proceeded smoothly in its initial stages. We met in Plenary Session in Northcote House at 10.30 a.m. when each of the Leaders made a formal introductory statement. Heath, as the host, welcomed us and stressed the historic nature of our meeting which he hoped would lead to a lasting peace. It could, he said, be both an end and a beginning. The Plenary Session continued until early evening, discussing briefly each of the main areas, identifying where agreement already existed and where further detailed discussion was required in sub-committees. It was quickly clear that most of the decisions on the structure of the Council of Ireland made at the Castle talks were generally acceptable. It was agreed that it should be a North/South institution with arrangements to protect the interests of the United Kingdom Government where these were involved. The fact that it never even occurred to Unionists to argue that it should be tripartite and that we would in fact have regarded that as weighting the whole structure against us may be illogical, but it underlines yet again how important it seemed for our security to have our future relationship with the Republic firmly in our own hands, and how unenthusiastic Westminster was thought to have become about Northern Ireland's position within the United Kingdom. I said we would agree, reluctantly, to a second tier Consultative Assembly, but I insisted that representation on this must be equal from

North and South. The SDLP supported me very strongly, and this was agreed.

We also agreed that there should be a small permanent staff to service the Council, and there was some good-humoured banter about where it should meet. Austin Currie proposed Armagh, which seemed to be the official SDLP line, but Paddy Devlin suggested Ahogill, a small County Antrim village which, because of its name, is drawn into many Ulster jokes. The only real problem area seemed to be on the 'executive and harmonizing' functions of the Council of Ministers. John Hume said he regarded harmonization of laws in North and South as very important, and Garret Fitzgerald pointed out that there was much duplication on each side of the border on matters such as tourism, electricity grids, agriculture, and industrial research which should be eliminated for reasons of economy. I said too much weight should not be given to the term 'harmonization', as we in Northern Ireland had to walk in step with United Kingdom legislation. Nor did I see the Council of Ireland having any independent executive power; everything must be delegated from Belfast and Dublin. Gerry Fitt weighed in to argue that if the Council of Ireland had no independent functions it was merely an exercise in propaganda.

This was in fact very near the truth of the whole structure argument. There seemed to be a lot of mystical nonsense surrounding the SDLP approach to the Council of Ireland, and their constant repetition of the word 'identification', but if this nonsense was necessary to bring their supporters along I did not see why we should be difficult, provided we could ensure that it meant nothing in practice. Thus all our efforts were directed towards ensuring that, however many tiers and secretaries the Council of Ireland might have, it remained essentially propaganda and in no way impinged on the powers of the Northern Ireland Assembly. I felt confident that Unionists, being basically practical people, would judge our final agreement on a practical rather than symbolic level. Later events were to throw considerable doubt on the traditional view that Ulster Unionists were less interested in symbols than their Nationalist fellow-countrymen.

We all agreed that this subject, especially the 'executive and harmonizing' functions, needed detailed discussion in sub-committee. Leslie Morrell and Reggie Magee represented us on this, and Leslie showed his skill at drawing up watertight verbal formulae, much to the chagrin of Garret Fitzgerald. I regarded the issues of recognition of Northern Ireland and co-operation against terrorism throughout the island of Ireland as by far the most important which the conference had to discuss and involved myself primarily in these discussions.

The question of status came up in Plenary Session just before lunch on the first day when Heath asked me to give our views. I took a tough line, attacking the continued existence in the Constitution of the Republic of clauses claiming jurisdiction over our territory. I recognized that a change in the Constitution required a referendum, but we needed a commitment that such a change would be attempted and, most important, a firm declaration recognizing not just the institutions of Northern Ireland, but the right of its people to order their own affairs. Oliver Napier supported me saying that Northern Ireland was part of the United Kingdom and must be recognized as such. Cosgrave said that a reciprocal declaration by the two Sovereign Governments should solve this problem. But when we came back to the subject again later in the afternoon he added the rider that they could not undertake to amend their constitution. I said that a declaration not accompanied even by a commitment to try to change the Constitution was inadequate.

This discussion was continued later by Cosgrave and myself in a subcommittee entrusted with the task of agreeing on the proper form of recognition, and Heath also took part. As a result of our discussions the Dublin Government agreed, after some resistance, to sign a declaration of firm recognition of Northern Ireland which, together with a declaration on self-determination from the British Government, would be registered with the United Nations and therefore would mark a real step forward in North/South relations. I proposed that the two Declarations should be printed side by side—which I was told by the lawyers reinforced the relationship between the Dublin Declaration and the British commitment to self-determination for Northern Ireland—and this was agreed. The Declarations read as follows:

The Irish Government fully accepted and solemnly declared that there could be no change in the status of Northern Ireland until a majority of the people of Northern Ireland desired a change in that status.	The British Government solemnly declared that it was, and would remain, their policy to support the wishes of the majority of the people of Northern Ireland. The present status of Northern Ireland is that it is part of the UK. If in the future the majority of the people of NI should indicate

a wish to become part of a
united Ireland, the British
Government would support
that wish.

We did not pursue our case for a written commitment to hold a referendum which would remove from the Constitution of the Republic the claim to the territory of Northern Ireland. But what amounted to a verbal commitment was given. Mr Cosgrave and his Ministers made it very clear that they regarded the claim as an anachronism and an irritant between North and South and that for them the only obstacle to an amendment of the offending Articles was political expediency. As they quite fairly pointed out, if a commitment was made to hold a referendum which the Government then lost—as was not unlikely if Fianna Fail mounted a 'sell out of our fundamentals' campaign—we would have achieved nothing; we would in fact have set back North/ South relations by years. The declaration of recognition, which did not have to be put to any referendum, was a concrete achievement marking a real move forward. It was precisely such a 'Binding International Agreement' which we had been mandated by our party to seek.

Two major topics came under the general heading of co-operation against terrorism—the problem of fugitive offenders, and police co-operation—and we decided to establish a sub-committee to deal with them as well. It quickly became clear at the Plenary Session that fugitive offenders and the related argument on extradition, common law enforcement, political offences, international legal conventions, and common courts was going to provide a technical paradise for the lawyers. I was confident that Rawlinson had a sensible attitude on these matters and would soon run a coach and horses through some of the more fanciful ideas of Costello, the Attorney-General from the Republic who was arguing for a Common Court, nominated by and legislated for by the Council of Ireland.

I pointed out that it did not make much sense to people in Northern Ireland to see murderers set free in Dublin Courts as 'political offenders'. It would, I said, be hard to convince the relatives of the dead and maimed that the perpetrators of these outrages deserved respect as 'political criminals'. The Dublin team said they were very aware of this, but they had political problems in handing over Irishmen to British courts and security forces which had been accused of 'torture'. It was agreed that the lawyers would get together and report, and Basil

McIvor, John Baxter and Professor Calvert, the three legal men on our team, represented us at its meetings.

Policing was the other major area where there were positive gains to be had from a Unionist point of view—minority co-operation with the RUC in Northern Ireland, and full co-operation against the terrorists from the Gardai. I decided to take part myself in these discussions. I was already alarmed by some of the wild suggestions which had been floated and I had to come down very hard against the proposals from Mr Cooney, the Dublin Justice Minister, that the Council of Ireland should control the police, North and South, through the respective Police Authorities. When I listed the areas in which co-operation was needed and asked him in what way joint control by the Council of Ireland would contribute to these, he seemed at a loss for an answer, until John Hume stepped in quickly with the 'identification of the minority with the forces of law and order' argument, which we had heard often before and were to hear many times again. Bradford joined me on the sub-committee for this issue, which turned out to be the most difficult of all, and assisted me very ably through the long hours of tough negotiation.

But first there was a social function to attend. The Prime Minister had laid on a dinner for the delegations at Downing Street on our first evening, and it turned out to be a very convivial occasion. A choir had been brought along for our entertainment, and sang a wide range of modern and classical music from Ireland and Britain while we drank our coffee and relaxed after our seven-course meal. Drink had been flowing freely throughout the evening and by the end of the choral performance some of those present were becoming more informal than I think Heath had intended. Loud calls of 'Give us a song, Paddy' were heard but Heath skilfully diverted any possible embarrassment by leading us into another room for more coffee and sober conversation.

Next day the sub-committees got down to work, drafting and re-drafting, discussing and arguing, while the press huddled in a building several hundred yards away wondering what was going on. Three times during that Friday we held brief Plenary Sessions to report back on the progress of the sub-committees and on each occasion most of them reported only limited progress. The structure of the Council was the first thing to be agreed and by late on Friday the form as eventually announced in the Sunningdale Communiqué was more or less worked out. We agreed on the general principles: achieving the best utilization of resources, avoiding unnecessary duplication of effort in the two parts of Ireland, and ensuring complementary rather than competitive effort where this was to the benefit of agriculture, commerce and industry. We specifically referred to the EEC context where North and South would have some common interests as peripheral areas.

On many of these matters there was already substantial co-operation between us, often from necessity. It was difficult to maintain our excellent record in animal and plant health if the only state with which we shared a land frontier had different standards and regulations, especially in view of the substantial cross-border trade in livestock. Similar considerations applied to most of the other areas. We did not see our agreement to this as constituting any massive shift in real practice since all powers delegated to the Council could be revoked or reduced by either the Dail or the Assembly at any time.

The lawyers were deeply absorbed in technical discussion on the extradition issue, but some progress seemed to have been made. At our last session on Friday, when we met in Plenary Session just before midnight to review progress reports, the policing sub-committee had to report almost complete deadlock. As Austin Currie said, 'We have so far disagreed on every section of the draft.' Nor was there any obvious solution. It seemed clear to us that if the SDLP continued to insist that 'identification' with the RUC by the minority could only be achieved by placing the police north and south under the control of the Council the negotiations would collapse on this issue. I was adamant that we were not prepared to concede on this and I would lead my delegation home if necessary. What we required was full co-operation between our two separate police forces, and full support for effective law enforcement inside Northern Ireland from the minority represented by the SDLP. It seemed reasonable to expect that this should be forthcoming inside a system where the SDLP were part of the Government, though I was convinced that if the Northern Ireland Executive itself controlled the RUC and legislated for the criminal law—instead of these being reserved to Westminster—we could achieve 'identification' more successfully. Bob Cooper suggested we sleep on the matter and consider it again the next day, and this we agreed to do.

On Saturday agreement was reached on everything except policing. We agreed our final draft on status. The lawyers agreed that in view of the legal technicalities involved in the different possible solutions to the problem of fugitive offenders a high-powered Law Commission consisting of leading judges from Britain, Northern Ireland, and the Republic should be set up to report urgently on the most practical means of bringing terrorists to justice.

But the policing sub-committee sat through the whole day from 9.15 a.m. without making any substantial progress and by the evening

Ted Heath's impatience was beginning to show. He had already had to leave the conference for a delayed meeting with the Italian PM at Chequers, after Sir Alec had filled in for him for several hours. Unfortunately Heath had not been involved to any extent in the Castle Talks and was not as familiar as was necessary with the intricacies of Irish politics. Francis Pym, being new to his job, was not able to exert the necessary pressure on Heath, and Frank Cooper was on the British side the main link with the background of Ulster politics.

Heath, always a rather headstrong man, impatient with obstacles placed in his way, clearly made up his mind that the Unionists would have to be made to concede the point if agreement was to be reached. As we continued to discuss through the night he began to exert increasing pressure on us to agree to a Council of Ireland link with the RUC. The sub-committee would meet briefly to discuss some new way out, and the members would then separate and go back to their respective party rooms, where we in fact spent most of the night. We were quite relaxed as we had decided that we could not accept the proposal which had been put to us and it was just a question of wearing the others down. The Alliance Party were supporting us during the night when we were meeting separately in our party rooms. James Allan, an Under-Secretary at the Northern Ireland Office, travelled from room to room taking the 'temperature', and when there seemed to be anything new to discuss the members of the sub-committee would get together in the main room. After every session of the sub-committee, in order to go back to our party rooms we had to pass through the hall-way where scores of increasingly tired civil servants were sitting around waiting for some hint of progress. One would have thought we were discussing whether or not to go to war the way expectant eyes were raised each time we emerged from the door.

Morale was good in our delegation and there was much humour and team spirit. Each party room was equipped with a fully stocked drinks cabinet but we decided not to imbibe lest it reduce our staying power as the all-night sitting progressed. Drinks in some of the other party rooms ran out early and we willingly donated ours to the messengers who arrived looking for spare supplies. Leslie Morrell kept our delegation supplied with polo mints which he had sent our press officer, Sam Butler, out to buy, and after Leslie's early comment on some of the drafts shown to us that they gave him 'butterflies in his stomach', it became a standard test for each new draft to ask Leslie whether it too gave him butterflies in his stomach. Most of them did.

Sometime after 2 a.m. Frank Cooper came to our room with a minor

verbal concession which he described as a 'great offer' from the SDLP.
We were unimpressed and made it clear he was wasting his time. He
went off and then came back again, this time with a 'major concession'
which was little different from the previous one. Once again we said no.
Then an Alliance Party representative came round and, much to our
surprise, supported Frank Cooper's argument. But our mind was made
up and we would not agree. It was after 4 a.m. when a grim Ted Heath
descended on our party room, clearly determined to sort us out.

Flanked by Frank Cooper he announced that we had done very well
indeed on the recognition issue and were therefore duty bound to agree
to give ground on policing. He made it clear that if the talks broke down
on this issue he would lay the blame on the Unionists in public. But we
were not going to be blackmailed in that way, and we said so, one by
one, until the whole delegation had spoken and the reasons for our conviction that putting the police under the Council of Ireland was a ludicrous and impractical idea had been exhaustively explained. Heath
argued with several of the speakers and grew quite irritated, raising his
voice heatedly, but by the time we had all spoken our determination not
to concede must have been unmistakable, for he lapsed into one of his
famous silences. After sitting for perhaps several minutes looking over
our heads he got up suddenly and walked out without a word. Frank
Cooper winked broadly in my direction as he followed Heath out.

When he had gone we discussed among ourselves the possibility of
breaking up the talks and going home. We were very well aware that
we would have been welcomed as heroes by our supporters. But we
would have been returning with only half an agreement, and as it had
been generally accepted since the beginning of the Castle Talks that until all was agreed nothing was agreed, we would be risking the complete
collapse of the Constitution and everything we had laboured for over
the previous six months. It might be possible to provide the SDLP with
some face-saving formula, we decided, but we would have to demand
some *quid pro quo* for providing it. The most useful thing, I argued,
would be to get a commitment on devolution to the Assembly of policing and criminal law matters as soon as possible. I remained convinced,
as I had been in March 1972, that these powers were important to the
credibility of any Government, and we had started to argue for them
earlier during the Conference. We now decided to push Heath hard for
a commitment on this, and Leslie Morrell discovered by some behind
the scenes politicking with Paddy Devlin that the SDLP were not
as completely opposed to it as was commonly thought. I met a very
tired-looking Paddy Devlin by chance in the corridor towards the end

of our all-night sitting and he said, 'Look, we mustn't let this police business break us.' I agreed, and he said that the SDLP's problem was the Special Branch. Would it be possible to split the Special Branch from the regular RUC, he asked. I expressed doubts, but suggested that Special Branch co-operation between North and South might help. The upshot of this conversation was an understanding that the SDLP would agree to support us on the devolution of policing matters if we would make some gesture to meet their 'identification' argument.

At 6.15 a.m. on Sunday Heath called a break in the talks and everyone went off to their rooms for a wash before an early breakfast. While I was sitting with my colleagues eating breakfast, and feeling a little revived by the food, Heath stopped by my chair on his way in and asked when I thought we should reconvene. As cheerfully as I could manage I said, 'After breakfast of course!' Heath shook his head with a look of absolute horror and wandered off without saying anything.

It was eventually decided to give people a few hours to catch up on sleep, and we met again for discussions in the afternoon. There were signs of a softening of the SDLP and Heath approaches and, although progress remained very slow, we began to believe that agreement could be reached. It was 8.21 p.m. when we reached complete agreement. Heath had, extremely reluctantly, agreed to write into the communiqué a Westminster commitment to devolve policing powers as soon as the security emergency came to an end. Because of our row over security control in March 1972 he seemed to regard this concession as a personal admission of error. But it was clear that the talks could collapse otherwise, and so he agreed. In return we agreed to a tenuous and, in practice, totally meaningless link between the police forces north and south of the border and the Council of Ireland.

For the RUC this meant that before the Secretary of State appointed the members of the Police Authority in Northern Ireland, he would ask the Executive for suggestions, and the Executive would in turn tell the Council of Ireland what names they were putting forward. There was no question of any obligation by the Executive to accept any alterations suggested in the Council of Ministers. As far as we were concerned it was simply a token link to cover the abandonment by Dublin and the SDLP of their earlier positions.

That Sunday evening all of us in the Unionist deputation were convinced that we had come off best at Sunningdale. We sat in our room for several hours talking and exchanging anecdotes and jokes. We felt elated and expected our success to be recognized. One member of our delegation remarked that Sunningdale would go down in history as a Unionist victory.

All this may seem in retrospect ironic and unreal. But I do not think if one examines the balance-sheet our conclusions can be shown to have been poorly judged. Formal co-operation against terrorism had been agreed for the first time and, although the lawyers had not yet produced any agreed means of closing the 'political offence' escape, we were confident that a high-powered joint legal commission would do so inside a few weeks. The agreement in principle on a common objective of eradicating terrorism we saw as the major step forward, and we had a firm commitment that there would be operational and intelligence co-operation from the Gardai.

In the other crucial area, recognition of the constitutional status of Northern Ireland, our achievement seemed even more decisive. We had for the first time since de Valera laid claim to Northern Ireland some forty years earlier achieved recognition by the Republic of our right to self-determination within our existing boundaries. We also had an informal commitment that the constitutional claim would be removed at the earliest opportunity.

The price we had paid for this progress—and one usually pays some price for progress in negotiations—lay in the structure of the Council of Ireland. The Council of Ministers had a valuable practical role in formalizing co-operation on security and social and economic matters. In a very real sense getting the Dublin Government to treat Northern Ireland representatives as equals on an inter-governmental body underlined their acceptance of partition. A similar scheme had been rejected by the then Dublin Government in the early 1920s on the grounds that it would have given legitimacy to Northern Ireland. But the other appendages of the Council—the Consultative Assembly, the Permanent Secretariat, the executive functions of the Council of Ministers—fell in my mind into the 'necessary nonsense' category. They were necessary to get the co-operation of the SDLP and the Dublin Government. But nothing agreed on at Sunningdale infringed on the powers of the Northern Ireland Assembly by which everything would have to be approved and delegated. Given the overwhelmingly Unionist composition of that body and the unanimity rule in the Council of Ministers we were satisfied that the constitutional integrity of Northern Ireland was secure.

The formal signing of the Sunningdale Communiqué and the press conferences followed rapidly on our final agreement. All the delegations were in optimistic mood, happy that the long hours of argument had produced an agreement which could mark a significant step forward in the relationships between Northern Ireland, the Irish Republic, and Great Britain. We were particularly pleased to note that the general verdict among the media men seemed to be that the Unionists had done well. Little did we realize as we returned to our province very early on a cold Monday morning the chain of misrepresentation, miscalculation and coincidence which was, over the next few months, to discredit much of what had been achieved.

18
The Power-Sharing Executive

The first ever power-sharing Executive of Northern Ireland took office on Tuesday 1 January 1974. The previous day there had been a slightly absurd little ceremony at Stormont Castle when we all received our 'Warrants of Appointment' from the Secretary of State, Francis Pym, on behalf of HM The Queen, after being sworn in by the Lord Chief Justice, Sir Robert Lowry. The oath committed us to uphold the laws of Northern Ireland and conscientiously to fulfil our duties under the Constitution Act in the interests of Northern Ireland and all its people. We had the choice of 'Affirming' or 'Swearing', but only Paddy Devlin Affirmed for what he described as 'personal reasons'.

The school prize-giving atmosphere at this ceremony, mildly embarrassing though it proved, was less important than the damaging impression given to the public that the Executive was the child of the Secretary of State. It was an important part of the loyalist argument that the new Constitution and the power-sharing Executive had been forced on Northern Ireland against the wishes of its population by British politicians and that the Executive therefore lacked any democratic status. We knew that the Executive was a freely agreed coalition of elected politicians, supported by a strong majority in the Assembly, but this appointment ceremony can, in retrospect, be seen as making the loyalist misrepresentation that little bit easier.

I moved into my offices in Stormont early on Tuesday morning and began to consult with the senior civil servants. That afternoon we had the first meeting of the full Administration. It was hard to believe, as we gathered in the former Prime Minister's room, how far we had come since I last sat there. There was a feeling of comradeship and trust between those of us who had been through hundreds of hours of negotiations, whether on the same or different sides of the negotiating table, and a sense almost of moral purpose. Many people believed that a government such as ours could not operate on a basis of collective responsibility. But not only did we take an early decision to operate totally within the principles of collective responsibility, we never during the life of the Executive had to criticize anyone for a breach or an attempted breach of them—except one person, and that a member of my own party. The coalition of Protestant and Catholic politicians really worked, but unfortunately at grass-roots level fear and, above all, violence were continuing to push the ordinary people of the Province apart. In time the lead we had given would have overcome these problems. The Executive needed to be able to show what it could do, to establish itself as an efficient form of provincial government which was creating social and economic progress, political stability and respect for law and order.

There were early indications of the practical benefits of the Executive. All the Heads of Departments (the designation given to us in the Constitution Act, but rapidly discarded—our civil servants found 'Good Morning, Minister' a much less embarrassing form of greeting than 'Good Morning, Head of Department') and their Permanent Secretaries met on 8 January for a full day to review policies and plans. We found the government machine in first-class condition and ready to tackle the ambitious social and economic plan which we had agreed at the Castle talks. A great deal of work remained to be done in sorting out priorities, liaising with the London Ministries and the Treasury, and preparing the necessary legislation. Discussions ranged over the whole range of activity for which the Executive was responsible, and even the SDLP members of the Administration, several of whom had been strongly critical of the Northern Ireland civil service over previous years, were impressed by the enthusiasm, ability and impartiality shown by the civil servants present. After the meeting I spoke to John Hume and Paddy Devlin who both agreed that on the basis of their first week in office and that day's meeting they were very willing to admit that the Northern Ireland civil service had been much maligned. This I regarded as an important sign of the moderating effect which the sharing of both power and responsibility could have in Northern Ireland, and I looked forward to its application in the field of policing when those powers were devolved to us.

A great deal of work went into the Social and Economic plan to ensure its feasibility and to tie in existing plans with it before publication on 21 January. There was much travelling backwards and forwards between London and Belfast by the Ministers, especially those dealing with roads, housing and industry, to ensure that our proposals meshed into overall United Kingdom policies. We found the Westminster Government extremely helpful in its attitude to the serious economic

situation in Northern Ireland, largely because everyone was so enthusiastic about making the new Executive a success. It was made clear to
us that, within reasonable limits, money was no obstacle. The battered
Ulster economy stood to gain a great deal from the existence of the
power-sharing Executive.

Early in February a reception for industrialists was held in the Ulster
Office in London. It struck me very forcibly how much more effective
our sales story was made for the 250 or so powerful men who came along
by the simple fact that Gerry Fitt and I were standing side by side at the
door to welcome them, and showing the same concern for jobs and living standards in the Province we now governed. The reaction of those
to whom we spoke showed that some at least of the enthusiasm we felt
had transmitted itself to them, and there were real prospects of an improvement in the hitherto dwindling amounts of new outside investment.

Executive members were covering the ground and being seen to be
active by the public. John Hume, in particular, at the Department of
Commerce seemed to have an enormous amount of energy. He was in
London discussing the energy crisis, in the USA on an industrial promotion trip (the first time such a thing had been done by an Ulster Catholic), in Brussels to open a new industrial promotion office, and in
Germany to discuss business prospects and visit our office there. Roy
Bradford, as the Minister responsible for liaison on EEC matters, also
visited the Continent. Leslie Morrell, at the Department of Agriculture,
had a crisis on his hands and was commuting backwards and forwards
to London—EEC regulations provided us in Northern Ireland with
very little scope for independent action. An important indication of the
international support and respect for the new Executive came from the
United States: it was made clear to Gerry Fitt and I that we would be
welcomed there as guests by the President. Plans for such a visit were
overtaken by events.

Many difficult policy decisions were taken in the Executive. The
SDLP had, as agreed at the Castle talks, paved the way for the formation of the Executive by a statement after Christmas calling on all their
supporters to end their rent and rates strike in response to the release
of sixty-five detainees by the Secretary of State at Christmas, the
announced intention to carry out a phased release of all detainees as
soon as the security situation permitted, and the entry of SDLP politicians into government in Northern Ireland. Now we had to decide how
to deal with those who continued the strike, and how to collect arrears
from others. It was a particularly difficult decision for the SDLP, but

they came through the test well, and after some argument for a delay, agreed to the imposition of a 25p per week surcharge from 20 May on those still refusing to pay and an increase in the amounts deductible from social security payments to meet rent arrears. Austin Currie himself at the Department of Housing, Local Government and Planning had to announce our decision in the Assembly on 3 April, and to implement it through his Department, and he shouldered the responsibility honourably. 'There cannot be an amnesty. Arrears must be paid,' Currie told the Assembly, and Michael Canavan, an SDLP Assemblyman from Londonderry, speaking on behalf of the SDLP backbenchers, supported him.

Basil McIvor came to the Executive after some weeks with proposals for a new method of reducing the segregation of Catholic and Protestant schoolchildren, which he called 'Shared Schools'. The Executive supported his proposals and because of its mixed Catholic/Protestant composition was able to put them forward without any fear of accusations of religious bias such as would certainly have greeted even identical ideas if they came from a wholly Unionist government. It took us two meetings of the Executive to reach agreement, as some of the SDLP members had reservations about the details of the scheme, but once the decision had been taken no one wavered from collective responsibility even when the Cardinal and the Catholic bishops launched a strong attack on the whole idea after publication. But the hopes of dealing with this important problem, like many other hopes for Ulster, died with the Executive.

All decisions were taken by only the eleven full members of the Executive, among whom there was a Unionist majority. There were many meetings of the whole Administration and on other occasions Heads of Departments were brought in to explain something relating to their particular department. But at no time was a controversial Executive decision taken with the whole Administration present. In any case there was never a vote. Our decisions were taken by consensus, as we all knew that we had to work together for the Executive to survive.

In terms of administrative efficiency I rated the Executive quite highly, though this has been exaggerated by some of its supporters. It was on average a younger government than those in which I had served at Stormont before and this, combined with the new complex blend of political and social attitudes, brought a welcome freshness of approach and an energy to the problems that faced us. The Executive was the nearest thing Ulster had ever had to a 'Government of all the talents', as it drew its members from three parties instead of one. I did not, during the first months, find that my role as Chief Executive required great feats of political gymnastics to hold the Executive together. I tried to play things straight down the middle and to sustain the confidence and respect of all my colleagues. The only constantly recurring problem was to get everyone to meetings on time! There seem to be two kinds of people in the world—the punctual and the unpunctual. We were supposed to meet every Thursday at 10.30 a.m. and at the first meeting of the Executive I made a point of stressing the need always to start our meetings on time. But the SDLP, apart perhaps from Austin Currie, clearly fell into the category of unpunctual men and tended to arrive at intervals after 10.30. Oliver Napier of Alliance was invariably early, while I always tried to make a point of arriving dead on time. This problem, however, never seriously threatened to bring down the Executive!

SDLP Ministers were determined to co-operate fully and always came to me when they received an invitation to appear on TV, so that we could discuss whether or not it was a good idea that they should accept at that particular time. On several occasions SDLP members of the Executive visited Dublin, but usually on specifically executive business, and never without my prior knowledge and consent. It seemed to me sensible that, as the SDLP had traditionally the best lines of communication with Dublin, they should be the persons we used to try to persuade both Government and Opposition in Dublin to agree to things which the Executive had decided. I can see now that there may have been too many of these visits from a political propaganda point of view. They allowed Paisley and Co. to tramp Northern Ireland saying that the SDLP were making regular trips to Dublin to get their instructions on what to do and to give away all the 'secrets' of the Northern Ireland Executive.

Perhaps the highest point in the Executive was reached in our talks on the content of 'executive and harmonizing' functions of the Council of Ireland before our meeting with the Dublin Government at the former Governor's residence at Hillsborough, County Down, on 1 February. The Dublin Government had sent us their proposals, as had been agreed at Sunningdale. Their ideas about the scale of the functions were very much more all-embracing than ours. They still wanted a full-scale Council of Ireland with a permanent headquarters and executive functions on matters as important as industrial development and planning. The SDLP were prepared to agree with us that this was unrealistic, and in three special meetings of the Executive in January we reached a unanimous position on what exactly the Council should do.

Thus I was able to go to Hillsborough with a united team. Eight of us—Leslie Morrell, Roy Bradford, Herbie Kirk, John Hume, Paddy

Devlin, Gerry Fitt, Oliver Napier and myself—faced eight representatives of the Dublin Cabinet as Ulstermen and took up a totally united position which at the end of the day had been accepted 100 per cent by Mr Cosgrave and his Ministers. The ever-talkative Garret Fitzgerald went on at great length about his ideas for the Council of Ireland, and eventually had to be silenced by Cosgrave when it was clear that we had made up our minds and would not be shifted. It was decided that Executive functions would be confined to the horse-racing board, drainage, fisheries, some aspects of tourism, animal health and various other politically insignificant matters where co-operation would be beneficial. There was also some discussion of cross-border security contacts, and we were surprised to find ourselves in the position of being told that not enough was being done north of the border to enforce the law. The tough-minded Minister for Justice in the Republic, Mr Cooney, lashed the British Government's security policies in the South Armagh area and said it had been allowed to come totally under IRA control. The army brief with which we had come proved woefully inadequate to answer his arguments.

In the meantime much was happening on the domestic political front and the loyalists had not been inactive. As soon as the Sunningdale Communiqué was published Paisley launched a major assault on the whole scheme as a 'sell-out' designed to push Ulster into a united Ireland. An Assembly debate shortly before Christmas showed the same bitterness, the same long strings of insults directed particularly against me, and the same determination to bring the whole system down by whatever means. While Paisley was busy trying to whip up hysteria, the Officers of the Ulster Unionist Council quite irresponsibly agreed to call a special meeting of the full Council to consider a motion from the dissidents led by Harry West and John Taylor condemning any Council of Ireland. The meeting was called for 4 January, only four days after the Executive took office.

It was one of the more unfortunate aspects of Sunningdale that it did not represent a final agreement. Too many things were left as 'unfinished business', providing too much scope for those who felt they wanted to amend, alter and generally interfere with the negotiations—without, in many cases, any real understanding of the issues at stake. Ulster has always had too many amateur politicians. At Sunningdale we had agreed that once the Legal Commission had reported and final agreement had been reached on the 'executive and harmonizing' functions we would meet again for a formal ratification conference leading to the immediate establishment of the Council of Ireland. But because there was still scope for manœuvre many, even of our own supporters, found it easier to say to their constituents, who were fearful because of the loyalist campaign, 'nothing is finally agreed yet, and we won't agree unless Dublin delivers the goods on co-operation against terrorism'. The final shape of the deal which we were supposed to be selling was still widely disputed.

It was impossible to expect that after only four days of this completely new form of government for Northern Ireland we could have effectively proved our value to the people of the Province. The 600 delegates to the Unionist Council would be coming up to Belfast with their views on Sunningdale influenced by the latest wild and newsworthy allegation by bitter and power-hungry loyalists. I was still hopeful that we would get a majority, if only a small one, who were prepared to give us a chance to show what we could achieve. I was disappointed when, after an extremely acrimonious debate, the Council supported West's motion by a majority of fifty-three votes.

Events at the Unionist Council that day showed again that it had become an archaic body, designed for a situation which no longer existed. It had among its members those who were also members of other political parties. I noticed once again that a well-known member of the Vanguard Party, Rev. R. Bradford, who was later to become one of its M Ps at Westminster, was on his feet in the hall, shouting. He was present as an Orange delegate, as were many of his party colleagues. It was so ludicrous that a major political party should have on its most powerful body members of hostile and competing political parties that I was convinced the Unionist Council had ceased to be a suitable organization for the propagation of Unionist policies in Ulster. There was no future for Ulster in the long series of repetitive party wrangles which we had gone through time and time again over the previous five years. I decided that I would have to resign from the leadership of the Unionist Party now that our policies had been rejected. After the meeting was over I held a brief press conference where, flanked by Roy Bradford who was strongly supporting me, I hinted that I would have to think of resigning.

During the weekend I thought deeply about my position in the party and consulted political friends to get their reaction. It was an important watershed in my career. I had been a member of the Unionist Party for twenty-eight years and had always tried, though with increasing impatience in recent years, to put forward my policies through its cumbersome structures. Now it seemed that out of fear and misunderstanding the party was rejecting the greatest opportunity it had ever faced. I could not at the same time lead the Executive forward and the Ulster Unionist Party backwards. Resignation from the leadership of the party was the only honourable course.

Early on Monday morning I sent a brief letter of resignation by hand to Tony Clark the Chairman of the Standing Committee, before going to Stormont for a meeting with my twenty Assembly party colleagues. In a long and serious meeting each of them spoke in turn after I had made a statement telling them of my decision to resign. There was for me, I told them, no going back and even if I found myself the only Unionist in the Assembly advocating the policies of partnership I would go on doing so. Two Assemblymen, James Stronge, from Armagh, and William Morgan from North Belfast said they could not go along with me on Sunningdale any longer, but the rest all reaffirmed their commitment to our policies and gave me their full support. I felt proud to lead these men, who were placing their concern for the future of Northern Ireland far above any immediate concern for their own political careers which were now clearly at risk. It meant that the Executive still had a large majority in the Assembly and could carry on.

I would have been prepared to establish a separate party immediately to give our supporters something to identify with and organize for. During the first week after my resignation many of the senior officers of the Unionist Party, including Sir John Andrews the President, resigned in sympathy and the morale of our supporters was high, but we needed a clear-cut organization to sustain that enthusiasm. Most of those closest to me were reluctant to believe that a final split from the old Unionist Party was inescapable and talked of forming a pressure group inside it. I allowed myself, against my instincts, to be pressed into adopting a gradualistic approach. Later I realized that during this period of indecision much of the initial enthusiasm drained away and we lost our momentum.

A few days after the Council meeting our troubles were added to when the Cosgrave Government's defence submission in the 'Boland Case' was published by the press. Shortly after the Sunningdale Agreement was announced Kevin Boland, one of the Ministers who had left the Fianna Fail Government at the time of the gun-running scandal, challenged it in the courts of the Republic as repugnant to the Constitution. He argued that the Articles claiming Northern Ireland as part of the national territory could not be reconciled with those sections of the Sunningdale Communiqué which expressed recognition of the status of Northern Ireland. This put the Dublin Cabinet in a very difficult position and they had to mount a technical defence claiming that they had not actually recognized Northern Ireland as being outside their jurisdiction. Naturally this caused a sensation in Northern Ireland where many people who had thought the recognition side of Sunningdale marked a real step forward now began to doubt if it had any value. I too was surprised and upset to read this in my newspaper and issued a warning that if Dublin was going to renege on the recognition agreed at Sunningdale we would have to reconsider our position.

Mr Cosgrave rang me the next day, 14 January, and it was clear that he in turn had been surprised by the strength of the Unionist reaction to the affair. He agreed that he should have talked to me about it before, but argued that our alarm was based on a misapprehension and that he and I should meet quickly to thrash out an understanding. I flew south in a helicopter two days later with Ken Bloomfield and Tommy Roberts, our pressman, and met Cosgrave at Baldonnell airfield. I told him that there had been some erosion of our position since Sunningdale, caused in part by his Government. The status issue, previously one of our trump cards, had been blurred, and the fact that fifteen suspected terrorists had been picked up by his security forces amid much publicity on the eve of the crucial Unionist Council meeting, and then released a day or two later, undermined confidence that he was determined to stamp out IRA operations in the Republic. Mr Cosgrave insisted that he stood by all that had been agreed at Sunningdale, including recognition of the status of Northern Ireland. He showed me copies of the controversial defence submission and explained that, for as long as their Constitution retained the claim to the territory of Northern Ireland, any form of recognition which he and his colleagues could agree to would have to be capable of a technical defence that it did not infringe the letter of the law, even if—as was inevitable and even desirable—it infringed the spirit.

It came down to the problem of the Constitution again, and I asked him if it were not possible to take early action to delete the offending Articles by referendum, as it seemed clear that the matter of status could never be satisfactorily resolved until this was done. But Mr Cosgrave was convinced that the time was not ripe for such a move, as his Government would lose the referendum, and I accepted his judgement. 'Look,' he said. 'We accept Northern Ireland as it is, and we want to co-operate with you, and that's all there is to it.' He promised that as soon as the court case was over he would put on record in the Dail a clear statement of his Government's position to try to reassure people in Northern Ireland. As always I found him honest and direct and I had a very great respect for him. He and I were both struggling with deeply rooted traditions which made it difficult for us to work together as we wished, but I never doubted his goodwill, and I believed that in time we could have overcome these obstacles.

The verdict in the Constitutional case was given in favour of the Government on the same day as our meeting at Baldonnell. But Boland immediately appealed, the matter was again *sub judice*, and Mr Cosgrave was not free to make his promised statement in the Dail until 13 March. By then the situation had deteriorated further.

The loyalists were cock-a-hoop about my set-back in the Ulster Unionist Council and the difficulties over the Boland case, and made plans to wreck the first Assembly meeting of the New Year. Members of the Executive were to take their places on the Front Bench to the right of the Speaker for the first time on 22 January, but Paisley boasted that none of us would make it to the Despatch Box. We did, but only after a prolonged display of hooliganism during which the Assembly had to be suspended five times to restore order and the police, acting on the instructions of the Presiding Officer, forcibly removed eighteen members from the Chamber. Many foolish things were done—such as Professor Kennedy Lindsay dancing on the Speaker's Table shouting through a microphone 'We have driven the money-changers from the temple' before chaining himself with a padlock to one of the benches, or the other 'loyalist' members who played pass-the-parcel with the Mace, the symbol of Royal Authority—but the ugliest scenes occurred when the police, acting on the instructions of the Presiding Officer, had to use force to remove those who were defying the authority of the Assembly. Five policemen were injured in the struggles at Stormont Buildings that day.

I and my fellow Executive members stood at one side of the Chamber while all of this was going on, trying to maintain some dignity in the playground atmosphere. Before he was removed from the Chamber the Professor came over and spat in my face as I stood there with my arms folded. Eventually the benches were cleared, the protesters were removed from the Chamber, and the Executive took its place. It provided an appropriate contrast with what had gone before when in our first Adjournment Debate the Executive, represented by Bob Cooper, was questioned by James Kilfedder on its intentions regarding the physically handicapped. This, it seemed to me, was what the Executive and the Assembly were all about—getting down to the task of providing a better way of life for all our citizens and dealing with the bread and butter issues which mattered to them.

Once the Executive was firmly established in the Assembly and the business of government began to move ahead the anti-Constitution parties were seldom seen. They rarely returned in force except to stage a walk-out or to try to disrupt the proceedings and intimidate the Presiding Officer. On 23 January they staged a walk-out after ten minutes. On 24 January Paisley orchestrated an hour-long series of points of order. And so it went on.

All the other backbenchers in Alliance, SDLP and the 'Pro-Assembly' Unionists were very active in putting down questions and keeping Ministers on their toes. Peter McLachlan in particular showed an immense capacity for constituency work and a wide knowledge of the affairs of government in putting down over 220 questions inside five months—though sometimes my Executive colleagues and their civil servants wished he was less energetic! Hugh Logue of the SDLP was nearest to him with 75 questions. The range of matters covered was considerable. For example, the Official Record for 30 January shows that Ministers answered Oral Questions on roads, the Urban Motorway, EEC, finance, water supplies, rates, sickness benefit, amenities, housing, the Porter Committee on rents, Small Claims Courts, government training centres, industrial relations, agriculture, new towns and the future of the Community Relations Commission.

The first business which the Executive put before the Assembly was a Motion of Confidence. As I said in proposing it:

> We want to establish, right from the start, to whom it is that we are responsible... We are not responsible to the Secretary of State—any more than our predecessors in Northern Ireland Governments were responsible to the Governor who appointed them—but to the people of Northern Ireland as represented by this Assembly.

We debated this motion over six days of Assembly time. Each member of the Executive spoke, outlining the plans of his Department in a wide-ranging and very constructive debate. William Morgan, a Unionist backbencher, proposed an amendment expressing support for power-sharing but opposing a Council of Ireland, which was eventually defeated by 41 votes to 3.

At the beginning of February a Westminster General Election was announced, and the date was fixed for the 28th of the same month. Gerry Fitt and I both put it strongly to Francis Pym before the announcement was made that an election at this time could do immense damage to the Executive, a completely new type of plant which had not had time to take root. In organizational terms I and my supporters were not ready to fight an election. The Executive had not had time to produce any legislation. Sunningdale was the subject of a constitutional challenge in the Republic where Boland's appeal was still dragging through the courts and the status issue was still blurred. If any of the parties in the Executive did badly in the election, which was under the first-past-the-post-system and would therefore exaggerate movements of opinion, it could undermine the credibility of the whole thing and stop us ever really getting off the ground. Pym and Whitelaw supported us, but found in the Cabinet that the Prime Minister and most of his colleagues had other priorities.

19
Election Aftermath

The result of the General Election was more disastrous than any of us had feared. The loyalists, working together now in an electoral pact called the United Ulster Unionist Coalition (commonly known as the UUUC), won 51 per cent of the votes in an exceptionally low poll and 11 of the 12 Northern Ireland seats at Westminster.

The election was an organizational shambles for the Executive parties. We were in difficulty from the start because it was not a practical possibility to ask our party workers to coalesce with the SDLP workers in an electoral coalition. We had been political opponents for over fifty years, and seven weeks of power-sharing was not enough to change the attitudes and traditions which had built up during that time. We therefore had to fight as separate parties, though in some constituencies we were able to give each other a clear run. We were also handicapped by confusion over our own position within the Unionist Party organization. In some branches my supporters dominated the official organization and our candidates got the nomination, in others we were working totally outside and had to put together a new organization. Roy Bradford got the nomination in North Down and fought a determined but unsuccessful campaign against the sitting member, James Kilfedder. Peter Utley, the well-known leader-writer from the *Daily Telegraph*, came to North Antrim as the Unionist candidate and courageously took on Paisley in his home ground, but again without success.

The Alliance and Northern Ireland Labour parties, with whom an electoral coalition was a real possibility, made things even more difficult by refusing to give our candidates a clear run against the UUUC in several crucial constituencies where only we stood any chance of winning. In South and East Belfast these interventions were important factors in the UUUC success.

During the campaign I made a tactical error when I gave an honest answer to an interviewer's question as to how I would cast my own vote in South Down. Willie Orr, the sitting MP, had declared himself against the Executive and the only candidate against him was SDLP representative Sean Hollywood. Orr and I were in theory committed to the same overriding political objective, the Union of Great Britain and Northern Ireland, but I was convinced that the policies he now espoused were the most certain way to destroy that objective and I felt it quite impossible that I could vote for him. So I said to the interviewer that I would probably abstain. Even this mild rejection brought howls of wrath on my head. It was seen as attempting to give the seat to the SDLP and many of my own supporters still preferred a hard-line Unionist to an SDLP candidate.

The pro-Assembly Unionists received 23 per cent of the votes cast in the seven constituencies we fought. The SDLP and Alliance votes were similar to those they had received in the Assembly elections. Gerry Fitt was the lone power-sharing supporter to be elected, as MP for West Belfast. It was our party which had lost votes. The UUUC had done well on their emotive and misleading slogan 'Dublin is just a Sunningdale away'. I saw it as a serious but not necessarily fatal blow to the Executive. It did, however, have an effect on my own backbenchers, who became increasingly nervous about implementing the Council of Ireland proposals. On 4 March an Assembly Party meeting at Stormont ruled out any immediate progress towards ratification of the Sunningdale Agreement, on the basis that Dublin had not yet honoured its commitments on recognition of Northern Ireland and on dealing with terrorism.

At 8.30 a.m. on the day Harold Wilson, as the new Labour Prime Minister at Westminster, moved into Downing Street I phoned him, congratulated him on his success, and said that the Northern Ireland Executive looked forward to working closely with his Government. I said that I knew it was not my business to tell him who to appoint as Secretary of State for Northern Ireland but I would be happy to work with the person who had been acting in that capacity as 'Shadow' in Opposition, Merlyn Rees. Wilson replied that I need not worry about the appointment, which he would be announcing very soon. It was clear from his phrasing that Rees was going to be the new Secretary of State, and so it turned out.

Rees was an earnest Welshman who sat for a constituency in Leeds and had visited Northern Ireland regularly over the past four years. I met him for talks within minutes of his arrival at Stormont Castle on 6 March. He assured me that he would give the Executive his full support and would not interfere in the conduct of its affairs. We agreed that the practice, introduced by his predecessor Francis Pym, of having a working lunch every Monday with Gerry Fitt and I after his weekly meetings with the GOC and the Chief Constable, should continue. The only other member of the new Northern Ireland Office team with whom I had much contact was Stanley Orme, the Minister of State. He had a history of supporting the Nationalists in the 1960s and so his appointment was viewed with apprehension by some Unionists. I did not always agree with his political judgements, but I found him an energetic Minister who, like the new Secretary of State, genuinely cared about people and their living conditions.

The Unionist members of the Executive decided that it was essential to respond in some way to the public fears highlighted by the election results. Something had to be done to make it clear that the Council of Ireland was not the massive Trojan Horse people were being led to believe. The impression that its structures were designed to provide the means whereby an inevitable but very gradual process of uniting Ireland outside the United Kingdom would take place had been spread by the UUUC. We had to reassure the voters that they would have control over the direction and pace of its developments and that its establishment would in no way compromise their position as citizens of the United Kingdom.

Oliver Napier joined us in pressing on the SDLP the necessity for amendments to Sunningdale. I had several private talks with Fitt, Hume and Devlin and some difference of emphasis between them soon became evident. The Belfast SDLP representatives tended to be less Dublin-orientated than those I called the 'country men'. The latter, who usually included the Derry representatives, were influenced by the Nationalist tradition. The former had a more practical labour-orientated tradition and were less interested in Nationalist dogma. It always seemed to me that Gerry Fitt did not really care if there was a Council of Ireland or not, but had to go along with it because his party was insisting.

We began formal discussions on a re-negotiation of the Council of Ireland in mid-March and put to the SDLP the proposition that there should be a two-stage implementation. In the first stage the Council of Ireland would be consultative only, and the transfer of 'executive functions' and the appointment of a permanent secretariat would proceed only if the next Assembly election endorsed the Executive. The SDLP were reluctant to agree to any amendments whatsoever and kept postponing a decision on the grounds that they needed to talk to their party. The result was that our discussions dragged on for some six weeks, diverting much of the energy and time of Executive members. At the end of April the Unionists decided that the political situation was continuing to deteriorate and the issue must be decided one way or the other.

Because of the need to operate under collective responsibility and to avoid prejudicing the discussions we could not inform the public that re-negotiation was taking place. So it appeared to many that we had not been influenced by the election results in any way and were carrying on regardless. Some hard-liners started to mutter that democracy was being ignored and other means of changing our policy would have to be tried.

There was some response to our pressure on the SDLP. A sub-committee consisting of Leslie Morrell, Roy Bradford, Oliver Napier, Bob Cooper, Paddy Devlin and John Hume was set up to discuss the staging of Sunningdale. But it made slow progress, and by the time a package had been agreed things had moved on to a final showdown.

Dublin appeared to be feeling some pressure from SDLP quarters to back up their line in the inter-Executive discussions, and Mr Cosgrave intervened with uncharacteristic clumsiness in April. Accompanied by Fitzgerald and Corish he held talks in London with Wilson and Rees, and these talks were sold to the media as 'pressing for ratification' of Sunningdale at an early date. The *Guardian* reported astonishingly in its headline 'Anglo-Irish talks clear the way for Sunningdale', and the *Financial Times* took the same line stating with apparent authority 'Sunningdale likely to be ratified in May'. We were aghast; it was almost as if the parties in the Northern Ireland Executive did not exist as an essential part of Sunningdale. It was a blatant piece of hustling which was badly miscalculated. We had not been consulted, nor were we a party to the London talks. It made my party even more determined that they would dig in their heels and secure changes in Sunningdale before it was signed. An Executive meeting agreed on a press release saying that none of us would agree to ratification until the Dublin and London Governments honoured the pledges they had made at Sunningdale. That meant that Dublin had to provide some clearer evidence of determination to co-operate against terrorism, and London had to move towards the ending of detention.

The new Labour Government made a bad start in dealing with the security situation. The IRA mounted a bombing blitz on the centres of Belfast, Bangor and Lisburn during two days at the end of March as a clear challenge to the new administration. A 500-lb bomb was planted outside the Army HQ in the Grand Central Hotel in Belfast's main shopping thoroughfare. It exploded, destroying the Army building and causing damage of some £1 million to the surrounding area. I visited the scene and found among the crowds intense anger against the terrorists and against the Government which was thought to be doing nothing to stop such things happening. I shared their feelings about the terrorists who were not only causing great suffering but also trying to wreck the most hopeful political developments the Province had seen. My response to press questions was, 'We will not be licked by these bloody murderers.' But since security was not devolved to the Executive there was little we could do about this in the short term other than try to create a political atmosphere in which the terrorists would feel increasingly isolated.

A week or so earlier I had arranged to fly to London for talks with Wilson and Rees on the general political situation and on the need for Treasury backing for our social and economic policies. The bombings meant that our talks, held on 1 April, dealt primarily with security and the plans of the new Government to deal with it. The main theme of my comments was that the Labour Government needed first to establish its resolution in the face of terrorism, and there should not therefore be any reduction in the number of troops at this time. The pros and cons of legalization of Sinn Fein, the publicity front of the Provisional IRA, and the UVF, a 'Protestant' murder gang, were discussed, and I urged very strongly that both organizations remain proscribed. There was a school of thought that one should give these people the opportunity to 'go political' and force them to acknowledge their lack of popular support, but it was not indicated that the Secretary of State or the Prime Minister took this line. My arguments that legalizing Sinn Fein in particular could be interpreted as preparing the way for a deal with the IRA seemed to be taken on board.

Wilson was at pains to impress on me the determination of his Government to stamp out terrorism and to prevent a recurrence of the bombings of the previous few days. He said that new measures would be taken to ensure that matters improved and these would be announced in the House in the forthcoming debate on Northern Ireland. I left the meeting feeling that at worst the Labour Government was not going to launch upon any newly disastrous policy and that there was a distinct prospect of an improvement, and I told the press I was pleased with the meeting.

I was not pleased, however, when three days later Merlyn Rees announced to the Commons a distinctly unimpressive policy. Sinn Fein and the UVF were to be legalized, the phased release of detainees was to be continued and combined with a scheme for assigning them after release to 'sponsors' who would seek to keep them on the straight and narrow. The press soon dubbed this last scheme 'take a terrorist home to tea' and it never came into operation because it was naïve and impractical in the extreme. The overall impression given to the people of Northern Ireland was one of wetness and incomprehension on the part of the new Government. It was a bad start which did nothing at all to strengthen the position of our battered Executive. The next of my usual weekly lunches with the Secretary of State at Stormont Castle was extended to two hours as I had rather a lot to say on security matters. I made it clear that the credibility and continued existence of any Northern Ireland Executive depended on firm action by those responsible for security. These powers had, against my advice, not been devolved and those who had insisted on taking responsibility for them, i.e. Westminster, must now do their duty in defending the citizens of Northern Ireland and not appear to be shuffling off responsibility with talk of a 'phased army withdrawal'. Merlyn seemed to accept the need to give some clear reassurance to the public.

Events over the next two days reinforced my arguments. The IRA had clearly decided that the new Government was a soft touch and a major effort from them could bring about desired changes in policy. Belfast was paralysed by a well-co-ordinated series of bombs and bomb hoaxes which closed all major roads to the city. Fifteen incendiary devices were found in Belfast businesses. Ten shops in the City of Armagh were burned down by incendiary bombs, causing damage of some £3 million. A retired UDR officer, Colonel Saunderson, was shot at the school where he taught in Derrylin, County Fermanagh, and his pupils found him dying in the school kitchen.

Faced with this response from the IRA the Government abandoned conciliation and acted against them: thirty-five Republicans were lifted in early morning swoops in Republican areas, releases of detainees were interrupted, and new pedestrian areas were set up in Belfast with entrances manned by civilian search units. On 17 April Wilson flew over and held talks with the security chiefs and with Merlyn Rees. He also met the Executive and made it clear to us that any change in the Sunningdale Agreement which we agreed between us would be acceptable to him and repeated that his Government would not soft-pedal in dealing with terrorism. But four days later another of the early Labour gaffes was made when Roy Mason, the new Secretary of State for Defence, expressed in public the opinion that there was a widespread feeling in Britain that troops should be withdrawn from Ulster. Everyone, including the SDLP, was appalled. The most fundamental factor in any anti-terrorist campaign, evincing the will to win, had been put in doubt. Gerry Fitt flew over to London on behalf of the Executive and met Wilson, who assured him that the statement did not represent any change in policy and issued a statement saying that troops would have to stay for as long as the security situation made them necessary. We were helped at this time by the fact that Mr Cosgrave's Government also believed that stability could only be guaranteed in the immediate future by the presence of British troops in Northern Ireland. It might have been a different matter had we faced a Dublin Government committed to the old Republican line of 'British troops out of Ireland' irrespective of the realities of the situation or the risk to life.

Parallel with these events there was a prolonged Assembly debate on the Sunningdale Agreement. It began on 19 March when John Laird, one of the 'Unpledged' Unionists, proposed on behalf of the UUUC a motion calling for complete re-negotiation of the constitutional settlement in the light of the election results. I proposed an amendment on behalf of the Executive parties stressing our public position that all commitments entered into at Sunningdale must be honoured and that if they were the constitutional arrangements could succeed, but not referring to our secret negotiations. It was frustrating to be put in this false political position but we could not do anything else until we had got a decision in the Executive.

I spoke for 36 minutes proposing our amendment and was interrupted 130 times by shouted insults, heckling and points of order. I stressed the relevance of the power-sharing experiment to the security problem: '... those who direct terrorism have stepped up their efforts in the short run because they well know that in the long run the success of this power-sharing experiment will leave them totally stranded...'

I argued that talking of an 'imposed' constitutional settlement was misleading; events had imposed the constraints under which we worked, not the British Government:

I will share with the Assembly a very deep fear. It is that by protesting all the while their determination to prevent a so-called sell-out to a united Ireland they may rupture the bonds of sympathy which have for so long tied us to the British Parliament and nation. . . . The ordinary voter . . . may find that he was right to be fearful but that his gaze was fixed in the wrong direction. . . . Would Parliament, having seen one settlement in the UK context set aside, patiently begin to frame another?

The debate dragged on for nearly two months after some successful delaying tactics in the Assembly by the UUUC who wished to prevent a vote they would obviously lose. In spite of all their talk of democracy this was one democratic exercise for which they seemed to have little taste. So they succeeded in intimidating the Presiding Officer, Nat Minford, into using a procedural ploy at the end of the allotted three days of debate to prevent a vote and allow a free-wheeling political discussion to continue over succeeding weeks. I was anxious for a vote to be taken so that the wishes of the Assembly and in particular of my party should be clearly made known and the views of the majority of Ulster representatives in the Assembly be seen on the side of the Executive. When it became evident very late on 2 April that the Presiding Officer had capitulated to UUUC pressure I made an angry but unavailing protest in the Chamber.

This debate provided Paisley, Craig and West with a good opportunity to make some political running. They were becoming aware that their own thuggish and unparliamentary activities had stimulated the organization of sinister forces on the fringe of the UUUC and so they concentrated on trying to restore their own political credibility by producing all kinds of proposals, some of them rather half-baked. Their 'Portrush Conference' at the end of April, noteworthy as the first UUUC function attended by Enoch Powell and as the first real policy conference of the three parties combined, produced some odd proposals for an Ulster federated to Britain, but it was never clear subsequently if any of the participants took these proposals very seriously. Certainly Enoch Powell did not, as he showed in a speech shortly afterwards when he was beginning to seek an Ulster seat in Parliament.

On Friday 26 April—several months later than expected at Sunningdale—copies of the Anglo/Irish Law Enforcement Commission Report were made available to the London and Dublin Governments and Merlyn Rees provided me with an advance copy, before it went officially to the Executive on 2 May. On 10 May there was a meeting between the Executive, Merlyn Rees, Orme, and the Attorney-General, Sam Silkin, to discuss the Report. Silkin did not think much of the arguments the Dublin lawyers had put forward against extradition and made this clear but he thought the compromise solution agreed as a second-best—peripatetic courts (described as 'extra-territorial courts') trying fugitives for a schedule of offences committed on the other side of the border and taking evidence on commission if necessary—was the best we could get and should be proceeded with. We agreed, although there was general disappointment in the Executive at the lack of any really effective agreed proposal. My party had hoped for something much more decisive in terms of showing the Republic's determination to tackle terrorism, and the lack of any retrospective provisions meant that the 30, odd murderers already wanted would remain free.

At the beginning of May our 'Pro-Assembly' Unionists group held its own conference in Portstewart to discuss our position within the old Unionist Party. After a long and thorough discussion of all the pros and cons we eventually agreed that a new party should be set up and the links with Glengall Street should be finally severed. I had been convinced for a long time that a more dynamic and positive party could be built up around the Executive supporters than could ever be achieved by returning to the old sterile wrangling of a diffuse Unionist Party organization with which we were now largely out of sympathy. Peter McLachlan and Fred Tughan were particularly strong in their support of me on this point. One notable absentee from the conference was Roy Bradford, who had flown off to a 'prior and pressing' engagement in Brussels and returned professing himself alarmed by our decision. This was further evidence of what we had suspected since the General Election—that Roy felt the political winds were not blowing in our direction and was repairing his fences with the West-led Unionists.

It was eventually decided in the Assembly that the vote on the anti-power-sharing motion would be taken on Tuesday 14 May, and this vote was being given considerable advance publicity. There were dark mutterings from some of the UUUC that if the Assembly ignored democracy—by voting against them—other means of changing policies would have to be tried. An organization called the Ulster Workers Council was threatening to call a strike against the Executive but few of us had heard much of this organization before and assumed it was a successor to the short-lived and not very successful 'Loyalist Association of Workers' which had early in 1973 called several strikes which rebounded on the organizers.

The Executive Amendment was put to the Assembly at 5.50 p.m. and carried by 44 votes to 28. The amended motion was carried by the same majority and the House adjourned at 6.07 p.m. amid cries of 'No Surrender' from William Beattie, Paisley's Deputy Leader.

20
The Strike

Thoughts of the strike were not uppermost in the minds of Executive members as we left Stormont that Tuesday evening. It had been announced to start at 6 p.m., but when we arrived at our offices the following morning there had been no significant evidence of support for it. Life in the Province was going on as usual.

As the day went on, however, it became clear there were new factors in this strike as compared to previous attempts. First there had been Harold Wilson's 'revelation' in the Commons the previous day of IRA battle-plans for a civil war which would include a scorched earth policy in much of Belfast. His thinking in giving these plans, recently found in a major IRA hide-out, such publicity was probably to impress people in Britain and Northern Ireland with the good intelligence of the security forces. Unfortunately it had the opposite effect in Northern Ireland. It alarmed people to think that such ambitious IRA plans could be treated seriously and raised tension rather than lowering it. More important than this was the widespread organization of the para-military forces, particularly the UDA, and the mobilization of support for the strike among the Province's power-workers. It soon became clear that the Government's response to these last two problems would be decisive.

There never seemed from the beginning to be any scope for talking out the strike threat. The UWC declared its objectives as the abandonment of Sunningdale and new elections to the Assembly. The Assembly had been elected only the previous June for a four-year term and the Executive had been in office less than five months. We could not allow the timing of new elections to be dictated by street action. We were well aware that the opponents of power-sharing could only hope to destroy it by nipping it in the bud and preventing it ever really getting off the ground. The Executive had had a difficult start but if it could have time to establish itself, to start producing legislation and give the public time to get used to the sight of Unionists and SDLP working together in government, and to show that men like John Hume and Gerry Fitt cared about the Province and were prepared to use their talents for its benefit, then there was little doubt that support would snowball and old suspicions and bitternesses could become a thing of the past. For our opponents therefore it was a question of now or never.

They were assisted by the fact that the Assembly vote was being over-simplified in the media as a vote to implement Sunningdale. It was not. It was a vote to allow the negotiating process to continue with Westminster and Dublin and within the Executive, but the slow progress of our sub-committee discussions was still preventing us from making this clear. In effect the strike was called while the public were under a misapprehension about the plans for Sunningdale and by the time we were able to announce final agreement our chance to correct this had been lost.

By Wednesday afternoon the UWC and their supporters had shown their hand. Gangs of para-military supporters were out on the streets building barricades and openly intimidating those going to their work. Men in para-military 'uniform', sometimes wearing masks and carrying cudgels, walked into shops and simply ordered shopkeepers to close. A lunchtime meeting of several thousand workers at Harland and Wolff's shipyard was told that any cars left in the car park after lunchtime would be burned. At the major engineering works of Mackies in East Belfast gunmen walked in and ordered the staff out. The evidence of Province-wide intimidation is now so well documented that supporters of the strike scarcely bother to deny it. As the strike progressed I began to receive more and more reports from people who had been threatened openly. In one County Down town all the shopkeepers were called together by the local strike committee and told the hours during which particular shops could open. At the end of the meeting two gunmen walked in, asked what had been agreed, said it would not do and ordered a more complete closure. All afternoon workers were going home and factories and businesses were closing down, while buses and lorries were being hijacked and used to block roads. One town, Larne, in County Antrim, had been totally taken over by uniformed UDA men and virtually cut off from the outside world.

It was very clear by Wednesday evening that this was not just another protest, but an organized challenge to constitutional authority. The loyalist politicians, some of whom had been doubtful about the strike tactic, were swinging behind the UWC. Craig had given firm support from the start, but West's supporters had been slower to move in and one of his Assemblymen had even condemned the idea of a strike. But as it gained momentum they were quick to align themselves with it.

What concerned us more than this was the fact that virtually nothing had been done all day to stop the intimidation and thuggery being seen on our streets. We could see the value of a low Army and police profile when it was hoped the strike was simply a damp squib which would fizzle out—a hope which the Secretary of State held much longer than the Executive—but we could not see the virtue of making them stand by and watch while this massive intimidation and disruption went on. I contacted Merlyn Rees and urged him to instruct the security forces to enforce the law.

Westminster was now well and truly hoist with its own petard. Having consistently resisted granting the transfer of policing and law enforcement powers to the Northern Ireland Executive they found themselves deeply involved in a crisis which they would have preferred to regard as a struggle between the Executive and its political opponents. The Executive was responsible for the government of the Province but it had no power to enforce its authority when challenged on the streets. We were entirely dependent on whatever action the Secretary of State, as agent of the Westminster Government, was prepared to take to maintain order. For Labour Ministers the problems of dealing with what purported to be a general strike were particularly agonizing. Merlyn Rees was a sensitive and liberal man steeped in the British traditions of 'softly, softly' while his main aide, Stanley Orme, was well known as a left-wing Tribunite in the Labour Party. They were more accustomed to viewing strikers sympathetically than taking action against them, and though it was more an attempted putsch than a strike in Ulster this background seemed to leave them confused and ineffectual in their response until it was too late.

Orme met a deputation from the loyalist politicians, accompanied by representatives of the UWC, at Stormont on Wednesday. He outlined the position which he and Rees were to maintain throughout the strike—there would be no negotiations. He put the message across in a typically robust and tough manner which annoyed the deputation, but we in the Executive would not have minded that if it had been backed up by equally robust action to maintain order on the streets. There was nothing negotiable in the strikers' demands, but they would still have to be beaten.

On the second day of the strike, Thursday 16 May, I chaired the usual meeting of the Economic Council. The strike and its crippling effect on the economy of the Province was the major subject of discussion. Representatives of the employers told us that up to 90 per cent of their employees were not at work. Everyone there, representatives of trade unions and employers alike, agreed that firm action would have to be taken to protect the right to work and to keep the economy going. Several speakers underlined the long-term damage such a stoppage could do to the chances of new investment and to the ability of firms to meet export orders. They underlined the fact that, whatever people thought about Sunningdale and power-sharing, most of them wanted to work and were being prevented from doing so by naked intimidation, and by the organized running down of power supplies.

I was heartened by the support and unanimity of this meeting but alarmed by the information as to the extent of the stoppage. I immediately set about taking the available steps to meet the strike by contacting Merlyn Rees again and urging action by the security forces, and by issuing a statement challenging the authority of the strike junta who were holding the whole community to ransom. 'Where do they come from? Who elected them? What is their authority?' I asked. I did not receive an answer.

There was not much reassurance forthcoming from Merlyn Rees, who just seemed to have gone into a flap. I was never sure later if his failure to give any leadership from the beginning was due to his hope that the strike would peter out, or to warnings from the Army that it should not get involved in a second front by taking on the para-military Protestants. I believe it to have been the latter. Throughout the strike we always found the Army making excuses for doing nothing and very slow to respond to any suggestions put to them. The GOC in Northern Ireland, backed up by the General Staff and the Ministry of Defence in London, seem to have grossly exaggerated to the Government the likelihood of getting involved in a shooting war with the UDA if they took action against the barricades and the roaming gangs. Merlyn kept telling me that he was going to have 500 extra troops, but I was getting increasingly exasperated because I could not see what they were going to do if the 16,000 troops already in the Province were not being used. In any case it was the police who should have been utilized first, backed up where necessary by the Army; the RUC, apparently without any clear instructions from Stormont Castle, were doing very little. Word was passed down to the men on the beat that they were to do nothing to 'provoke trouble'. There were a few cases where RUC men showed sympathy with the strikers, which only proved that policemen are human and have feelings about the community they come from. Without any leadership it was inevitable that they would play it by ear, and that the tune would differ from one policeman to another. The RUC was and is a highly professional force and its general failure to take a firm attitude to intimidation and barricades during this strike was due to the lack of clear instructions and to the general unpreparedness for dealing with this kind of problem rather than to bias. Whatever the reason, the strike supporters were delighted and surprised to find themselves almost unopposed and ordinary citizens felt abandoned by authority and defenceless against the bullying of the new rulers of the streets of Ulster. What point was there in risking their necks trying to go about their business when all over the Province they could see evidence of the security forces standing by and watching lawlessness flourish? During those first crucial days the Government lost its authority and the junta at Hawthornden Road, the UWC headquarters, established theirs.

The power workers too were being subjected to intimidation. There was certainly organized support for the UWC among the operators in Ballylumford, the power station from which some 70 per cent of the Province's electricity came. On the first day of the strike there had been power cuts by early afternoon and by the second day these were seriously affecting the capacity of industry to operate. Those people who managed to avoid the barricades and UDA men and get in to work were often finding that there was little they could do for long periods when power was not available. But at the Economic Council meeting on the 16th the Chairman of the Northern Ireland Electricity Service (NIES) told us that his middle management were capable of keeping sufficient power going and willing to do so if they were given protection. I later spoke to Jim Smyth, the Chief Executive, who confirmed this, and so I pressed Merlyn Rees to see that the necessary protection was provided. But he refused point-blank to do so.

Meanwhile, Orme had been threatening in public that if the UWC tried to run down power the forces would be sent in to run the power stations and, since most people were unsure at that stage whether or not they had the technical capacity to do so, the strikers withdrew a threat of a total shutdown and agreed to keep a minimal supply going. But as the strike went on, members of the Executive became increasingly sceptical of the Secretary of State's reassurances that the forces had experts who could meet any emergency. There was an important shift in the attitude of the middle management and engineers at Ballylumford after the first few days of the strike when it became clear that the Government was not going to give them protection and that the streets of the Province had been abandoned to the para-military without a struggle. By the 19th they were telling Smyth that they would not agree to work alongside sappers from the Army and the Navy if they were sent into the stations. As with many others across the Province, their will to resist was collapsing.

The extent to which power could be kept flowing through the grid was unclear for some time, partly because we did not know how far the strike supporters in Ballylumford were prepared to go in shutting down the machinery, partly because of the shifting attitudes of the middle management, and partly because the technical information reaching us was often confused and contradictory. The two coal-fired stations in Belfast had been closed down due to lack of coal supplies quite early in the strike, and there was some argument as to whether we ought to step up the supply from the Coolkeragh plant in Londonderry which was manned largely by Catholics who were not, of course, supporting the strike. John Hume thought we should use it, but most of the rest of the Executive thought this would be a dangerous development which could set Catholic worker against Protestant worker, and the NIES management agreed. Hume thought that with Coolkeragh we could keep 60 per cent of normal supply running, and without it only 30 per cent, but these figures were in any case dependent on assumptions about Ballylumford which we were in no position to make. The future electricity supplies of the Province and therefore the ability of people to carry on a normal life were dependent on what happened there.

From the beginning the strikers had, quite shrewdly, sought to use the fact that John Hume was Minister of Commerce and therefore responsible for power supplies to their advantage. Their advertisement on the 14th had said, 'All essential services will be maintained, and only action by Mr John Hume will rob the housewife, the farmer, and essential services of power.' This was of course complete nonsense, but it was consistently repeated by the UWC and their supporters throughout the strike with some embellishments. When Craig and Barr (a Vanguard Assemblyman from Londonderry who was also a UDA leader and one of the main spokesmen for the UWC) met Orme on Friday the 17th they demanded that industry be cut from the grid, and when he refused said that any shortage of power from hospitals and homes was not their responsibility. It was not in fact possible to cut industry from the grid, nor did we feel inclined to accept the dictation of this self-appointed junta to close down industry. To do so would have required the declaration of a State of Emergency by Rees and the issuing of instructions to all industry to cease operations.

The Executive held a meeting on the morning of the 17th, with a six-point agenda which did not specifically include the strike, though inevitably this was one of the major points of discussion. We were asked to consider the final agreed report of the sub-committee on the re-negotiations of Sunningdale, arrangements for rehabilitation of detainees after release, proposals from Bob Cooper at Manpower to change the trade union political levy from opting in to opting out, the re-organization of secondary education, the collection charges for rent and rates strikers, and the Ministry of Commerce proposal for the setting up of Emergency Petrol Depots to ease distribution. We agreed the basis of our new approach to the Sunningdale Agreement, and decided to consult our Assembly supporters and discuss the timing of any announcement at our next meeting. John Hume reported on the struggle to maintain power supplies and the threat that Ballylumford would be completely closed down if we kept the plant at Coolkeragh working. It was agreed to back the Minister of Commerce in his refusal to react to the threat, and he was asked to represent the Executive at a meeting which the Secretary of State had requested that morning. On his return from Stormont Castle at noon Hume reported that Rees was completely firm in his refusal to concede to the strikers and was 'prepared to take alternative steps to ensure minimum essential supplies of electricity if the system broke down completely'.

Over the first weekend there was much planning and preparation for the next week. I spent the whole two days at my office in Parliament Buildings studying shoals of reports about the situation across the Province, and at meetings with Rees and his staff at Stormont Castle. Many hypothetical developments were examined and contingency plans drawn up, but one possibility in particular haunted us—the total collapse of power supplies. From quite early in the strike, officials in Roy Bradford's Environment Department and Hume's Department of Commerce were drawing up 'Doomsday' plans for dealing with hospitals, food supplies and public health in such an eventuality. The news on the power station front was uniformly depressing, and when we heard of the change in the attitudes of middle management at Ballylumford we decided to prepare for the worst. On Sunday Merlyn Rees declared a State of Emergency to allow instructions to be issued to industry to cease using electricity if the power on the grid dropped to dangerously low levels.

A rather unrealistic scheme for getting people back to work also began to take shape over the weekend, and Merlyn Rees told me about it. Some trade union leaders, anxious to restore their authority with working people in the face of the challenge from the UWC, suggested holding 'back to work' marches on a specified day and bringing over the TUC General Secretary, Len Murray, to head them. Rees was delighted with the idea and very enthusiastic, but I told him that unless adequate security measures were taken to allow people to go to work the march would be a waste of time. In the Executive the idea was treated with some levity and regarded as another example of the sad incomprehension with which our well-meaning Secretary of State and his Ministers were approaching the whole affair.

On Monday morning 20 May there was another upsurge of barricading of roads and intimidation of anyone travelling to work. The earlier barricades had been taken down by the para-military themselves before the weekend for tactical reasons. They had already effectively challenged authority and there were signs that the security forces were being moved in belatedly to clear some of the main roads. But the hold of fear was sustained by the simple expedient of human barricades of strike supporters who parted when the security forces appeared and closed up again behind them when they passed. There had been little opportunity for people to start drifting back to work. This Monday morning I was told by the police that there were so many barricades on roads between my home and Stormont that I would have to be flown in by helicopter. My Private Secretary, Sinclair Duncan, contacted the Northern Ireland Office and, after an argument with a civil servant there who suggested I travel by a fifty-mile detour, had an army helicopter laid on.

As we travelled across County Down I could see beneath me the evidence of para-military activity. Near Moneyrea the road was blocked by a sawn-down telegraph pole and a long queue of vehicles was waiting in front of it. I asked the pilot to hover for a few minutes and watched as the gang manning the barricade turned away the cars and sent them home. Even at Stormont as we came in to land I could see a barricade within sight of Merlyn Rees' office. I went straight in to the Secretary of State's office and demanded angrily that something be done to remove all the barricades, but he insisted at first that the security forces had the problem under control and that roads were in general clear. I ended the argument by taking him to the window and pointing to the barricade at Dundonald House, and in some agitation he hurried to instruct his officials to have it cleared. Shortly afterwards a bulldozer arrived and pushed the obstruction aside, but an hour or so later it was up again at the same spot. It was much the same all across the Province as half-hearted and ineffectual attempts to clear main roads were treated with derision by the strikers. The Secretary of State's information appeared to be largely inaccurate, and he kept producing maps and pointing out roads claimed to be free of obstruction but which I knew to be blocked.

Later that morning the Executive met for a situation report. I said it appeared that in the event of a complete breakdown of power supply essential services could be maintained for two to four days without serious danger to public health, but at some risk to life among the elderly and the sick. The Minutes record that 'Ministers agreed that, alarming as the situation was, it would be wise not to enter into any deal with the strikers but to support the trade unions and as an Executive to try to reach agreement on the Council of Ireland as a matter of gravest urgency'. It seemed to be all we could do, apart from continuing to press the Secretary of State to take action on the streets and hoping the strike would lose its momentum.

At 2.30 p.m. we gathered again to meet the Secretary of State. He read the statement which Stanley Orme was to make at Westminster at 3 p.m., reiterating that the UWC demands were not negotiable and expressing the hope that 'those who are bravely standing out against bullying and intimidation will rally the mass of the people of Northern Ireland to the path of reason'. All necessary steps, it said, would be taken to maintain order and to keep essential services going. But when he spoke to us Rees had no clear plans for carrying out this promise. Extra troops were on the way, he said vaguely, and the Westminster Government was absolutely determined to stand firm in support of the Executive. He went on to refer to the Council of Ireland re-negotiations which he felt should be dealt with as a 'matter of extreme urgency'. Any agreement should be announced immediately, he suggested, or else it would be seen when it appeared as a victory for others. He promised to make a statement on the 23rd on the Law Commission Report on cross-border co-operation against terrorism, agreeing to urgent legislation to implement its proposals.

Meanwhile the Province was at a standstill. The UWC was issuing new instructions 'requesting' chemists shops to remain open, post offices and food shops to open only between 2 p.m. and 6 p.m., and all others to 'stand firm' in support of the stoppage. Farmers had lost thousands of gallons of milk which had to be poured down the drain because it could not be collected and distributed, but their early concern and anger was reduced when the Milk Marketing Board announced that it would be providing full compensation. Farmers and businessmen formerly totally opposed to the strike were turning to the UWC, as the only body apparently able to get things done, with requests for special concessions. The media, and particularly the BBC, were carrying every statement and 'request' from the UWC as if it were a Royal Proclamation, which was causing increasing anger in the Executive. There was little we could do in publicity terms to counteract this; we simply wanted people to go about their normal business but, lacking any power to take measures enabling them to do so, there was little point in going on the radio with mere exhortations. An exasperated Leslie Morrell suggested, half in jest, that we should commandeer the BBC and use it entirely for official announcements and soothing music, and there were times when some of us wished that was a practical possibility. Glen Barr was exaggerating only a little when he boasted, 'We are in a position to set up a provisional government.'

On Monday evening 20 May the 'Back to Work' march was announced for the following morning organized by trade union officials and led by Len Murray who had just flown in from London. The Northern Ireland Office backed the march, promising to clear roads, and asking employers to respond by making sure that all factories and places of work were open. The UDA responded by saying that all main roads would be blocked from 6 a.m. and that people would be well advised to stay at home and make no attempt to go to school or work.

Tuesday morning showed that the UDA's threats were more effective than the Government's promises. Troops and police were out in force and most major roads were cleared of barricades, but residential areas remained almost completely cut off and few people could get as far as the main roads. Only about two hundred people, most of them trade union officials, turned up at Queen's Quay for the 'Back to Work' march and though they completed their gesture by walking into the shipyard in the face of jeers and a barrage of rotten vegetables hurled by 'pickets' it was a futile display of courage. There was nothing anyone could have done when they got to work, because there was no power available for industry. This fiasco simply provided another victory for the UWC and another humiliation for authority.

Payments started that day under the new 'Emergency Benefit Payments' system which had been agreed by the Executive on the suggestion of Paddy Devlin, Minister of Health and Social Security. Normal systems of unemployment benefit, sickness benefit and supplementary benefit could not be operated in the existing state of near anarchy, and so we decided to suspend them and institute temporarily a more streamlined system to alleviate the vast hardship which seemed likely if the strike continued. Under the law, as in Britain, we were required to pay benefit to people unable to work after one week, and to the dependents of strikers, and Paddy Devlin was quite determined that no one was going to accuse him of imposing hardship on Protestant workers. Queues hundreds of yards long rapidly formed outside payment centres, and it subsequently emerged that there was fraud on a massive scale involving funds estimated at up to £5 million.

Events were taking their toll of Executive members and their unity was coming under some strain. Roy Bradford had broken ranks at the weekend by issuing a statement calling for talks with the UWC without consulting or informing any of his colleagues either of his opinions or his intention of going public. When he followed this up with a radio interview the SDLP, who had for some time regarded him with great distrust, were furious and there was a major row in the Executive involving demands that he be sacked. The rest of us sympathized but I could see the kind of political game that was afoot and when Bradford offered his resignation I refused to accept it. I was not going to provide such an easy way out of a tight corner and further comfort for the UWC.

On the other hand Paddy Devlin had written out a letter of resignation because of the Executive's determination to press ahead with the imposition of collection charges for rent and rates strikers. It was a typically unpredictable and emotional action apparently due to massive pressure in his constituency where there were probably more rent and rates strikers, and more families of internees and convicts, than anywhere else in the Province. I had always got on very well with him and respected his down to earth common-sense. At Executive meetings he sat beside me on my right and always kept me informed about what he was doing. He told me in advance about his resignation decision, and I formed the view that he would have second thoughts and realize the dangers of resigning at this time. In the event the shock news of the Dublin bombings led him to freeze the resignation, and he never got the opportunity to warm it up again.

Flushed with their success on Tuesday morning the UWC decided to tighten the screw, and announced a complete embargo on petrol and oil, previously regarded as 'essential supplies'. They designated a certain number of petrol stations throughout the Province (many of them run by UDA leaders) as supply points for essential users, as defined by their representatives on the spot. It was clear that all petrol tankers from the refineries and depots were intended to be diverted, with or without the co-operation of the drivers, to these stations, and I immediately urged Rees to provide escorts for all tankers. He seemed to agree, but over the next forty-eight hours nothing was done and petrol supplies gradually dried up. By the end of the week even Government Departments were running out of petrol and Ministers' cars were being kept running by borrowing from Army supplies.

The UWC also started issuing passes at Hawthornden Road and at other provincial towns for 'essential services', without which no one would be allowed through barricades. A civil servant from my own office was having difficulty getting to Stormont from his home in North Down and so he approached the local UWC organizers telling them he was involved in emergency benefit payments and was immediately given a pass. He told me about this with great glee when he arrived at the office, but it did little to lift the gloom now settling over Stormont. Gerry Fitt, Ken Bloomfield and I had lunch with the Secretary of State and his Permanent Secretary at Stormont House. We ate off gilt-edged government issue dishes, but our menu was baked beans on toast.

The endless round of meetings, reports and doomsday planning continued. The IRA had been untypically quiet since the beginning of the strike, and we were pretty sure that they were watching with delight as the UWC did more in a few days to sap the British will to remain in Ulster than they had been able to do in five bloody years. The first real evidence of this came with the news from Londonderry that the IRA had warned all Catholics employed at Coolkeragh power station that any of them found going to work would be 'knee-capped'. We discussed the Coolkeragh situation at the Executive meeting in the afternoon, but it was clear we might soon have to shut it down.

Discussions continued on the handling of the Council of Ireland re-negotiations. Some SDLP Ministers thought it would be a mistake to announce anything until the strike was over lest it be represented as a concession and a sign of weakness. But most of us believed that the time was long overdue for putting the record straight, so that people would at least have the opportunity of knowing what they were actually supposed to be striking against. Eventually we all agreed that the best prospect of defeating the strike now lay in a combined security and political initiative and that the issue of the statement, designed to reassure those concerned about the Council of Ireland, must therefore be dependent on a parallel initiative by the security forces designed to break the street gangs. I stressed to the Executive that time was running out and that if any benefit was to accrue from the new agreement it would have to be announced soon.

The next day, Wednesday 22 May, it became clear that we could expect no effective initiative to restore order, although some barricades were removed in the early hours of the morning on main roads, and we decided to go ahead with our announcement. The SDLP Executive members had a meeting of their backbenchers to secure final approval, but when they came back they were more disappointed than I had ever seen them. 'I'm sorry,' said Gerry Fitt. 'We can't get them to agree.' It seemed as if the Executive was about to break up on this issue, as neither Alliance nor ourselves were prepared to go back on what had been agreed. I got up from the Executive table and said, 'Well, if that's the case I am afraid it means the end of the Executive. I am going in to the Assembly to announce the resignation of the Executive because of the failure to agree on the re-negotiation of the Council of Ireland.' I was at the door when Gerry Fitt stopped me. 'Give us another half an hour and we will try again, Brian,' he said.

It was about an hour later that Fitt and his colleagues returned looking more cheerful. 'We had another vote and a majority have agreed,' he said. I went straight in to the Assembly and announced the new proposals. It later transpired that Orme had been rushed up from Stormont Castle to address the SDLP backbenchers, and had played a major part in changing their attitude.

The proposal now agreed was for a phased implementation of Sunningdale, and marked a major change in approach which, announced at any time before the strike, could have done much to take the heat out of the Council of Ireland issue. Phase One, to be implemented immediately, involved the establishment of the Council of Ministers as a body for consultation and co-operation. Phase Two, bringing the transfer of some executive functions in the areas agreed at Hillsborough, the establishment of a permanent headquarters and the election of the second tier Consultative Assembly from the Northern Ireland Assembly and the Dail would be implemented only after a test of opinion of the electorate at the next Assembly elections in 1977/8, and then only if the Assembly approved. In effect all the most controversial aspects were being postponed until people had had a chance to see a more modest form of cross-border co-operation working.

In the event the announcement had little effect on the situation. The UWC and the UUUC politicians rejected it and the media, having seen the successive victories of the strikers, regarded it as a desperate attempt to turn back the strike. Our insistence that it was the product of long negotiations which were virtually complete before the strike began were treated with cynicism and the papers the next morning covered it as 'capitulation' to the demands of the UWC, and 'too little too late'. It was clearly too late, but if the junta at Hawthornden Road had not already scented victory and seen the desperate straits of the Government I do not believe it would have been too little. The UWC were now determined to accept nothing less than the heads of the Executive on a platter.

The rest of that week the tide was flowing strongly against the Executive. The strikers started to polish up their public relations, dismantling the barricades which had now become unnecessary, distributing fairly generously their 'passes' for essential services and petrol, promising farmers that feedstuffs would be kept in supply, and generally providing the basic necessities which the Government seemed unable to guarantee. People who had previously urged us to stand firm against the strike were now urging us to talk to the UWC. Our 'no negotiations' stance accompanied by no effective action was being made to look like pigheadedness and petulance which was more to blame for the state of the country than the actions of the UWC.

That Wednesday evening the Executive met again and decided to play the only card which seemed to be left to it. The Ministry of Commerce had for some time had an oil contingency plan ready for any energy crisis which might occur, involving the take-over of petrol supplies and distribution by officials through a selected number of petrol stations. Hume brought this before the Executive, and we adopted it in principle, agreeing that the Minister of Commerce should submit it to the Secretary of State immediately to get his backing. We knew that without support from the security forces the plan could not be implemented. I reported to the Executive that Rees had readily agreed to our proposal of the previous day for the establishment of a Standing Committee of Ministers under the chairmanship of the Secretary of State or the Minister of State to co-ordinate the civil and security aspects of the emergency, and the first meeting would be held the following morning. The Executive would be represented by the Ministers of Commerce, Environment, and Manpower Services, with full discretion to call in other Ministers as required. This was in fact simply a formalization of the rather *ad hoc* basis of co-operation which had existed during the strike so far, with an interminable series of poorly co-ordinated meetings. Before the strike there had been a system of weekly meetings between Northern Ireland Office civil servants and the Northern Ireland Civil Service, and since the beginning of the strike a Committee of Permanent Secretaries had been meeting under David Holden, Head of the Northern Ireland Civil Service, in addition to the daily meetings of effective Ministers and their Permanent Secretaries at the Castle with Stanley Orme.

When the new Standing Committee met on the morning of Thursday 23 May the Army Chief of Staff and Frank Cooper attended. Hume requested, on behalf of the Executive, that the Army should go in and run the power stations and there was talk of naval sappers being gathered up from Malta and various other places and flown in to help. We were not told that the forces could not keep power supplies going. Hume also put forward the oil plan with a request that it be implemented immediately. Once again the response was vague expressions of determination to do whatever was necessary but no agreement on any clear line of action. This new Committee never really resolved the problems of liaison between the Executive and the Secretary of State's Office.

The Executive met twice on Thursday to discuss the Government's attitude and the increasing pressures from industrialists for negotiations. At a meeting before lunch we examined the oil plan again and agreed that, as there was no acceptable alternative means of demonstrating our determination to govern, strong pressure should be put on the Secretary of State to give us the necessary support. After lunch I met representatives of the CBI and the ICTU who stressed how serious the situation had become and urged that some initiative be taken to break the impasse. I spoke to Rees and asked him to give me a decision one way or the other on the use of troops to maintain essential supplies by 4 p.m. At 3.30 p.m. the Executive met again and discussed the changing attitudes of leaders of industry and commerce. Roy Bradford repeated his view that we should have talks with the UWC, but others pointed out that the whole purpose of the strike was now to end power-sharing and destroy the Constitution Act and therefore must be resisted. Towards the end of the meeting Ken Bloomfield gave us a message from Frank Cooper saying that a decision was likely to be received later in the day and would be in support of the Executive. The delay was simply due to the fact that the British Government wanted to be perfectly sure of the course they were taking and the extent of troop involvement. We decided that if the Government would not back the oil plan we would have to resign. There would be no point in keeping in office any longer an ineffectual charade.

At 6.30 p.m. John Hume met Orme at Stormont Castle and told him on our behalf that if the oil plan were not supported we would resign. Rees was in a Cabinet meeting in London where the matter was obviously under discussion and soon after we received a telephone message inviting us to Chequers for discussions with Wilson and his Ministers the following day. It seemed that at last some decisive action was being planned, and Fitt, Napier and I flew over on 24 May with more hope than we had had for some time.

Harold Wilson received us cordially and Mason, Silkin (the Attorney-General), and Rees joined us for our talks. I explained the situation as we saw it, and underlined dissatisfaction concerning the absence of any response by the security forces. 'What can we do now?' Wilson asked, and we put forward the oil plan as the only means of restoring petrol supplies. Wilson said that of course he could not commit the Cabinet and there would be a meeting that night at Downing Street, but he would let us know immediately what the decision was. He told me privately that he would be recommending that our proposal be supported, and Merlyn Rees arranged to telephone me. If he said that everything was OK I would know they were going to put the plan into operation. The Northern Ireland Ministers assumed that this meant the next day. The idea of a Prime Ministerial broadcast also arose during this meeting and it was agreed that Wilson and I should both broadcast the following day.

We flew back to Belfast late in the afternoon in optimistic mood and at 7 p.m. reported to a meeting of the Executive. I told my colleagues that it was our clear impression that the Prime Minister was firm in his desire to do whatever was necessary and within his power to stand by the Executive. The Minutes record:

> Ministers discussed further the possibility of some move towards opening a channel of communication with the strikers through an intermediary. Ministers decided that they must assume Mr Wilson and his colleagues were aware of all the implications of the oil plan. They should defer any move to initiate talks until action on the oil plan had taken place.

Around midnight Rees rang me at home and said, 'Everything is OK'. To me that meant the implementation of the oil plan by Sunday at the latest, and I was very pleased.

But the next day nothing happened, and the strike went on as before. Rumours abounded of disagreements between members of the Westminster Cabinet. I was working on the text of my broadcast for that evening and about 2 p.m. I received a courtesy copy of the text Wilson was going to use. I was surprised and alarmed when I read it, because it merely seemed to lump everyone in Ulster together as reprobates and insult them to no purpose. They were 'sponging on British democracy' the text said.

I made strong representations to Rees, and he promised to speak to the Prime Minister about it, though he stressed that he could give no guarantees that anything would be changed. When the recorded broadcast went out at 9 p.m. some of my objections had been met, but the 'sponging' section remained. I broadcast immediately after, urging people to return to work, but immense damage had been done by Wilson's broadcast which had brought out Provincial feeling against him and vastly increased popular support for the strike. During the next few days strike supporters were proudly displaying small pieces of sponge pinned on their lapels. The broadcast of Francis Pym, then Conservative Spokesman on Northern Ireland, the following evening, was more sensible, but by then the damage had been done.

On Sunday 26 May the Executive parties met separately at Stormont. I was told by a civil servant that the SDLP were preparing to issue a twenty-four-hour ultimatum to Rees to implement the oil plan or they would resign. No reason for the delay in implementing what had been agreed at Chequers was given to any of us, and we felt that we had been let down. The SDLP took their decision on their own and communicated it directly to Rees. Wilson had returned to the Scilly Isles to complete his holiday, and we heard that Rees had flown to Cornwall to see him. Later in the day the Secretary of State's office contacted me and said that the oil plan would be implemented the next morning. We immediately set about the planning of this, and John Hume as Minister of Commerce did most of the co-ordinating with the security forces. No other Minister knew the details of the twenty-one petrol stations which were to be commandeered, but to reduce further the risks of any leak he changed the plan at the last minute.

In spite of this the information was clearly leaked to the UWC who took measures to disrupt the operation by such methods as the mixing of fuel tanks at the stations concerned. The information was obviously passed on by an official sympathetic to the strike. But this was only realized after the troops had moved in at 5 a.m. on Monday and it became clear that the operation had led to a diminution rather than an increase in the availability of petrol. The UWC accused the Government of provocative action and announced a total shutdown of all services, including the power stations. Doomsday seemed to have arrived.

At Stormont that Monday morning I had a sombre meeting with all our senior civil servants. I had asked my Private Secretary to get Ken Bloomfield out of a meeting of Permanent Secretaries to see me, and Ken suggested that I ought to hear what they had to say. I agreed, and was given a detailed report on the situation by David Holden and his colleagues. It was a very black report indeed as they pointed out how hospitals might soon have to stop functioning, and how if the sewage pumps stopped working there was a real probability of raw sewage flooding the streets of low-lying parts of Belfast. It was an entirely factual report, but it brought home to me more graphically than ever before the dire situation in our Province.

At 4.45 p.m. the Executive met. Our morale was very low and we could see that the situation was moving out of control. Over the week-end it had been admitted for the first time by Rees that the forces were not capable of running the power stations without the assistance of the middle management, who were not now prepared to co-operate. I told the Ministers that messages were coming in from an increasing number of sources—employers, the Ulster Farmers Union and others asking that there be some communication with the strikers. I told them about my meeting with the Permanent Secretaries, and said we now needed to look ahead. 'It is my view that we should consider the use of some independent person or body to establish the facts of the situation and the attitudes of the people involved to see if some way out cannot be found,' I said.

The Minutes record that:

It was generally agreed that some way should be found to communicate with the strikers but it was emphasised that care must be taken to ensure that the Executive did not seem to be weakening the position of the Secretary of State nor paving the way for the IRA to press successfully for talks with the Executive.

The SDLP were still reluctant to agree to communication with the strikers and our meeting broke up in a pessimistic atmosphere after we had agreed to get more reports on the electricity situation and make a final decision the next morning. In the end we were to fail to agree and the only vote taken in five months of working together was to be the last decision taken by Ulster's power-sharing Executive.

21
Reflections

The power-sharing Executive, brief though its existence was, marked a new departure in Ulster politics. It was my proudest moment to be able to chair such an Executive, and it is my main regret that it was brought to a premature end.

It did not succeed because we left too much unfinished business, because we presented it inadequately, because the IRA was able to step up its terrorist campaign, and because neither the Irish nor the British Governments was prepared to take difficult decisions and give us consistent backing when it was most needed. But we will come back to this point again. It may be called coalition, or partnership, or community government—but, whatever the name, Ulster people will realize that unless Protestants and Catholics, Unionists and Nationalists, can find a way of working together in government for the good of the Province there will be no political stability, no economic progress, and no end to violence. The only real alternative to working together is to live separately. That means repartition and a form of sectarian apartheid which will bring shame on the name of Ireland. Being an optimist and a firm believer in the basic common-sense of Ulster people I am convinced that co-operation will win through. In the power-sharing Executive we showed the way and others will follow.

Since the collapse of the Executive there have been further unsuccessful attempts to make political progress. The Labour Government held elections for a Constitutional Convention to give Ulstermen themselves an opportunity to agree on their own constitution. The UUUC won an overall majority in the Convention, which met during the latter half of 1975 and failed to reach agreement. The UUUC forced through a majority report by 42 votes to 31, calling for a return to simple majority rule in Ulster on the basis of a federal constitution. They were elected by people who thought they would be able to drive a hard bargain and who were badly let down when it was discovered they could produce no bargain at all. Both major parties at Westminster predictably refused to implement such a one-sided report, arguing that it did not show sufficiently widespread agreement to provide a stable basis for devolved institutions. My own supporters, organized as a separate Unionist Party of Northern Ireland (UPNI), were decimated in the Convention elections and I led a group of five members in the Convention. We were able to play only a limited watching role as the SDLP struggled without success to reach a compromise with the UUUC.

Since the ending of the Convention there have been desultory political talks, but no signs of any agreement have emerged. They have failed for the same reason the Convention failed: the politicians are now operating in a false framework. Westminster, having had its fingers burned over its high-profile involvement in Sunningdale, has rushed to the other extreme and adopted a 'sort yourselves out, it's nothing to do with us' attitude. The UUUC in particular took this to mean that all alternatives were now open and proceeded to present their first. For as long as both sides believe they have a prospect of having their first options implemented they will not settle for the second choice, which is the only possible basis for agreement. The UUUC will continue to demand simple majority rule, and assert the unsuitability of anyone with an aspiration towards Irish unity, however long term and whether or not qualified by acceptance of the principle of democratic consent, for a place in a Northern Ireland Government. The SDLP will feel obliged to counter this by assertion of the importance of an institutionalized Irish dimension and a constitutionally guaranteed place in any future government. Both will remain extremely sensitive to any swings in British opinion and devote much of their effort to attempting to secure, and telling their supporters they are securing, support among significant sections of British opinion.

If progress towards political agreement is to be made in Northern Ireland it is vital that a clear framework be established by Westminster politicians, preferably on a bi-partisan basis, so that Northern Ireland politicians have an understanding of the basis on which they are holding discussions. The failure of the Government to do this prior to the election of the Constitutional Convention—except in terms so ambiguous as to be almost meaningless—was the major reason for its failure.

The constitutional talks of late 1972 and 1973 operated against the understanding that Westminster would not agree to set up devolved institutions unless they were of a type acceptable to leaders of both the Catholic and Protestant communities. This understanding, combined with a strong conviction of the importance of restoring government of

Ulster by Ulstermen at an early date, helped provide an impetus towards agreement. Whatever criticisms may be made of the details of
the agreement we reached, I have no doubt that it, or something very
close to it, was the only deal available at that time.

Today the deal does not have to be the same one. The SDLP, supported by the Dublin Government, may now have a deeper understanding of loyalist sentiment and be prepared to be more flexible. But the
same principle—that the agreement of both sections of the Ulster community is essential—must form the basis of discussions. Westminster
needs to spell this out in unequivocal terms.

Democracy has shallow roots in Ireland, north and south of the border.
England ruled Ireland by force for centuries. The Irish Republic
achieved its independence after a series of rebellions and a bitter civil
war. Northern Ireland secured its separation from the rest of Ireland
by force and the threat of force. Over the last seven years the appeal to
force has been made again, with incalculable consequences for the
future of everyone in these islands, and for the future of our children.

'Ulster will fight and Ulster will be right' was the slogan coined by
Lord Randolph Churchill and adopted by Ulster Unionists during the
Irish Home Rule crisis at the beginning of the twentieth century. I
believe they were right to stand together then against the threat of incorporation in an all-Ireland 'nation' whose political ideals and symbols, sense of identity, and way of life were alien to them. They were
threatened with forcible expulsion from a nation to which they and
generations before them belonged by birth and by loyalty. Were the
same threat to face Ulster today it would call for the same response. But
there is no such threat.

A 'united Ireland' could not come about in 1912 because the hearts
and minds of those who lived in Ireland were not united. It is not a possibility today for the same reason. The sense of difference has, if anything,
increased. Yet at the same time the conditions for a constitutional settlement on a basis of mutual respect and peaceful co-existence have
improved.

When Irish Nationalists were fighting for independence they saw
Ulster Unionists merely as an irritating extension of the traditional
English enemy, rather than as a people in their own right with deep roots
in Irish soil and traditions which ought to be taken into account. Today
most Nationalists realize that one million Unionists can not be wished
out of existence nor subjugated by force. Ever since the first faltering
steps towards a good neighbourly relationship in the 1960s the growth

of a modern way of life on both sides of the border has been making the old Cold War between North and South look increasingly anachronistic. In a world where Germany, France and Britain, for centuries rivals in Europe, can live in peace and friendship, building a common future for their citizens, it is an obscenity that we in Ireland should go on killing each other. I have no doubt that this is a conviction which has long been held by the majority of Irish Nationalists and Ulster Unionists, that 'moderate majority', the 'ninety-nine-point-nine per cent' who have so regularly been invoked over the past seven years but who have increasingly become the subject of scepticism and ridicule as the violence has continued. Yet the failure of this reasonable majority to make its influence effective in no way makes me doubt its existence; rather does it highlight the failure of those of us in all parties who are democratic politicians to stand together and provide convincing and consistent leadership. The men of violence have been allowed so to retain the initiative that civilian morale has collapsed and there has been a reversion to the tribal groups where people feel safest when threatened.

Blame for the past and the present in Ireland lies on all of us— Dublin politicians, Ulster politicians, both Unionist and Nationalist, and British politicians.

Dublin politicians deserve blame for maintaining a divisive and meaningless claim to the territory of Northern Ireland, a claim which many young men, untutored in the distinctions between theory and practice, have died while trying to enforce. They are to blame for failing for too long to recognize the realities of Northern Ireland's existence and of Unionist opinion, and for conducting policy on Northern Ireland as if one million Ulstermen did not exist. They built a society and a state which made only token concessions to the existence in Ireland of any significant tradition other than Catholic nationalism. In the early years of the present crisis they fanned the flames of violence through political opportunism and carelessness about anything other than domestic political gain. More recently they failed to take and implement tough political decisions when the power-sharing Executive was fighting for its life.

The Nationalists in Northern Ireland are to blame for persistently looking to the South instead of seeking a realistic accommodation with their fellow-Ulstermen. They indulged for so long in the politics of boycott, obstruction and wrecking that when a genuine urge for participation arose it was treated merely as a new ploy from those irreconcilably opposed to the very existence of the State. They have too often taken the easy way out by attacking the security forces and criticizing their methods, without first making a convincing commitment towards the enforcement of the law and the defeat of terrorism.

The British establishment is to blame for its wilful ignorance about Irish affairs, in spite of the central role Britain has played, and will continue to play, in them. Distaste has too often been disguised under the old cliché. 'The English can never really understand the Irish,' which is in any case totally untrue. They are to blame for combining this attitude in what might be thought a 'typically Irish' fashion, with easy assumptions of superior knowledge about what ought to be done after only the briefest acquaintance with the Irish problem. They are to blame for their inconsistent policies during a terrorist campaign in which consistency was vital, and for their persistent ambiguity about their ultimate intentions. Ambiguity has fed insecurity, which in turn has fed violence.

I believe the suspension of the Stormont Parliament to have been a fundamental error in the handling of the Northern Ireland situation. One cannot simply sweep away at the stroke of a pen a system of government which has existed for over half a century without causing very deep political upheaval, particularly if this is done in the middle of a savage terrorist campaign. Given consistent backing Stormont could have evolved a system of community government without arousing the deep fears among Unionists and the quite fantastic hopes among Nationalists that Britain was on the verge of adopting a policy of 'uniting Ireland'. Political and social systems are living organisms which cannot be changed simply by adopting constitutional blueprints and panaceas. They need tending and developing within a stable framework.

Unionists are to blame for their lack of generosity when it lay in their power to be generous, for being frightened and negative in their politics when a positive approach could have tapped the potential of the whole Ulster community. We too easily allowed sectarian traditions to hem us in and dictate what was politically possible. We failed to make the effort to understand the aspirations and the frustrations of the Nationalist community, and the need to make them feel involved in the running of the State and confident of receiving their share of its benefits. We allowed provincialism and small-mindedness to go unchallenged for too long, so that people became almost incapable of looking ahead when it was vital that they should do so.

In the pages of this book I have tried to relate as accurately as memory and inadequate records will allow my role in the post-war political history of Northern Ireland. I have not tried to reinterpret everything I did in the light of the views I now hold. It has seemed more valuable to set out my reasoning at the time for taking particular actions, whether or not I would now go along with that reasoning. We are all—politicians particularly—children of our time. My account of events is by no means comprehensive: it omits aspects of Ulster politics which other people are better qualified to explain.

Looking back on events I feel now that in my early political career I did not question sufficiently the traditional religious divisions in Ulster affairs. I and my colleagues accepted far too readily the advice of those who said 'Don't stir things up'. We knew there were many things wrong with our society, but we had a deep sense of the need to give our relatively young state a period of stability which would allow the evolution of more ideal conditions. We made a pragmatic assessment of the political limitations on us and got on with the job of trying to govern as well as possible. If I had had a more rebellious youth I might have questioned the old dogmas more readily, but the Unionist politicians I met through family and friends seemed a civilized group of men from whom I was inheriting an honourable tradition.

I regret now that when Unionists of vision, such as Brian Maginnes MP, and Sir Clarence Graham tried to stimulate new thinking and broaden the appeal of Unionism in the 1950s and early 1960s I did not come out in support of them. I did not think they were achieving anything useful and I preferred then, as I have always done, to aim for the possible. But we should have spent more time watering the roots of tolerance. We did not take the initiative in reforming our society until events forced change on us. Politically, though not industrially, the 1960s were a wasted decade for the Ulster Unionist Party. I allowed myself to become too compartmentalized at the Ministry of Commerce and did not pay enough attention to the wider political perspective. Whether I could have done any better had I become Premier in 1963, or even in 1969, I do not know. But by 1971 we were reacting to events rather than controlling them and one was always conscious of running very fast merely to make up lost ground.

It is hard to evaluate one's own political career, with its weaknesses and strengths, its sins of omission and commission. Ulster politics is a harsh school and one has to be prepared to take a lot of hard knocks. That has never worried me greatly. In fact one of the things I enjoy about politics is a good hot political meeting where quick thinking and giving as good as you get can carry the day. I do not think I bore any grudges against opponents, and when I attacked them it was for what they did rather than who they were. Issues are always more important than personalities.

As a politician I have always enjoyed a good professional relationship with the media. I was schooled in the ways of newspapers from the beginning due to my good fortune in having as a neighbour Jack Mansfield, a reporter for the *Belfast Telegraph*. He taught me always to issue a script for my meetings and to build up confidence among journalists that whether they could attend my meeting or not, I would use this script. My first script had 'A. B. D. Faulkner' across the top, but Jack soon convinced me that I should replace that with 'Brian Faulkner' if I wanted people to regard me as a friend. Television and radio too I enjoyed and tried to develop some expertise in. On one occasion when I arrived at the BBC studios in Belfast to do a radio link-up with London late in the evening I found the studio staff had not yet arrived. Having seen it done so often I was able to switch myself through to London where they were waiting, and had finished recording the interview when the Belfast journalist got to the studio. The media will usually treat another professional fairly and, though I have received apologies for what were regarded as unfair or biased interviews, that has never been as a result of complaints from me. Criticism is an inevitable part of public life and one has to survive it as best one can.

This does not mean I was untouched by all criticism. However thick one's hide it was hard not to be hurt by the unjust things that were sometimes said. Persistent accusations that I was 'ambitious' and 'devious' I felt particularly strongly about, though they were not the sort of things an active politician could easily refute. In one sense I have been ambitious in wishing to be good at my profession of politics and to get things done. But the criticisms may derive from the way I went about my work. I have always been healthy and energetic, and my years in industry taught me to ignore the details in which far too many politicians get completely bogged down nowadays and to take decisions on the important matters. I was unaware that anyone regarded this as unusual until one day when a senior civil servant, explaining a delay in the production of some work I had asked for, said that out in the office they referred to the 'Faulkner white heat' and found it difficult to keep up. In Northern Ireland, where politics was often a part-time occupation, there were those who thought that this kind of behaviour could only be explained by an all-consuming ambition to reach the top. And devious? I hope not, for one of the personal qualities I value most in friends is honesty and directness. As a practical politician one certainly has to make many compromises, but I hope that through time many of those who have opposed me will come to realize that I was telling people the truth more often than they had been prepared to admit. My political career has been consistently devoted to the overriding belief that Ulster's place is within the United Kingdom and that everything must be done to strengthen that position.

A politician should be judged by what he has done, and what he has tried to do, rather than by other people's guesses at his motives. I hope that my political activities can stand that test.

Today violence continues in Northern Ireland at a depressingly high level. At the time of writing (1977) the death total is approaching 1,700 and the past year, 1976, has been the worst since 1972. Knee-cappings, the brutal method of terrorist punishment for those incurring the displeasure of various organizations, are as high as ever. Mafia-style operations have been growing as para-military organizations on both sides of the sectarian divide use their ill-gotten gains to buy themselves into semi-legitimate 'front' operations. 'Protection' rackets proliferate. Bank robberies are running at the rate of £$\frac{1}{2}$ million a year. The Province is virtually unrecognizable from that which we governed in the 1960s, when we had the lowest rate of 'ordinary' crime in the United Kingdom.

In the middle of all this sordid violence and lack of political leadership a massively supported 'Peace Movement' has been initiated by the women of Belfast. It represents a cry for sanity and for help but it is also born out of desperation. It has shown beyond doubt that it enjoys massive support, that the 'moderate majority' desiring above all freedom from violence does exist, and yet it seems sadly futile. In the last analysis what can marching women, however courageous, do to gangs of armed killers—short of confronting them physically themselves? It is for such tasks that the legitimate forces of law and order exist, and while a peace movement can do much to destroy the morale and the (already very limited) support of the terrorists, it is the security forces who must carry through the campaign against terrorism to a successful conclusion, and who require the participation and support of all who desire peace.

Ireland and Great Britain are knotted together in their past, present and future, for better or for worse. When British soldiers, and British politicians, grapple with British responsibilities in Ulster they are not fulfilling some remote 'colonial' responsibility, they are defending their own homes and their own democratic institutions. The Irish Sea may be the boundary of the interest of many members of the British public, but it does not form a very substantial barrier against the spread of violence, anarchy and social upheaval. If Britain abandoned her responsibilities in Ulster it is quite conceivable that in the ensuing civil war one or both of the combatants would turn for assistance to a foreign power which was not well disposed to the NATO Alliance.

We need a new relationship between Ulster, Britain and the Republic of Ireland. Seven years of violence has been horribly and completely futile. It must be implanted in the minds of this generation as never before that the Irish problem can never be solved by violence. The responsibility lies on politicians to prove that democracy can solve it. The relationship between Ulster and the Irish Republic must be moved on to a basis which clearly recognizes democratic mechanisms as the only legitimate means of securing constitutional change. Only when we have neutralized the much-talked-of 'Irish dimension' can democracy begin to deepen its roots in Ireland and our people, of all religions and none, get on with the task of providing a decent way of life for themselves and their children.

Epilogue

Below is a letter from Lord Faulkner to a colleague, Reginald Magee, written on 18 February 1976, a few weeks before his death:

Dear Reggie,

I have received over 400 letters during the past six weeks. They have all been kind, many generous, all very pleasant to read ... you have greatly reassured my own mind, with your interpretation of events and your conviction on the rightness of our policies. I made many mistakes during that 1973/4 period. I assumed, too readily, that the public would come along with our actions. Obviously there was need for much more explanation in order to bring support.

I should have tried harder, during the Assembly Election and afterwards to keep all the Official Unionists together. After all if we had been able to total 32 instead of 22, I would not have had any problems in securing a large overall majority of Unionists in the Executive. The sight of 2 SDLP, 1 Alliance and the remainder Unionists could have brought a quite different public response. As it was I had, as you know, a difficult task in getting acceptance from the Government for a Unionist majority at all.

Certainly I was convinced all along that the outcry against Council of Ireland was only a useful red herring—the real opposition was to sharing of power.

However all this is hindsight. Nevertheless I shall grieve till my dying day that we did not succeed.

If we had done so the rewards for Ulster would have been beyond our brightest expectations. There would have been strong support for our Government from virtually every country in the world. That would have brought in its train a readiness to strengthen our economy from Britain, from North America and from Europe.

Terrorism could not have flourished on this island. For the first time there would have been an all Ireland watch for men of violence with both police forces co-operating and with complete community support.

Will there ever be an opportunity to get a worthwhile devolved government established? I cannot, at present, see it. The two sides are growing away from each other. I would fear a break up of SDLP into old Nationalists, old Republicans and a Civil Rights rump. The present leadership has nothing to offer supporters with no prospect of an administration so there is no encouragement for them to forget their all-Ireland outlook and work within the UK.

Britain will be slow to make a move. They are in trouble enough with Scotland and if they ever do give devolution to Scotland it will be a pale shadow of Stormont.

It is a long time since that day when we lunched at the Ulster Club. I wonder if you would have taken on a Constituency if you had been able to see the road ahead? I think you would and I hope you feel that the adventure with Faulkner was, at least, exciting.

Yours ever,

Brian.

APPENDIX I
Speech

A lunchtime address by Brian Faulkner at the church of the Corporation of London, St Lawrence Jewry, next Guildhall, Tuesday 19 November 1974

It is natural that I should think of the term 'those in authority' in a political sense, for that is the sphere I know best. I am conscious that in dwelling on this aspect I am doing something of an injustice to those in authority in many other spheres—education, trade unions, the Church, for example—who have a marked effect upon different facets of our national life. Yet I am sure that they, too, will agree that in our democracy it is in the political, particularly the governmental, sphere above all that the character, the nature of that national life is on the one hand expressed and on the other hand formed. This two-way interaction is essential in a democracy, but it is my basic thesis today that the balance needs to be moved in the direction of the formative influence of national life which can, and should be, exercised by those in authority.

It is axiomatic, but all too often overlooked, that leaders must *lead*. In these days of public opinion polls, public relations, and policies packaged for maximum consumer appeal there is a great danger of politics being aimed more and more at the lowest common denominator in the electorate. And before anyone rises to accuse me of being an elitist, a fascist, or the implacable enemy of socio-economic classes four and five or whatever, let me say that to me the dangerous lowest common denominator in political terms is simply the person who takes a short-sighted view of situations. The politically myopic are not restricted to any one class or group in society—indeed they are spread right across all the usual boundary lines in terms of which people in this country are accustomed to think—but they are extremely numerous and, it seems to me, have increasingly engaged the attention of the politicians, to the detriment of the overall public interest. The over-simplifications of complex issues, the giving of short-term 'goodies' at the expense of long-term interests, the choice of the soft option at the expense of principle, the echoing articulation, instead of the correction of narrow-minded prejudices—all these have been seen, not just in the political party, but on all sides, in recent years and they have been damaging to the common weal.

I believe that leaders should not always be looking over their shoulders at those with a short-sighted perspective. They should set out their problems and their objectives clearly and fully without gimmicks or gloss—the electorate at large is far more sophisticated than the politicians give it credit for. The growth in cynicism about politics in general can, I feel sure, be linked to a widespread feeling of resentment by the public against what they take to be attempts by the politicians to talk down to them or lead them by the nose.

But what the public is entitled above all to expect of those in authority is that they should not shy away from questions of right and wrong. By that I don't mean right and wrong answers to the management of the economy—important though such considerations undoubtedly are—but right and wrong in their now almost outdated moral meaning. Even to recall such concepts in a political context is nowadays to run the risk of being dubbed a reactionary bore, yet can it be coincidence that the decline of these concepts has been accompanied by a general loss of purpose and a general lack of confidence? Can anyone deny that the very cement of our society, the rule of law, has dramatically and even dangerously weakened at an alarming rate? And I am not just talking about rising crime rates, which are but symptoms of a much deeper malaise—I am talking about the advance of expediency and the retreat of principles in so many aspects of our life.

So far, I have refrained from quoting concrete examples of the type of political action I have described, lest I be accused of meddling in the affairs of parties here—though I have no doubt that you will not be too hard pressed to think of examples of my general points. You will forgive me if I turn from the general to the particular in the case of Northern Ireland, about which I feel I have not only a right, but a duty, to talk in this context. For it is in the tragedy of Ulster that we have seen most dramatically the dangers of government—and I am not blaming one party more than the other—which has not confidently and unswervingly pursued policies founded on principled commitment. In their anxiety 'not to take sides' leaders of both main parties in Britain have appeared to be anxious, as one observer has put it 'to do neither wrong nor right'. The results have been the spread of doubt, indecision, an air of open-endedness about the future—the very environment in which the ruthless, fanatical terrorists thrive and increase in strength.

Victory against the IRA will never be achieved in terms of capturing the last member—it can only be achieved when those in authority, by the consistent demonstration of their determination, convince the IRA that in the battle of wills the government is *not* going to give in, or hedge its bets, or keep its options open, or radically reappraise its policies, or otherwise seek to welsh on its moral obligations and that the IRA, or any other terror organization, simply is not going to win. The fundamental battle in Ulster is one between terrorism and democracy—all the other many complications of the situation must not be allowed to obscure that basic fact. And if, because of the violence and destruction wrought by a minority with no mandate from anyone, the United Kingdom Government were ever, God forbid, to treat Northern Ireland in any less favourable a way than any other part of the country, or, worse still, seek to weaken the ties that, with the full consent and at the express desire of the overwhelming majority of her people, bind Northern Ireland to Great Britain, that would be not only an immediate catastrophe for Ulster but ultimately a crippling self-inflicted blow into the body of British national life.

I can understand that very many people in Great Britain look on the Ulster situation as something unique—something growing out of the history of Ireland and something which 'couldn't happen here'. True, the circumstances are peculiar to Northern Ireland, but the principles involved could well apply to many other externally different situations which one could foresee here without too many flights of fancy. Prejudice, ruthlessness and selfishness are not in short supply anywhere and those in authority must be prepared to take their stand against them.

I am enough of an optimist to believe that if governments are prepared to use their power justly, confidently and unswervingly, they will evoke respect and support from the much-maligned but vitally important silent majority and thus retain the capacity to hold off the growing challenge from those who would undermine our society.

It is not in my remit today to dwell on what can be expected of society—the other side of the coin—but I am sure that it is fundamental to the future health of democracy that the public be prepared to support those in authority, who carry responsibility. We must never lower our guards against tyranny, but we must give democratic government the power needed for an increasingly difficult task. I believe government can obtain such power—not just Parliamentary power and power through the statute books, but power through the support of the people—if its leaders demonstrate their will to pursue a principled and consistent course.

APPENDIX II
Chronology of Events

1920	23 December	Government of Ireland Act, providing for separate Home Rule Parliaments in Belfast and Dublin, receives Royal Assent.
1921	18 February	Arthur Brian Deane Faulkner born at Helens Bay, Co. Down.
	7 June	Parliament of Northern Ireland first meets in City Hall, Belfast.
1932	16 November	Parliament Buildings, Stormont, opened by Prince of Wales.
1949	10 February	Brian Faulkner wins first election to Stormont Parliament for constituency of East Down.
1956		Becomes Chief Whip.
1959		Becomes Minister of Home Affairs.
1963	25 March	Terence O'Neill succeeds Lord Brookeborough as Prime Minister of Northern Ireland.
	27 March	Brian Faulkner becomes Minister of Commerce.
1965	14 January	Sean Lemass, Premier of Irish Republic, visits Stormont.
	4 February	Brian Faulkner pays official visit to Dublin.
1968	5 October	Civil Rights march in Londonderry.
1969	24 January	Brian Faulkner resigns from O'Neill Cabinet.
	28 April	O'Neill resigns.
	1 May	James Chichester-Clark appointed Prime Minister.
	3 May	Brian Faulkner becomes Minister of Development.
	13 August	British Government agrees to send troops on to streets of Londonderry.

1971	20 March	Chichester-Clark resigns.
	23 March	Brian Faulkner becomes Prime Minister.
	22 June	Brian Faulkner proposes new political deal with opposition.
	16 July	SDLP and Nationalists withdraw from Stormont in protest at Army action.
	9 August	Internment of terrorist suspects.
1972	31 January	Thirteen people shot by Army during riots in Londonderry—'Bloody Sunday'.
	24 March	Direct rule of Northern Ireland from Westminster announced by British Prime Minister, Edward Heath.
	31 July	'Operation Motorman' by Army ends 'No Go' areas.
	24 September	Darlington Conference.
1973	21 March	White Paper on constitutional proposals published by British Government.
	28 June	Elections for new Northern Ireland Assembly.
	22 November	A power-sharing Executive Designate appointed after long negotiations with Brian Faulkner as Chief Executive.
	9 December	Sunningdale Communiqué signed by British and Irish Prime Ministers and by representatives of the Northern Ireland parties in the Executive Designate.
1974	1 January	Executive takes office.
	28 February	Westminster General Election.
	16 May	UWC General Strike begins.
	30 May	Power-sharing Executive collapses when Brian Faulkner and colleagues resign.

APPENDIX III

Members of the Northern Ireland Government, March 1972

(As they appear in illustration nine, front row, left to right)

JOHN BROOKE (Minister of State at Finance)
NAT MINFORD (Minister of State at Development)
HERBIE KIRK (Minister of Finance)
(LORD GREY, Governor)
BRIAN FAULKNER (Prime Minister)
JOHN ANDREWS (Deputy Prime Minister)
WILLIAM LONG (Minister of Education)
BASIL MCIVOR (Minister of Community Relations)

(back row)

BASIL KELLY (Attorney-General)
(SIR HAROLD BLACK, Secretary to the Cabinet and Clerk of the Privy
    Council)
WILLIAM FITZSIMMONS (Minister of Health and Social Services)
ROBIN BAILIE (Minister of Commerce)
HARRY WEST (Minister of Agriculture)
ROY BRADFORD (Minister of Development)
G. B. NEWE (Minister of State, Prime Minister's Office)
(KEN BLOOMFIELD, Deputy Secretary to the Cabinet)

APPENDIX IV

Members of the Power-Sharing Executive

(As they appear in illustration eleven, left to right)

PADDY DEVLIN (Health and Social Services)
OLIVER NAPIER (Office of Law Reform)
BRIAN FAULKNER (Chief Executive)
JOHN HUME (Commerce)
BASIL MCIVOR (Education)
JOHN BAXTER (Information)
AUSTIN CURRIE (Housing, Local Government and Planning)
HERBIE KIRK (Finance)
GERRY FITT (Deputy Chief Executive)
ROY BRADFORD (Environment)
LESLIE MORRELL (Agriculture)

Index